USING
Microsoft Works 3.0
for Windows

More Software Application Tutorials from McGRAW-HILL

FOR FULL TERM APPLICATION COURSES . . .	SCHMITZ	*Practical DOS! 2nd Edition (2.0 - 5.0)*
	FREDERICK/YASUDA	*Using Windows 3.0/3.1*
	LARSEN /HYDRUSKO	*Using WordPerfect 6.0 for Windows*
	LEEBURG/LARSEN	*Using WordPerfect for Windows*
	CLUCK	*Using Word for Windows*
	LEEBURG/PURVIS	*Using WordPerfect 6.0 for DOS*
	O'DONNELL/PHILLIPS	*Beginning WordPerfect 6.0 for DOS*
	O'DONNELL/PHILLIPS	*Advanced WordPerfect 6.0 for DOS*
	PITTER/PITTER	*Using Lotus 1-2-3 for DOS Release 3.1+*
	WILLIAMS/WILLIAMS	*Beginning Lotus 1-2-3 Release 2.2*
	WILLIAMS/WILLIAMS	*Advanced Lotus 1-2-3 Release 2.2*
	WILLIAMS/WILLIAMS	*Beginning Lotus 1-2-3 for Windows*
	WILLIAMS/WILLIAMS	*Advanced Lotus 1-2-3 for Windows*
	AMOROSO	*Decision Making Using Lotus 1-2-3: Building Quality Applications*
	SHUMAN	*Using Microsoft Excel 4.0 for Windows*
	PITTER/PITTER	*Using Microsoft Excel 4.0 for Windows: The Basics*
	GRAUER/BARBER	*Database Management Using dBASE IV and SQL*
	SHUMAN	*Using dBASE IV*
	REISS	*Using Paradox 4.0*
	REISS	*Using Paradox for Windows*
	EAKINS	*Desktop Publishing on PC Compatibles and the Macintosh: Pagemaker 4X*
	FREDERICK/YASUDA	*Using Microsoft Works 3.0 for DOS*
	FREDERICK/YASUDA	*Using Microsoft Works 3.0 for Windows*
	YASUDA/FREDERICK	*Using Microsoft Works 3.0 on the MAC*
FOR A QUICKER PACE OR BRIEF INTRODUCTION . . .	SCHMITZ	*First Look at DOS 6.0*
	SCHMITZ	*First Look at Windows 3.0/3.1*
	ELLIS	*First Look at Macintosh and System 7*
	LEEBURG/PURVIS	*First Look at WordPerfect 6.0 for DOS*
	CLUCK	*First Look at Microsoft Word for Windows 2.0*
	LARSEN/HYDRUSKO	*First Look at WordPerfect 6.0 for Windows*
	SMITH	*First Look at Lotus Release 4 for Windows*
	SKINNER	*First Look at Lotus 1-2-3 for DOS Release 3.1+*
	SKINNER	*First Look at Harvard Graphics 3.0 for DOS*
	SKINNER	*First Look at Lotus Release 2.4*
	ROSNER	*First Look at Quattro Pro for Windows*
	ELLIS	*First Look at Paradox for Windows*
	PRICE	*First Look at dBASE 1.5/2.0 for DOS*
	LARSEN/LEEBURG	*First Look at NetWare 2.2*
	PITTER	*First Look at Works 2.0 for the Mac*
	PITTER	*First Look at Works 2.0 for the PC*

USING
Microsoft Works 3.0
for Windows

Vivian Frederick
Phyllis Yasuda
with Judy Yamada and Ann Koda

McGRAW-HILL

New York St. Louis San Francisco Auckland Bogotá Caracas
Lisbon London Madrid Mexico Milan Montreal New Delhi Paris
San Juan Singapore Sydney Tokyo Toronto

"One must learn by doing the thing;
Though you think you know it,
You have no certainty until you try."
Sophocles, circa 450 BC

McGRAW-HILL
San Francisco, CA 94133

Using Microsoft Works 3.0 for Windows

3 4 5 6 7 8 9 0 SEM SEM 9 0 9 8 7 6

ISBN 0-07-015693-X

Sponsoring editor: Roger Howell
Editorial assistant: Rhonda Sands
Technical reviewers: Fred Hanzelin and Sally Ann Hanson
Production supervisor: Leslie Austin
Project manager: Terri Schiesl, Shepherd Inc.
Interior design: Graphics West
Cover designer: Tom Trujillo
Composition: Shepherd, Inc.
Printer and binder: Semline, Inc.

Library of Congress Card Catalog No. 94-76038

Brief Contents

Detailed Contents

CHAPTER 4   Word Processing 3   64

CHAPTER 5   Word Processing 4   78

CHAPTER 6   Spreadsheet 1   95

CHAPTER 7

Spreadsheet 2   119

CHAPTER 8

Spreadsheet 3   140

Preface

Using Microsoft Works 3.0 for Windows is a hands-on, comprehensive tutorial designed to introduce Microsoft *Works 3.0* to students of varying backgrounds. With an encouraging and gentle approach, this text assumes some experience with the Windows operating system but little or none with Microsoft *Works* software. Each chapter contains one or more activities that lead students through the creation and alteration of documents using this powerful software's numerous features.

FEATURES OF THIS BOOK

Comprehensive, Hands-on Introduction—covers commonly used features of the word processing, spreadsheet, database, and draw modules of Microsoft *Works 3.0* software. Appendix A discusses the features of the *Works* Communications module.

Step-by-Step Tutorials—instructions for action appear in blue type, screen displays monitor student progress, exercises build gradually upon themselves, and section headings provide quick, convenient reference.

Real-Life Applications—exercises are built around a business scenario. Students create and edit documents for The Fun Factory, a retail toy store.

Student Reinforcement—learning objectives, chapter summaries, and end-of-chapter review questions and exercises reinforce and support each chapter's lessons. Answers to review questions are given in the back of the book.

Student Data Disk—available to adopters (packaged with the Instructor's Manual), it contains practice files that students will use to complete the exercises. Preview the "README" file before using the disk.

A comprehensive Instructor's Manual includes teaching hints and sample solutions to all end-of-chapter exercises.

HINTS FOR GETTING THE MOST FROM THIS TEXT

Read ahead! Read each section before you begin to follow its instructions. Experience has shown that students who read only as they go along miss the action taking place on the screen—and with any computer, that's half the fun! Reading computer screens is also the best way to learn to use any computer program.

Take your time as you progress through the activities, and review the material frequently. The original document will usually appear on your data disk so that you can start over again whenever you wish.

Feel free to experiment with the various operations of *Works* after you have completed each chapter. Try not to worry about making mistakes. In fact, we've found that people learn more from making mistakes, trying to figure out what went wrong, and then making the necessary corrections. So don't hesitate to jump right in!

If you get stuck, try one of these methods:

- Browse through the various options displayed on the menu; experienced computer users often learn a new program this way.
- Use the built-in Help facility or the Cue Cards if they are available on your system.
- Ask your classmates or instructor.
- Read the manufacturer's manual, *Microsoft Works 3.0 User's Guide*, which accompanies Microsoft *Works 3.0* software. (*Note:* The goal of this book is to teach you enough to get started with Microsoft *Works 3.0*. It is not designed to replace the manual.)

Above all, enjoy your experience with using the computer to become more productive.

Of the hundreds of students who have used this material during its development, one stands out for her ability to express our goals for this book in poetic fashion. When Sylvia Riveness began using this material, she suffered from an advanced case of "computer phobia." Her following original poem describes her progression through the course.

MY GOD! That's a computer that is staring back at me
I really think it's sneering in superiority.
My hands are feeling clammy and my head begins to throb.
Oh surely I could find a nice new *un*computer job?!

The teacher says it's time to start;
I summon up my nerve;
I meet the mighty IBM
My courage doesn't swerve.

I double check the manual;
Stare at the sketch that's drawn;
I take a breath and push a switch—
OH LORD—I've turned it on!

I'm in the lab for 2 straight hours;
The struggle is intense.
Please let me do just *one* thing right.
My pride would be immense.

And FINALLY I'm on Page 10,
Reviewing what I've done.
It did just what it said it would—
You know—this *might* be fun!

COPYRIGHT 1988 S. RIVENESS

ACKNOWLEDGEMENTS   The authors wish to express their appreciation to the reviewers for their contributions to the development of the text:

Fred Hanzelin of South Suburban College, Homewood, Ill.

Sally Ann Z. Hanson of Mercer County Comm. College, Trenton, N.J.

You, Your Computer, and WORKS 3.0 for Windows

OBJECTIVES

When you finish this chapter you will be able to

- *identify the preferred computer configuration for running WORKS 3.0 for Windows*

- *understand how to use this book*

- *recognize the special symbols used in this book*

- *list the modules contained in WORKS 3.0*

- *understand the introductory screens of WORKS 3.0*

- *use the on-line Help features of WORKS 3.0*

WHAT YOU SHOULD KNOW BEFORE YOU START

This book assumes that you have a working knowledge of the Windows environment. You should be able to

- start the computer
- use the Windows operating system version 3.1
- select commands from the menus
- make selections from dialog boxes
- use the mouse to point, click, double click, and drag
- use the mouse to maximize, minimize, restore, and resize windows
- use the mouse to scroll windows both horizontally and vertically
- launch *WORKS 3.0*
- format and copy a floppy disk
- shut down the computer

HARDWARE AND SYSTEM REQUIREMENTS

This book is based on the assumption that you will be working with a computer with one internal hard disk and one internal floppy disk drive. If your computer configuration does not conform to that assumption, the instructions will need to be adapted.

You will need the following:

- A Windows 3.1-based computer with mouse, keyboard, hard disk, and internal floppy disk drive
- Windows 3.1 installed on the hard disk
- Microsoft *WORKS 3.0* for Windows installed on the hard disk (the program requires at least four megabytes of space for minimum installation and 15 megabytes for complete installation)

- A minimum of two megabytes of RAM in your computer for running *WORKS 3.0*, although four megabytes is highly recommended
- A printer
- Access to the practice files that go with this book. A data disk containing those files is packaged with the Instructor's Manual that is given to every teacher who adopts this book. Your teacher may decide to store the practice files on a hard disk accessible to all students or may simply give each student a copy of the data disk.

In order to standardize instructions, we will assume that you have your own data disk. There is enough room on that disk for you to store the results of the chapter activities, as well as the end-of-chapter exercises. If you must use the data files directly from the hard disk, you will have to adapt the instructions accordingly. You will also have to obtain a floppy disk (new or used, as long as the data currently on the disk is no longer needed) suitable for the computer you are using so you will have a place to store the results of the chapter activities, as well as the end-of-chapter exercises.

HOW TO USE THIS BOOK

This book consists of a series of hands-on activities designed around a central scenario, which introduce you to the features of *WORKS 3.0*. The most effective way to use this book is to read each chapter before attempting the step-by-step instructions using your computer. That way you will know what to expect and will be able to concentrate on what's happening on the computer screen while you are doing the activities. The text includes both explanatory material and hands-on lessons. A mouse icon precedes all hands-on activities. Often, the explanatory material is interspersed throughout the lessons. The lessons consist of numbered steps that tell you each keystroke or mouse movement needed to achieve the desired result. Even if you are an inexperienced computer user, you can easily get started by simply following the explicit instructions in the lessons.

Take time to observe the computer's screen after each step to see what happens. Then compare your screen with the figures in the book. The appearance of your screen should be quite similar, if not identical, to the screens in the figures.

If time permits, you can also use the tutorial found in the HELP menu as a form of review for the various applications.

SIGNPOSTS TO GUIDE YOU

IT'S YOUR TURN

A mouse symbol like the one to the left signals hands-on activities that you can do on the computer. Hands-on activities are highlighted to make them easy to identify. The steps are numbered, unless there is only one step. Throughout the body of this text you are instructed to use the mouse as much as possible to carry out the activity steps. Alternate keyboard strokes to accomplish many of the same functions are given in the Command Summary appendix at the back of the book.

An arrow like the one to the left marks the appearance of a helpful hint.

CAUTION

The caution block alerts you to a warning that you should read carefully.

Bold italics	Denote important terms, the definitions of which can be found in the glossary.
UPPER CASE ITALIC	Will be used for filenames, names of directories, and drive designators.
PLAIN UPPER CASE	Will be used for menu titles. Menu commands will be Capitalized.
SMALL UPPER CASE	Indicates buttons found in dialog boxes.

WHAT IS WORKS 3.0?

WORKS 3.0 is the latest and most powerful of an evolving integrated software package that was first introduced in 1987 and that still exists in earlier versions.

WORKS 3.0 is an integrated productivity tool that runs under Windows 3.1. It includes four different modules, which are explained in the following list.

- Word processing with an included draw package allows you to electronically store, edit, and manipulate text and drawings.
- Database with reporting allows you to maintain collections of related information about specific topics, as well as generate reports that include all or selected subsets of the database.
- Spreadsheet with charting allows you to arrange data and information in a matrix and perform calculations on it.
- Communications allows you to electronically send and receive information to and from other computers.

As a user, you can work with any one or all of these modules as you need them. You can, of course, cut and paste between modules as you will do in the integration chapters. However, the draw feature is only accessible from the word processing and database module.

In this text, you will be led through exercises using all *WORKS 3.0* modules except for the communications module. That module is covered as an appendix, since many users will not have the equipment necessary to use the communications tool.

IT'S YOUR TURN

It's now time to take a look at *WORKS 3.0.*

1. Launch *WORKS 3.0.*

   You may see the Welcome to Microsoft Works dialog box shown in Figure 1-1. If so,

   a. Click the button labelled START WORKS NOW.

   The Startup dialog box shown in Figure 1-2 may appear. Continue with step 2.

2. Look at the dialog box.

The dialog box is divided into four main sections: The buttons on the left, the action buttons in the upper right corner, the buttons in the Create a New section in the middle of the screen, and the file list box in the lower

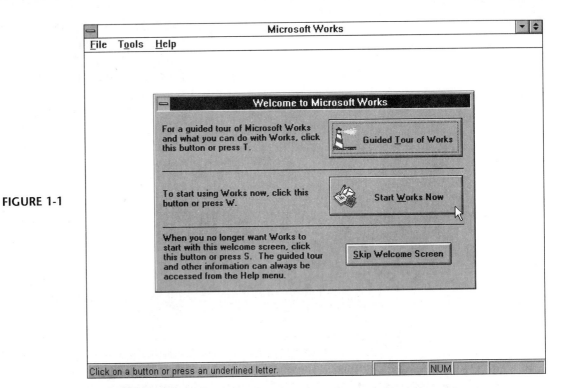

FIGURE 1-1

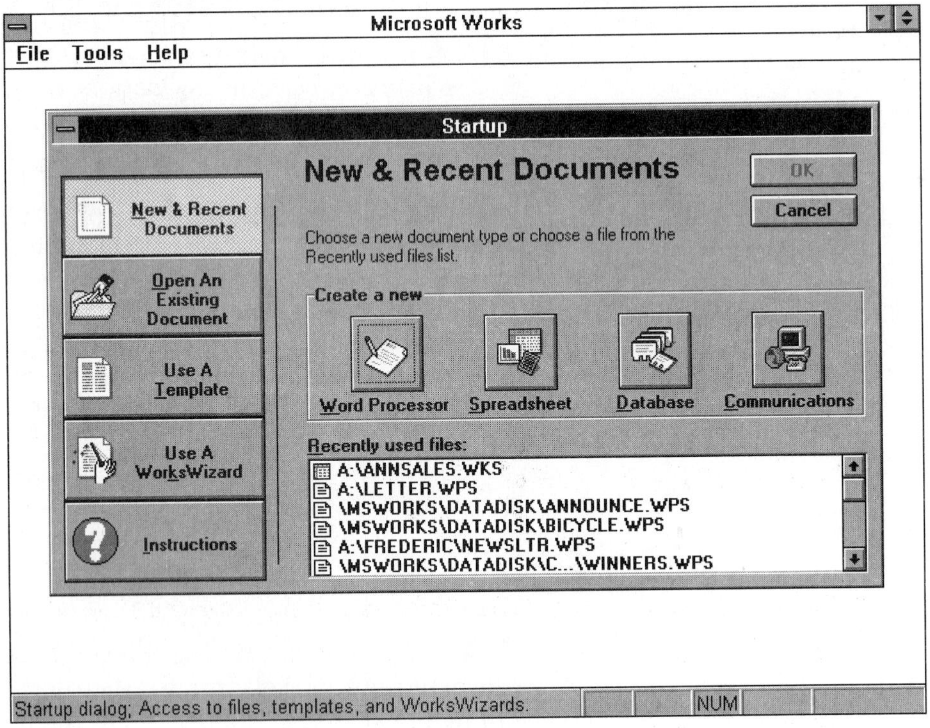

FIGURE 1-2

right side. The buttons on the left-hand side give you the following options:

NEW & RECENT DOCUMENTS

This button is active when the Startup dialog box first appears. The rest of the dialog box pertains to this choice. Note that the instructions in the middle of the Startup dialog box tell you what you should do. If this is the first time *WORKS* has been used, the Recently Used Files section will be empty; but after *WORKS* has been used, the program keeps a history of the most recently used files, so you can open one of them directly from this dialog box. If you wish to create a new file, you simply click on one of the module buttons in the middle of the dialog box.

OPEN AN EXISTING DOCUMENT

This button is used to bring up the *WORKS* Open dialog box which allows you to open any *WORKS* compatible file.

USE A TEMPLATE

When you click this button, you are presented with a list of already prepared documents that you can customize for your own purpose. Templates will be covered in a separate section.

USE A WORKSWIZARD

When you choose this button, you will see a list of documents that you can prepare with the help of *WORKS 3.0*. The program will ask you a series of questions and, based on your responses, will complete the document for you. You may want to experiment with WorksWizards in your spare time. You will use one of the WorksWizards in Chapter 5.

INSTRUCTIONS

This button gives you short instructions for the other buttons.

---

3. Insert your data disk into the floppy drive.

4. Click the OPEN AN EXISTING DOCUMENT button.

    An Open dialog box similar to the one shown in Figure 1-3 will appear.

5. Click the down arrow on the right side of the Drives box.

    The drives list, similar to Figure 1-4, will drop down.

6. Click the drive label that corresponds to the drive containing your data disk.

    On our system, this is drive A, but yours may be different.
       The contents of the dialog box will now reflect the files contained on your data disk found in the floppy drive. Your screen should be similar to the one shown in Figure 1-5.

    The filenames you see in the List box are files you will be using as you work through the activities in this book. The Directories list box also displays the three directories—*ARTWORK, CONTEST*, and *EXERCISE*—that are contained on the data disk.

7. Double click on the *EXERCISE* folder or on the directory name.

File Name Text Box   Current Directory   Directories List Box

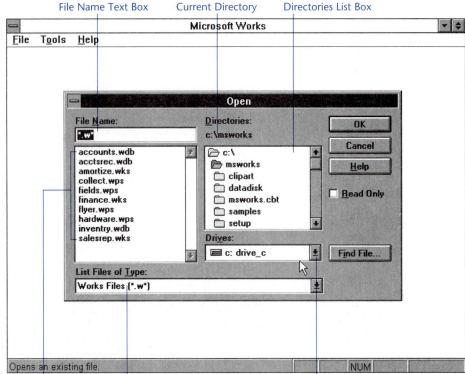

FIGURE 1-3

File Name List Box   List Files of Type Scrolling Box   Down Arrow for the Drives List Box

FIGURE 1-4

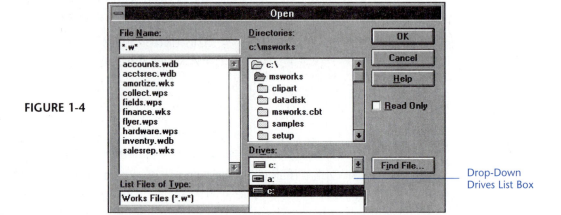

Drop-Down
Drives List Box

FIGURE 1-5

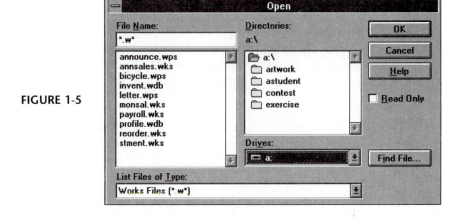

A:\EXERCISE now appears in the Directories line, and the File List box on the left now shows the names of all *WORKS* documents contained in the *EXERCISE* directory. If there were no *WORKS* documents, the File List box would be empty.

8. Double click on the open folder (above the Exercise folder) labelled with the drive designator containing your data disk.

    The list box changes to show the entire contents of the disk in that drive again.

To see only the names of word processing files in the Files list box,

9. Click anywhere on the box at the bottom labelled List Files of Type.

    A scrolling list box drops down, as shown in Figure 1-6. The arrow on the right-hand side of the List Files of Type box is the visual clue that this box controls a scrolling list box.

FIGURE 1-6

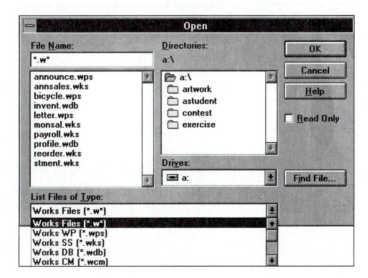

10. Click the line labelled Works WP (*.wps) and watch the File Name list box change to show only files with the extension .wps, which indicates they were prepared with the word processing module.

11. Open the List Files of Type list box and choose *WORKS* spreadsheet files (.wks), then database files (.wdb) and finally, communication files (.wcm).

    There are no communication files on your data disk, but you should see the File Name list box change as you select the other file types. When you had the List Files of Type list box open, you may have noticed that there were other file types listed there besides *WORKS* files.

Just to satisfy your curiosity,

12. Open the List Files of Type list box again.

13. Move the pointer to the bottom arrow on the vertical scroll bar and hold down the mouse button.

    You will see that there are over 20 additional file types listed. All of these file types can be opened by *WORKS 3.0* for Windows, even those that were created in other programs. As you can see, *WORKS 3.0* can open files that were created in many different formats.

14. Scroll back up to the beginning of the List Files of Type list box and click on *WORKS* Files (*.w*).

The File Name list box will once again contain the names of all the files on the data disk.

You are not going to open any files yet, so

15. Click the CANCEL button in the upper right corner of the Open dialog box.

You will be returned to the Startup dialog box.

16. Click the CANCEL button in the Startup dialog box.

Your screen now contains the blank *WORKS* window with no module window open. Note the three menu titles in the menu bar.

FILE	Contains commands that allow you to create new files, open existing files, access WorksWizards and Templates, save workspaces, and exit *WORKS*. This menu also contains the names of some of the most recent files used so the user can open them easily without having to go through the Open dialog box. Most of these functions are available in the Startup dialog box you have already used.
TOOLS	Contains the Options command that allows you to set certain global characteristics of *WORKS 3.0*. You will use the Options command in the next section.
HELP	Contains commands referencing the *WORKS* Help feature, which is more fully explained later in this chapter.

SETTING SOME GLOBAL WORKS OPTIONS

It is important that your computer have the same options selected as are used for the activities in this book. In this section, you will check the settings of your computer and change them, if necessary, to make them match the settings used for this book.

IT'S YOUR TURN

1. Click the TOOLS menu.

It drops down to show only one available command. Note that the command name Options is followed by an *ellipsis* (. . .). The ellipsis indicates that if you select the command, *WORKS* will present a dialog box asking for further information. Selecting a command that contains an ellipsis will cause a dialog box to be displayed.

2. Click the Options command.

The Options dialog box shown in Figure 1-7 is displayed. Check your dialog box with the one shown in Figure 1-7 to be sure that your dialog box matches. The Communication block may vary from the figure because of your system configuration.

FIGURE 1-7

```
┌─────────────────────────────────────────────────────────────┐
│ ▭                     Microsoft Works                    ▼ ▢ │
│  File   Tools   Help                                          │
│  ┌─────────────────────────────────────────────────────────┐ │
│  │ ▭                      Options                           │ │
│  │  ┌─Units──────────┐ ┌─When starting Works─────┐ ┌──────┐ │ │
│  │  │ ⦿ Inches       │ │ ☐ Use saved workspace  │ │  OK  │ │ │
│  │  │ ○ Centimeters  │ └─────────────────────────┘ └──────┘ │ │
│  │  │ ○ Pica         │ ┌─In Word Processor───────┐ ┌──────┐ │ │
│  │  │ ○ Points       │ │ ☐ Overtype             │ │Cancel│ │ │
│  │  │ ○ Millimeters  │ │ ☒ Typing replaces sel. │ └──────┘ │ │
│  │  └────────────────┘ │ ☒ Automatic word sel.  │ ┌──────┐ │ │
│  │                     └─────────────────────────┘ │ Help │ │ │
│  │  Speller:           ┌─Spreadsheet and Database┐ └──────┘ │ │
│  │  [American English▼]│ Default number of decimals: [2]    │ │
│  │  ☒ Show status bar  └─────────────────────────┘          │ │
│  │  ☒ Use 3-D dialogs  ┌─Communications──────────────────┐  │ │
│  │  ☒ Drag and drop    │ ┌Dial type┐ Modem port:         │  │ │
│  │  ☒ Helpful mouse... │ │ ⦿ Tone  │[COM1 - Available ▼] ┌Send mail┐│ │
│  │  ☐ Printer's env.   │ │ ○ Pulse │                     │○ Text   ││ │
│  │    feeder installed │ └─────────┘                     │⦿ Document││ │
│  │                     └─────────────────────────────────┘  │ │
│  └─────────────────────────────────────────────────────────┘ │
│  Sets units of measurement and other Works settings. │ │NUM│ │ │
└─────────────────────────────────────────────────────────────┘
```

3. Make adjustments in your dialog box if necessary.

4. When finished, click the OK button to return to the blank *WORKS* screen.

USING THE ON-LINE HELP FACILITY

WORKS 3.0 has an excellent on-line Help system, which you will explore in this section. It allows you to get assistance on all aspects of *WORKS 3.0*. Dialog boxes all have a HELP button that you can click for assistance on how to use the dialog box. There is even a special Help section that explains how to use Help! The Help menu is the last menu on the right in every menu bar.

IT'S YOUR TURN

With the blank *WORKS* window on your screen,

1. Click the HELP menu.

   The menu will open similar to Figure 1-8.

2. Click the Works Overview command.

   The menu will close and the Works Overview screen shown in Figure 1-9 will appear.

CAUTION

In the future, the selection of commands given in steps 1 and 2 may be summarized as: "Choose Works Overview from the HELP menu." Whenever you see such an instruction, it means to open the designated menu by clicking on the menu name and then selecting the designated command by clicking on the command name.

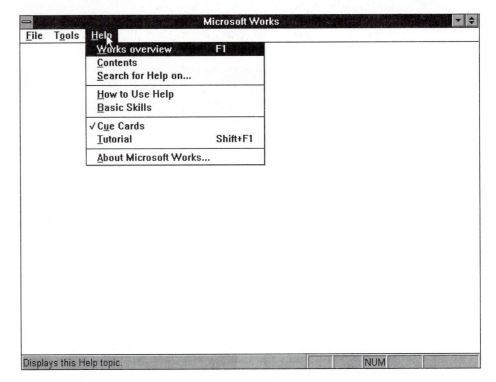

FIGURE 1-8

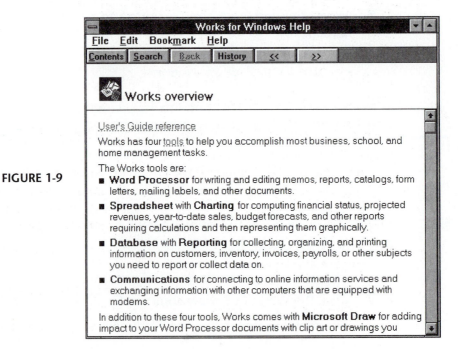

FIGURE 1-9

NAVIGATION BUTTONS

Note the navigation buttons across the top of this screen under the menu bar. Some of them are dark and others are light gray. The dark buttons indicate activities that you can currently access, and the gray buttons mean that the activity is not available at this time. Don't try to use the buttons just yet; instead first read the following explanations about what they can do for you.

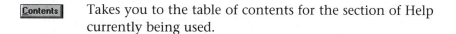 **Contents**	Takes you to the table of contents for the section of Help currently being used.
Search	Lists all the available topics in a new scrolling window. You can use SEARCH to jump directly to a specific topic.
Back	Takes you to the previous screen viewed, regardless of the page order in the Help system.
History	Opens a window containing a list of every Help topic you have viewed since opening Help, with the most recent topics listed first. You can jump directly to any topic by double clicking on it. Of course, the window can be moved and closed just like any other window.
<<	Allows you to examine the preceding topics in the current Help section in page order. Called the BROWSE BACK button, this button is a valuable addition to Help windows. If it is absent or dimmed, there are no preceding topics to browse.
>>	Allows you to examine the succeeding topics in the current Help section in page order. This is called the BROWSE FORWARD button. Like the BROWSE BACK button, if the BROWSE FORWARD is absent or dim, there are no succeeding topics to browse.

IT'S YOUR TURN

1. Read the Works Overview section.

When you get to the end of the screen,

2. Use the vertical scroll bar to display the rest of the material on this topic.

When you finish reading the topic, note the list of underlined items at the end of this section. If you are working on a color computer they will appear in green underlined text. You can jump directly to any one of these items to find out more about *WORKS*.

3. Move the mouse until the pointer is over the line entitled "How to Use Help."

When the mouse is in the proper position, the pointer will turn into a small pointing hand.

4. Click the mouse.

The How to Use Help window will appear. You will investigate it in the next section; but for now you will experiment with a couple of the navigation buttons.

5. Click the BACK button.

You are returned to the Works Overview window.

6. Click the HISTORY button.

The *WORKS* Help History window shown in Figure 1-10 appears with a list of the Help topics you have used.

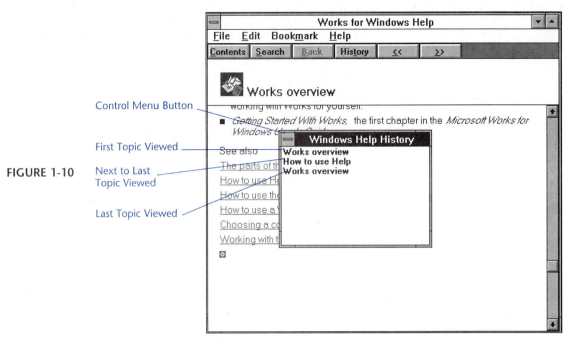

Control Menu Button

First Topic Viewed

FIGURE 1-10

Next to Last
Topic Viewed

Last Topic Viewed

To close the Help History window,

7. Choose Close from the CONTROL menu. (The CONTROL menu is accessed by clicking the button in the upper left corner of the Help History window.)

HOW TO USE HELP

In this exercise you will investigate the special Help section that tells you how to use the Help feature.

IT'S YOUR TURN

From the Works Overview window,

1. Click the topic, "How to Use Help."

You see the window shown in Figure 1-11.

FIGURE 1-11

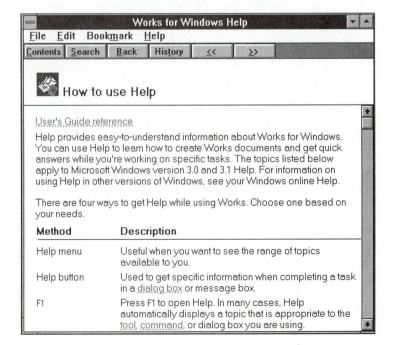

Notice that the first line contains a green, dotted underlined item: "User's Guide reference." Also notice that there is another green, dotted underlined item further down on the page: "dialog box." You may also be able to see more items of this type on your screen. Items displayed in this manner indicate that more information is immediately available to you as described below.

2. Click the "User's Guide reference" item once.

A pop-up screen appears referring you to the page number in the User's Guide for more detailed information on this topic.

3. Click the mouse once anywhere on the screen to put away the pop-up screen.

The pop-up screen disappears.

4. Click the "dialog box" item once.

This time the pop-up screen contains the definition for dialog box.

5. Click the mouse once anywhere on the screen to put away the pop-up screen.

6. Take the time to explore Help as much as you wish.

When you are ready to continue,

7. Click the CONTENTS button.

The Works for Windows Help Contents screen shown in Figure 1-12 will appear.

FIGURE 1-12

THE HELP MENU BAR   You may have noticed that the Help windows have their own menu bars. Whenever Help is active, you can select options from the FILE, EDIT, BOOK-

MARK, and HELP menus. Among the options available to you in these menus are ones that allow you to

- open and print Help files
- set printer options and print topics
- mark topics for future reference
- add your own notes to topics
- copy from Help topics and paste into another document

 CAUTION

Your computer configuration may be set up in such a way that the files needed to complete the next two sections are locked. If so, simply read the sections without attempting the keyboard activities.

USING BOOKMARKS

Just as you place bookmarks in a book to identify favorite passages, so can you place a bookmark in a Help topic to which you refer frequently. When you add a bookmark to a topic, Help adds the topic to the BOOKMARK menu. Then when you want to go to a topic you have marked, you can choose it from the BOOKMARK menu. Suppose you want to have the *WORKS* for Windows Basic Skills section available to you in the BOOKMARK menu. (You should be in the table of contents screen shown in Figure 1-12.)

IT'S YOUR TURN

1. Click the Works for Windows Basic Skills topic.

A screen similar to the one shown in Figure 1-13 will appear.

FIGURE 1-13

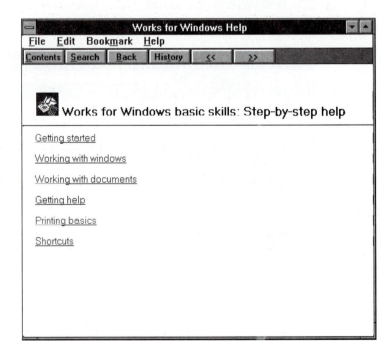

To place a bookmark in this topic,

2. Choose Define from the BOOKMARK menu.

A dialog box similar to Figure 1-14 will appear on your screen.

Note the proposed name that is highlighted in the Name box. If you wish to use another name for this bookmark, you can type it now and

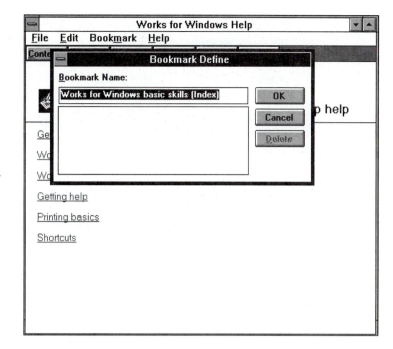

FIGURE 1-14

it will replace the proposed one. However, since this is a good, short, descriptive name, you should accept it as it is.

3. Click the OK button.

The dialog box will disappear, and the name will be added to the BOOKMARK menu options for later use.

To convince yourself that the name has been added and will work the way you want it to,

4. Click the BROWSE FORWARD [>>] button at the top of the Help screen several times until you are at a different topic.

5. Click the BOOKMARK menu.

The menu will drop down, revealing the options shown in Figure 1-15.

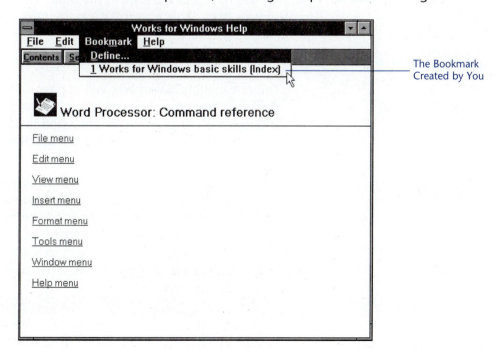

FIGURE 1-15

6. Choose Works for Windows Basic Skills from the BOOKMARK menu.

You will be immediately returned to that Help topic.

You can have as many as nine bookmarks listed on the BOOKMARK menu. As your proficiency with *WORKS 3.0* grows, you may wish to delete some bookmarks. To delete this bookmark, Help must be active.

7. Choose Define from the BOOKMARK menu.

The Bookmark Define dialog box (see Figure 1-14) will appear again with a list of all defined bookmarks. Note that since there is only one bookmark defined, the Works for Windows Basic Skills bookmark has already been inserted into the Bookmark Name text box.

Remember, however, that you may have a list of up to nine bookmarks; so the first thing you would normally do is

8. Click the name of the bookmark you want to delete.

The name you click will become highlighted.

9. Click the DELETE button.

The bookmark name will disappear from the dialog box.

10. Click the OK button.

The bookmark will no longer appear in the menu.

To check that it is indeed gone,

11. Click the BOOKMARK menu to drop it and verify that the bookmark has disappeared from the menu.

12. Click anywhere inside the window to close the menu.

ANNOTATING A HELP TOPIC

You can add your own comments to a Help topic. When you make an annotation, Help places a paper clip icon at the beginning of the topic to remind you that you have added a note to the topic. You should still be at the Works for Windows Basic Skills screen. This is the topic you will annotate.

IT'S YOUR TURN

1. Choose Annotate from the EDIT menu.

The Annotation dialog box will appear with a vertical line blinking in the blank text box. The vertical line is known as the *insertion point*, and it marks the position where typed material will appear. Note that none of the buttons except CANCEL is active since there is nothing to SAVE, DELETE, COPY, or PASTE.

When you type the comment below, do not press the [ENTER] key, even if you think it will take more than one line. Word processing programs automatically move words to the next line if there is insufficient space for them on the present line; this is called *wordwrap.* Do not press [ENTER] unless you wish to start a new paragraph or leave space at that point. If you make a mistake, press [BACKSPACE] and then type the new text.

2. Type: Every student should go through each of these topics at least once.

As you can see from Figure 1-16, the SAVE and COPY buttons are now active.

FIGURE 1-16

3. Click the SAVE button.

   The dialog box goes away, and the paper clip icon appears at the beginning of the Help topic to indicate that it has been annotated (see Figure 1-17).

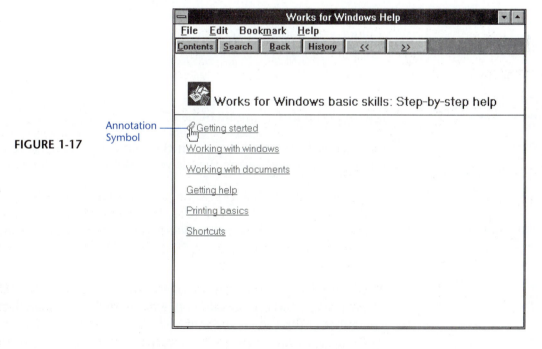

FIGURE 1-17

To display an annotation, you must be in the topic containing the annotation. The paper clip icon acts just like a glossary item. When the mouse is moved to point to it, the cursor changes into the pointing hand icon, as shown in Figure 1-17.

4. Click the paper clip icon.

The Annotation dialog box will appear, showing the annotation. This time the DELETE button is also active.

Since you do not need this annotation, and seeing it would confuse the next student using the computer,

5. Click the DELETE button.

The annotation will be deleted.

FINISHING UP

Usually you will find that you need help when you are working on a project. When this happens, Help is always available to you through the menu bar. Feel free to use it anytime you wish. Meanwhile, explore Help as much as you can at this time. When you are ready to continue, come back to this section.

IT'S YOUR TURN

1. Choose Exit from the FILE menu on the Help window.

You will be returned to the empty *WORKS* window.

2. Choose Exit Works from the FILE menu.

You will be returned to the Windows environment.

3. If the group window containing the Works for Windows icon obscures your screen, minimize it to get it out of the way.

4. Remove your data disk from the floppy drive and store it in a safe place.

5. If you are ready to quit for the day, quit Windows and shut down your computer as directed by your instructor. If not, you can continue with your exploration of *WORKS 3.0*.

SUMMARY

In this chapter you have learned what experience you need to use this book and what computing equipment you need to use *WORKS 3.0*. You have explored the Open dialog box of *WORKS 3.0*, and you have explored and experimented with the Help topics. In the following chapters, you will create and modify documents using the many capabilities of *WORKS 3.0*.

REVIEW QUESTIONS

True/False

1. An ellipsis after a command in a menu indicates that a dialog box will appear when the command is chosen.

2. The extension *.wps after a filename indicates that it is a spreadsheet document.

3. When you choose the OPEN AN EXISTING DOCUMENT button in the Startup dialog box, the files on your data disk will appear.

4. You can find an explanation or definition of any underlined word or phrase on the Help screen by clicking on it.

5. You are allowed only one bookmark in the BOOKMARK menu.

EXERCISES

EXERCISE 1-1   Viewing filenames

1. Launch WORKS and click the CANCEL button when the Startup dialog box appears.

2. Insert your data disk.

3. Open the Artwork directory from your data disk.

4. What extension do the files in this folder have?

5. Click the CANCEL button.

6. Quit *WORKS*.

EXERCISE 1-2   Using Help

1. Launch *WORKS* and click the CANCEL button when the Startup dialog box appears.

2. Choose Basic Skills from the HELP menu.

3. Choose the Working with Windows topic.

4. Choose The Parts of the Works Window topic.

5. Scroll down to the Descriptions section and click on the words Status bar. What menu and dialog box controls the Status bar display?

6. Close the Help window and quit *WORKS*.

CHAPTER 2

Word Processing 1

OBJECTIVES

When you finish this chapter you will be able to

- open and close a word processing document
- insert text
- select and align text
- delete lines
- change fonts and font sizes
- use the Undo option
- move text
- use the Save As option
- use the Print Preview screen
- use Page Setup
- print your document

INTRODUCTION

This chapter introduces you to the word processing module of *WORKS 3.0*. In order to complete the hands-on activities, you will need the practice files from the *WORKS 3.0* data disk that accompanies the Instructor's Manual for this text.

WHAT IS WORD PROCESSING?

Word processing is perhaps the easiest application to understand, as well as the most widely used. A word processing program enables you to use the computer's ability to save text and keystrokes in memory, thus allowing you to make changes before printing a final copy. Correcting typographical mistakes is no longer difficult, and you are able to concentrate on the purpose of writing—to communicate ideas. Revisions are no longer chores but opportunities to improve.

Since 1984, the combination of computers, printers, and word processing software has allowed us to print documents using varied typefaces, styles, and sizes, including headers (text that automatically appears at the top of each page), footers (text that automatically appears at the bottom of each page), and personalized form letters. The *WORKS 3.0* word processor module is versatile and powerful. It includes many of the features found in stand-alone word processing programs. Some of those attractive features allow you to view two parts of the document at one time, format text in columns, incorporate graphics into text, check spelling, and use a built-in thesaurus to check word usage.

An extremely useful feature of word processing programs is that they facilitate collaborative writing. For example, this book was written by several authors, each using the same word processing program. Files were edited and revised until no one had any sense of ownership of any individual part of the manuscript.

SETTING THE SCENE

PROJECT 1   The Announcement

In this and the following chapters, you will be using *WORKS 3.0* to edit or create documents for The Fun Factory, a retail toy store that you own and operate. The Fun Factory is almost ready for business, and you want to distribute a flyer (see Figure 2-1) to announce its grand opening to the neighborhood. You have created a rough draft of the flyer, but you need to make changes in it. The draft is stored on your data disk under the filename *ANNOUNCE*.

FIGURE 2-1

INTRODUCING A NEW
NEIGHBORHOOD TOY STORE

THE FUN FACTORY

Grand Opening
May 4, 1994
1:00 p.m. to 4:00 p.m.

241 Broadway
Evergreen, CA 99999

GETTING STARTED

It is a good idea to organize your hands-on activities and end-of-chapter exercises in a special directory, so you will now create a new directory on your data disk using your last name for the directory name. If you are not using an individual data disk you will need a blank, formatted disk for storing these items. Since this book assumes that you are familiar with Windows 3.1, you should be able to accomplish this task yourself; however, if you need some reminders, follow the steps listed below.

IT'S YOUR TURN

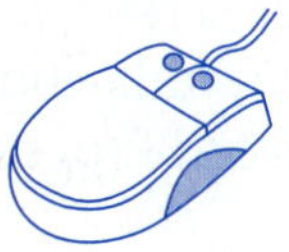

1. Insert your data disk into the floppy drive.
2. Open File Manager from the Main Group of Windows 3.1.
3. Click the drive icon for the drive that contains your data disk.
4. Choose Create Directory from the FILE menu.
5. Type your last name into the Name text box of the Create Directory dialog box.
6. Click the OK button.

    An additional directory will appear on your data disk named with the first eight letters of your name.

7. Remove the data disk and use a felt tip pen to write your name on the disk label.

To put away the File Manager,

8. Choose Exit from the FILE menu.

To put away the Main group window,

9. Click the MINIMIZE button.

OPENING THE FILE

The following instructions for opening a file assume that you are using an individual data disk. If you are not, you will need to adapt the instructions to your particular circumstances.

IT'S YOUR TURN

1. Launch *WORKS 3.0.*

    The Startup dialog box will appear on your screen.

2. Insert your data disk into the floppy disk drive.

3. Click the OPEN AN EXISTING DOCUMENT button.

    The Open dialog box will appear on the screen with the drive containing the *MSWORKS* directory selected.

To open the Drives drop-down list,

4. Click the Drives box.

When the Drives drop-down list appears,

5. Click the drive designator for the drive containing your data disk.

    The dialog box will change to show the files stored on your data disk.

6. Double click the *ANNOUNCE.WPS* filename in the File Name list box.

| CAUTION | In the future, whenever we want you to open a file we will not itemize the steps as we have done in steps 2 through 6 above. Instead, we will abbreviate these steps into the statement, "Open the *XXXXXXXX* file from your data disk." |

The file will open into a Word Processing window, and your screen will be similar either to Figure 2-2, with the Cue Cards window overlaying the Word Processing window or to Figure 2-3, with only the Word Processing window showing.

7. If your screen looks like Figure 2-2, read the next paragraph and follow steps 8 and 9. If it looks like Figure 2-3, read the remainder of this section for your information only—do not perform the steps.

Cue Cards are part of the Help system. They offer step-by-step instructions for basic tasks. When you need them, you can follow the instructions

FIGURE 2-2

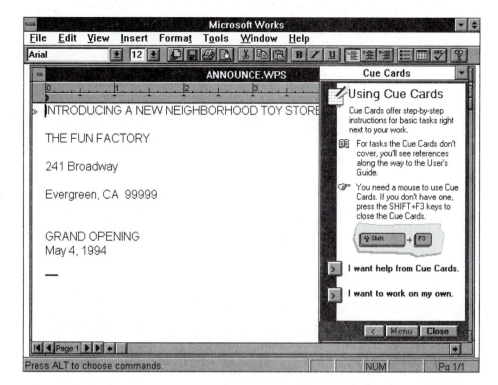

FIGURE 2-3

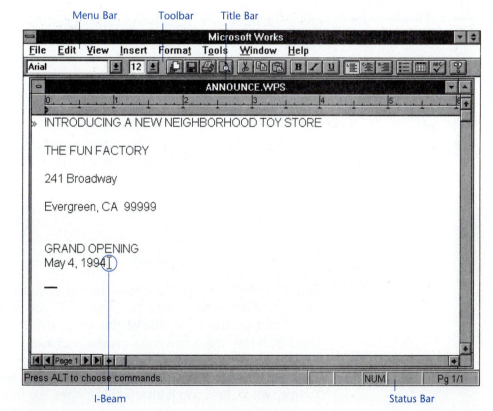

in a Cue Card as you work in a *WORKS* document. Since you will not be using Cue Cards for the activities in this text, you will now turn them off, as follows.

8. Click the HELP menu.

    The menu will drop down, showing the options available. Note that the Cue Cards option has a checkmark in front of it.

To turn off Cue Cards,

9. Click the Cue Cards option.

The checkmark goes away, the menu closes, and the Cue Cards window disappears. Your screen should now look like Figure 2-3.

CAUTION | Depending upon the previous user of your computer, you may or may not see certain special characters displayed on your document. When the All Characters command (see the VIEW menu) has a checkmark in front of it, your document will display paragraph symbols (¶) representing the number of times the [ENTER] key was pressed, dots between words representing the number of times the spacebar was pressed, and right-pointing arrows for each time the [TAB] key was pressed (your ANNOUNCE file did not use any tabs). If this command is turned off, only the beginning of document symbol [»] and the end of document symbol (short dark line) will display. This command stays on or off for all word processing documents until it is changed. None of the figures in this chapter show these characters.

INSERTING TEXT

As you can see from Figure 2-3, the Grand Opening hours were omitted from the announcement. Follow the instructions below to add the open hours, 1:00 p.m. to 4:00 p.m., below the date.

IT'S YOUR TURN

1. Move the I-beam (it marks the present position of the mouse and is shown in Figure 2-3) to the right of the date in the last line, and click once.

If you have the All Characters command on, the insertion point should be blinking before the ¶ symbol. It marks the position for your next action.

To add another line to the file,

2. Press [ENTER] once.

The insertion point moves to the next line.

Before typing the numbers, look to the bottom right of your window. If you see NUM in the Status bar, you can type numbers by using the numeric pad on the right side of the keyboard. If NUM does not appear in the Status bar, the arrow keys on the numeric pad can be used to control cursor movement just like the separate arrow keys. The NUM mode is controlled by the [NUM LOCK] key on the numeric keypad. [NUM LOCK] is a *toggle switch.* Pressing it alternately causes the numeric pad to enter NUM mode and record numeric data input; or leave NUM mode off and record cursor movement. If you do not have separate cursor movement keys, you should turn off NUM mode so you can use the numeric pad for cursor movement and use the numbers above the alphabet keys for numeric input.

3. Type: 1:00 p.m. to 4:00 p.m.

4. Press [ENTER] once.

SELECTING AND ALIGNING TEXT

The announcement would look much better if all the lines were centered. Across the top of the screen, *WORKS* provides a ***toolbar*** containing a button that enables you to do just that. If you do not see the toolbar just above the title bar, as in Figure 2-4, the toolbar has been turned off.

FIGURE 2-4

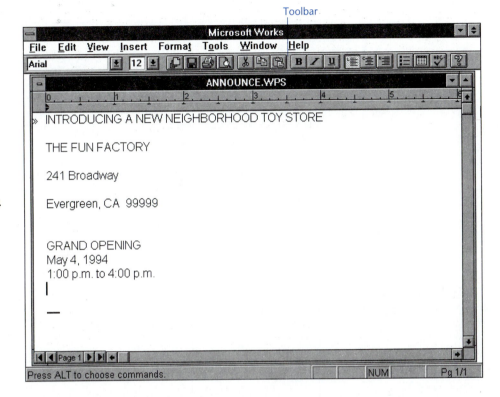

IT'S YOUR TURN

1. If the toolbar is not displayed, pull down the VIEW menu and choose Toolbar.

    The toolbar will appear above the title bar. The toolbar also contains buttons used for changing fonts and font sizes; saving files; printing and previewing files; cutting, copying, and pasting text; changing the text style; inserting bullets into a list; creating tables; invoking the spelling checker; and jumping to the *WORKS* Startup dialog box or the Learning Works dialog box.

In order to perform actions such as centering sections of text, you must first select (or highlight) the section to be affected. You can select text for editing in several ways.

To Select This:	Do This:
A character	Drag (hold down the mouse button while you move the mouse) over the character to be selected
A word	Double click on the word
A line	Click in the left margin beside the line. (When the cursor is in this area, the I-beam changes to an arrow pointing to the right. You can select more than one line by holding down the mouse button and dragging the pointer [arrow] down.)

To Select This:	Do This:
A paragraph	Double click in the left margin beside the paragraph.
An entire document	Choose Select All from the EDIT menu or hold down the [CTRL] key and click in the left margin.

CAUTION	You will not see a difference between selecting lines and paragraphs in the *ANNOUNCE* document because each line is a paragraph. A paragraph in word processing is defined as text ending with an [ENTER].

To center the document,

2. Select the entire document. (Either choose Select All from the EDIT menu, as shown in Figure 2-5, or hold down the [CTRL] Key and click in the left margin.)

FIGURE 2-5

The entire Announce document will become highlighted. Your screen should resemble the one shown in Figure 2-6.

FIGURE 2-6

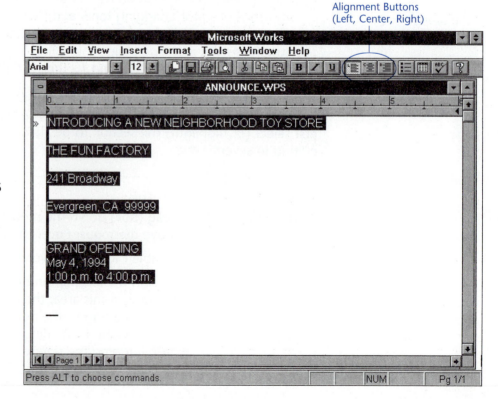

3. Move the I-beam up to the toolbar.

The I-beam will become a left-pointing arrow when you move off the document work area and into the toolbar area. Note that the I-beam and the arrow perform the same function—to indicate the location of the mouse. When the pointer is in the working area where you type, it is an I-beam. Anywhere else, it is usually an arrow. Also note that as you point to a toolbar button for a few seconds, the name of the button is displayed.

There are three buttons in the alignment group. They control the following:

Left alignment	Text appears flush against the left side with a ragged right side
Center alignment	Text appears centered horizontally in the print area with ragged left and right sides
Right alignment	Text appears flush against the right side with a ragged left side

WORKS provides another alignment option—full justification—in which text appears flush against both left and right sides with spaces added within the text. To access the Full Justification option, you must select Paragraph from the FORMAT menu and select the Justified option under Indents and Alignment.

4. Click the Center Alignment button.

Notice that when you clicked the button, it became selected and each line of the document was immediately centered.

5. Click anywhere on the screen to deselect the text.

Your screen should resemble the one shown in Figure 2-7.

FIGURE 2-7

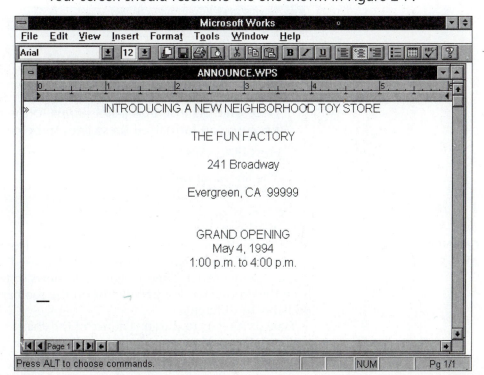

Step 5 is very important. If any key is accidentally touched while text is selected, the selection will disappear and be replaced by the inadvertently touched key. The section on the Undo option presented later in this chapter will explain this in more detail.

DELETING LINES

The blank line between the street address and the city/state lines should be removed.

IT'S YOUR TURN

1. Move the I-beam anywhere on the blank line between the street address and the city/state (see Figure 2-8).

FIGURE 2-8

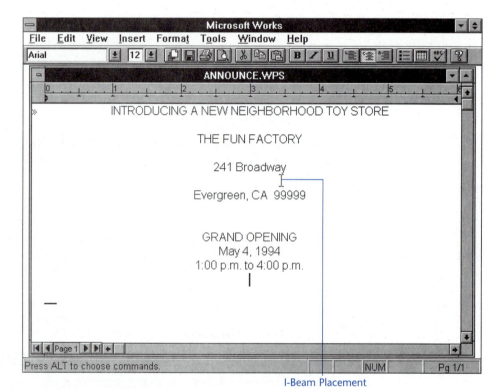

I-Beam Placement

2. Click to place the insertion point.

   Note that the insertion point jumps to the center of the line. This is because you formatted these lines to be centered in the last section.

3. Press [BACKSPACE].

   The line disappears.

CHANGING FONTS AND SIZES

The styles and sizes of typefaces (called fonts) depend upon your system's capabilities. The term *font* refers to the design used to print characters (for example, Courier, Arial, Times). Figure 2-9 shows some common fonts available from the drop-down Font Name list on the toolbar. Your Font name list will probably be different.

Type style refers to the appearance of the characters (**bold**, *italic,* underline, and ~~strikethrough~~ are available in *WORKS 3.0* for Windows). Bold, Italic, and

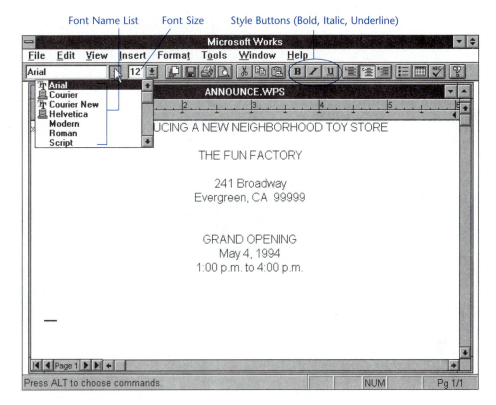

FIGURE 2-9

Underline styles can be created by clicking buttons on the toolbar. Strike-through can be accessed by choosing Font and Style from the FORMAT menu.

Type size refers to the height and width of a letter. When choosing the size, the larger the number you choose, the larger the print. Type size is measured in points. One point is equal to $1/72$ of an inch. When you choose a 12-point type size you are choosing type that requires a line height of $12/72$ or $1/6$ of an inch. The width of the type varies with the font. The available sizes will vary according to which font is chosen. Font sizes are listed in the drop-down Font Size list on the toolbar.

To add a little variety to the announcement, you will now change the type-face of the first line and increase the size of the text. The Font Name and Font Size buttons on the toolbar always show the current font settings for selected text. If the selected text contains more than one font and size, the buttons are blank. If no text is selected, the font name and font size of the word in which the insertion point rests is shown. If you select a different option, it will only be applied to the selected text. You can change font, type style, and size anywhere within a document. You do not have to use the same font for an entire document.

IT'S YOUR TURN

1. Select the first line. (Drag to select, or move the I-beam into the left margin beside the line containing the word "Introducing." When the I-beam becomes a right arrow, click once).

2. Choose any font you like from the Font Name drop-down list on the toolbar.

    Do you see the change in the type? If you don't like the one you chose, you can try another font. Keep changing the font style until you find one that pleases you. (We chose Times New Roman.)

With the line still highlighted,

3. Choose 18 or 24 from the Font Size drop-down list on the toolbar.

    The line now appears in large letters and may appear on two lines.

4. Click the BOLD button on the toolbar (see Figure 2-9).

    Figure 2-10 shows the announcement using 24 point Times New Roman font for the heading. Note that the heading is still selected.

FIGURE 2-10

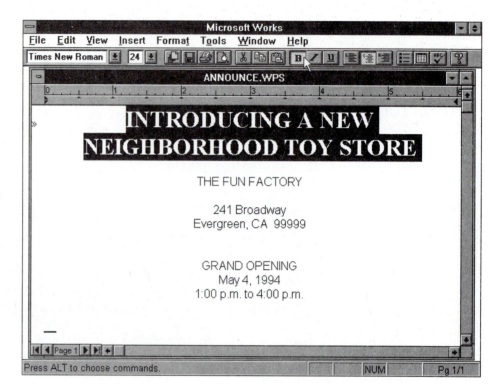

5. Leave the heading selected for the next section's activity.

USING THE UNDO OPTION

It is very important that you deselect text after you reformat it. Here's an exercise to illustrate a problem that may occur if you don't. First, the introductory line should still be selected (highlighted).

IT'S YOUR TURN

1. Select the introductory line again if it is not already selected.

2. Press [BACKSPACE].

    The entire heading has disappeared! But don't panic; you are still formatting the selected text, so undoing the damage is easy.

3. Choose Undo Editing from the EDIT menu.

    The introduction line reappears. You will find the Undo command extremely helpful. Whenever you do something you wish you hadn't, simply use the Undo command before you do anything else.

KEYBOARD SHORTCUTS

Shortcut keys are key combinations that can be used to achieve the same result as mouse selections. Experienced users of programs often use the shortcuts for frequently used menu options instead of the mouse. These shortcuts are sometimes shown on the menu to the right of the command. To carry out a shortcut such as [CTRL] + B (to bold text), hold down the first key ([CTRL]) while typing the second (the letter B). The keyboard shortcut for Undo (as in step 3 above) uses [CTRL] + Z.

MOVING TEXT

Another advantage of word processing is the ease with which text can be moved. How many times have you written something and wished that you could erase it and insert it elsewhere? Word processing programs handle this problem easily through a process called ***cut and paste.*** To illustrate how simple the process is, you will move the address lines of The Fun Factory to the end of the announcement.

IT'S YOUR TURN

1. Move the cursor into the line above 241 Broadway and drag down to select that blank line and the following two lines of the address.

   These are the lines to be moved. Your screen should resemble the one in Figure 2-11 after you have made the selection.

FIGURE 2-11

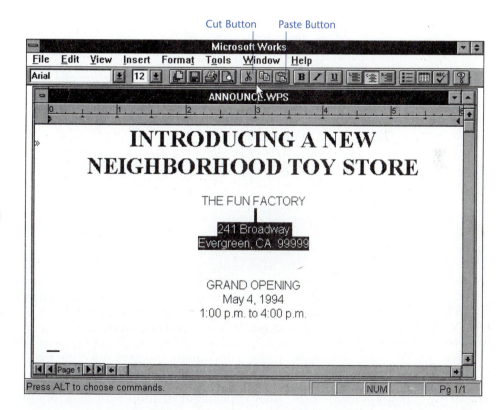

2. Click the CUT button on the Toolbar. (It's the button with a picture of a pair of scissors on it.)

   The lines disappear, but don't worry; they are still stored in the computer in a special memory area known as the ***clipboard.***

3. Move the cursor to the last line of the announcement (below the Grand Opening hours) and click to place the insertion point.

4. Click the PASTE button on the Toolbar. (It's third from the left in the Edit group and has a picture of a clipboard on it.)

The address lines are pasted in from the clipboard.

SAVING A FILE UNDER A DIFFERENT NAME

At the present time, your revision exists only on the screen and in the memory of your computer. If the power goes off, you have to start over with the original version of Announce, because the computer does not automatically save a file as you edit it.

When you view the FILE menu shown in Figure 2-12, you will note that *WORKS* presents you with two save commands: Save and Save As.

FIGURE 2-12

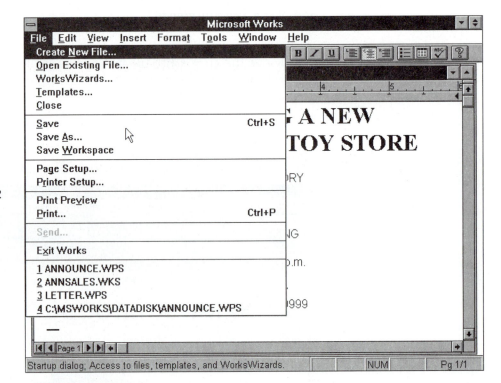

The Save command should be used only after a new document has been given a permanent name with Save As. It is used to save the currently active document. If changes were made to a stored file, the current version replaces the old document.

The Save As command is used to

- name a document and save it for the first time
- rename a document
- save a document in a different directory or on a different drive
- save documents as templates (a special *WORKS 3.0* format that can easily be reused)
- save documents in special formats compatible with other applications

By completing the following steps, your revision of *ANNOUNCE* will be saved with a different filename in your name directory on your own data disk so that the original file will remain unchanged in case you want to repeat this section at another time. You will name the new file *ANNOUNC2* to conform with the requirement that filenames be limited to eight characters.

IT'S YOUR TURN

1. Choose Save As from the FILE menu.

    The Save As dialog box shown in Figure 2-13 appears with the drive designator of your data disk displayed as the current directory. The Directories List box should also include the name directory that you created earlier in this chapter.

FIGURE 2-13

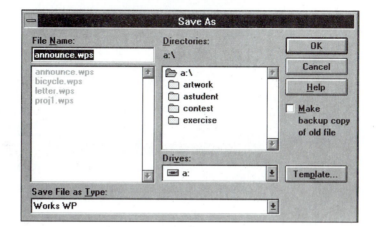

2. Double click your name directory folder if it is not already listed as the active directory.

    It will open and will become the currently active directory.

3. Click to place the insertion point immediately following the word "Announce" in the Filename text box. See Figure 2-14.

FIGURE 2-14

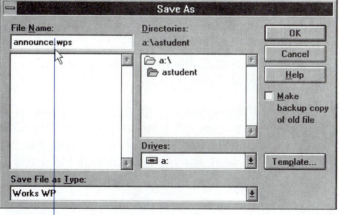

The Insertion Point Should Be Blinking
Immediately Following the "e"

4. Press [BACKSPACE].

5. Type: 2

    The filename is now *ANNOUNC2*. The Save As dialog box should look like Figure 2-15, except that the directory name will be the first eight letters of your name. (*Note:* You could have simply typed out the filename *ANNOUNC2*. It is not necessary to type the extension, as *WORKS* automatically does that for you).

Print Preview Button

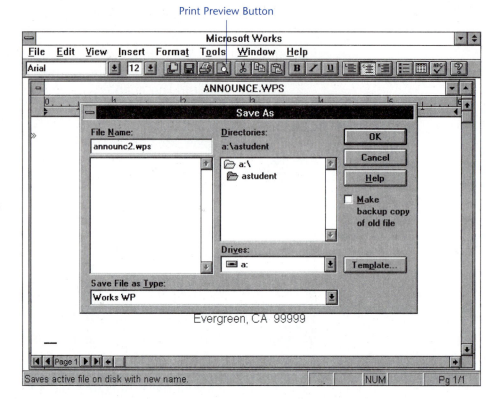

FIGURE 2-15

To complete the save,

6. Click the OK button.

    A Warning dialog box appears asking if you will be saving to a floppy
    disk other than the current one.

Since your data disk is already in the drive,

7. Click the NO button.

    Note that the status bar (bottom left) shows the saving progress in
    percentage.

When the saving is complete, the filename in the title bar of the document
on your screen will have changed to *ANNOUNCE2.WPS*. The revised announcement now exists on your data disk, as well as in the computer's
memory. Also, the old **ANNOUNCE** file is still intact on your data disk.

USING PRINT PREVIEW

Before you print your announcement, it is a good idea to see how it will look
on paper. *WORKS* includes a Print Preview option that allows you to examine
the appearance of your document before printing it.

IT'S YOUR TURN

1. Choose Print Preview from the FILE menu or click the PRINT PREVIEW
    button on the toolbar (it's the button between the one with the pair
    of scissors and the one with the printer in Figure 2-15).

    The Print Preview screen shown in Figure 2-16 will appear showing
    your document as it will look when printed.

FIGURE 2-16

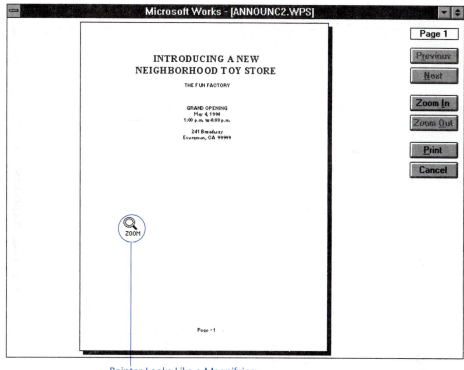

Pointer Looks Like a Magnifying
Glass When It Is on the Document

2. Move the mouse to place the cursor on the document portion of the screen.

   The cursor will change into a magnifying glass when it is on the document portion of the screen.

3. Move the magnifying glass until it is over some text that you would like to examine more closely.

4. Click the mouse when the magnifying glass is in position.

   Your screen will change to show the enlarged text.

5. Click the mouse again.

   When you use the magnifying glass, the magnified screen will automatically be positioned to show the portion of text that was under the magnifying glass when you clicked. You can scroll the magnified screen, as you will do in step 6, to see other parts of the document.

   The text is now in its full size. If you click again, it will revert to the original print preview screen.

But, before you do that,

6. Use the horizontal and vertical scroll bars to scroll up and down the page and from side to side.

   You can examine the entire full-size document and see how it will look when it is printed.

When you are finished,

7. Click with the magnifying glass cursor one more time.

The screen now displays the original Print Preview document.

8.   Look at the buttons on the right side of the screen.

Button	Use
PAGE 1	Tells you that you are on page 1 of this document.
PREVIOUS	Is used in multi-paged documents to turn back to the previous page; it is not active for this single-page document.
NEXT	Is used in multi-paged documents to turn forward to the next page; it is not active for this single-page document.
ZOOM IN	Selecting this button causes the document to be enlarged to its next larger size. When the document has reached its full size on the screen, this button becomes inactive.
ZOOM OUT	Selecting this button causes the document to be reduced to its next smaller size. When the document has reached its smallest size on the screen, this button becomes inactive.
PRINT	Selecting this button causes the document to be printed directly from the Print Preview screen.
CANCEL	Selecting this button causes the Print Preview screen to be closed and returns you to the Word Processing window.

9.   Click the CANCEL button.

Now you are back in the word processing document.

USING PAGE SETUP

The Page Setup option in the FILE menu allows you to

- select paper size and source
- print horizontally or vertically
- change page margin sizes
- set the first page number
- print footnotes at the bottom of each page or at the end of the document

When you save a document, *WORKS* stores your Page Setup settings with the document. In general, this dialog box enables you to choose paper size, select margins, print vertically or horizontally, and control page numbering and footnotes.

Page margins determine the page area available for text and graphics. You can reset page margins at any time by using the Page Setup command in the FILE menu. The margins you set affect the entire document.

CAUTION

Page margins are a different concept from left and right indents, which are set using the Paragraph command from the FORMAT menu and which affect only selected paragraphs. You will work with left and right indents in Chapter 3.

When you start *WORKS*, the page size is preset for letter-size paper, 8.5 by 11 inches (or 21 centimeters by 29.7 centimeters), and page orientation is vertical (upright or portrait). You will not change these settings unless you are certain they need changing.

After viewing your printed announcement, you decide that it would probably look better if it were printed horizontally (also referred to as **landscape,** sideways, or broadside). Therefore, some options need to be changed before printing. When you choose the horizontal orientation, the width of the paper changes to 11 inches instead of 8.5 inches. To center the announcement and maintain the current line endings, you will change the left and right margins. The ruler just below the title bar shows that your document is six inches wide. This means that you have five inches to divide between the left and right margins (2.5 inches for each margin).

IT'S YOUR TURN

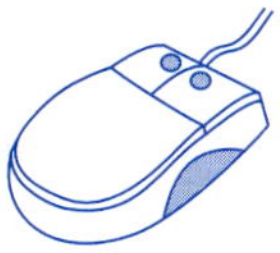

1. Choose Page Setup from the FILE menu.

FIGURE 2-17

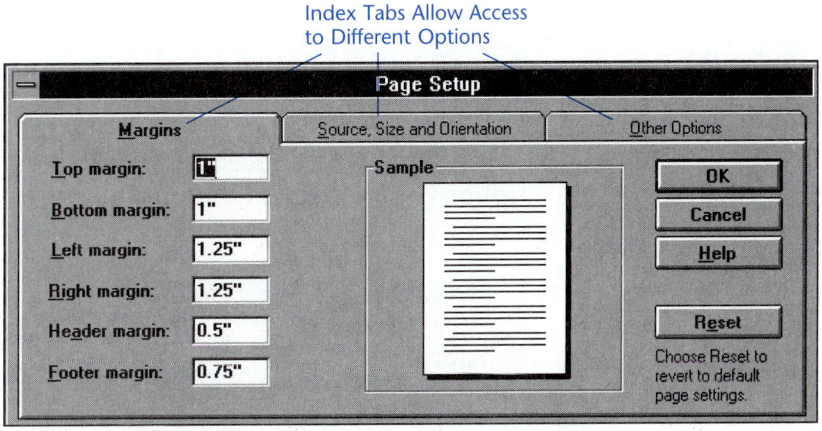

Index Tabs Allow Access
to Different Options

Page Setup

| Margins | Source, Size and Orientation | Other Options |

Top margin: 1"
Bottom margin: 1"
Left margin: 1.25"
Right margin: 1.25"
Header margin: 0.5"
Footer margin: 0.75"

Sample

OK
Cancel
Help

Reset
Choose Reset to
revert to default
page settings.

To change the orientation,

2. Click the index tab marked "Source, Size and Orientation."

3. Click Landscape in the Orientation block

   Note that the paper size did not change, but the width and height did change.

Now, to change the margins,

4. Click the Margins index tab.

5. Double click the Top Margin box.

   It will become highlighted so that anything you type will replace its current contents.

6. Type: 2.5

7. Double click the Left Margin box.

8. Type: 2.5

9. Double click the Right Margin box.

10. Type: 2.5

11. Click the OK button or press [ENTER].

HINT   To avoid any misunderstandings, this book tells you specifically which dialog box buttons to click. However, you should be aware that you can press [ENTER] to accept the broadly outlined option buttons, such as OK in step 9. This is especially helpful when you are already using the keyboard, as you are in this sequence.

12. Use Print Preview to examine the document again.

It is possible for you to print from the Print Preview window; however, for this first time, you will use the menu.

13. Click the CANCEL button to return to the document.

PRINTING A FILE

As you are preparing a document, it is good practice to use Print Preview frequently. When you are finished and ready to print to paper, there will be no surprises. To print your announcement,

IT'S YOUR TURN

1. Turn on your printer and be sure it is ready to print.

2. Choose Print from the FILE menu.

You will see a Print dialog box similar to Figure 2-18. It offers many options. The options that are currently selected are clearly marked.

FIGURE 2-18

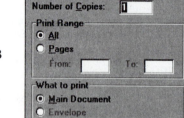

3. If the dialog box on your screen does not show the same selected options as those in Figure 2-18, click the appropriate buttons on your screen to make the boxes agree.

Don't worry if you make a mistake. Nothing happens until you click the OK button in the next step.

4. When your dialog box is correct, click the OK button.

Be patient—it may take a few seconds for printing to begin. You will see the printing message before printing begins.

FINISHING UP PROJECT 1

Now that you have printed your revised announcement, you should save it on disk, put the file away, and quit *WORKS* if you are through for the day.

IT'S YOUR TURN

1. Choose Save from the FILE menu since you have already named it with the new filename.

The file will be saved together with the changes to margins and page orientation.

Note: If you are continuing with the exercises for this chapter or going on to the next chapter, do not exit *WORKS*. Otherwise,

2. Choose Exit Works from the FILE menu.

    Both *WORKS 3.0* and your file will be put away properly.

3. If necessary, minimize the group window containing the *WORKS* for Windows icon.

4. Remove your data disk from the floppy drive and store it in a safe place.

5. Exit Windows and turn off the computer, or leave the computer as directed by your instructor.

SUMMARY

Congratulations! You have learned a lot while working on your announcement flyer. You should now be able to open and close word processing files, use *WORKS 3.0* menus and dialog boxes, insert and delete text, center text, change type size and style, save files, use the Print Preview option, and print documents.

REVIEW QUESTIONS

True/False

1. A checkmark next to a command in a menu means that the option is on.

2. When dots and paragraph symbols appear between characters, choose UNDO from the Edit menu to remove them.

3. To select text for editing, you must first highlight it.

4. The Undo option is found in the FORMAT menu.

5. It is possible to initiate printing from the Print Preview window.

6. The larger the font size number, the larger the print.

7. When you "cut" selected text, you have removed it from its current location.

8. When you use the Save As option, you are replacing the original file with the edited one.

9. When you close a file, you have exited from the *WORKS* application.

10. The clipboard is a temporary storage area in the computer's memory.

EXERCISES

EXERCISE 2-1 Modifying the INVITE file

(Change text styles and sizes, center lines, add text, change margins)

1. Open the **INVITE** file from the *EXERCISES* directory on your data disk.

2. Change the size of the first two lines to 14 point, make them bold, then center both lines.

3. Add the following closing after the last sentence. Leave one blank line between the last sentence and the closing. Press [ENTER] four times to leave three blank lines between the closing and your name.

Sincerely yours,

(Type your name)

4. Use the Page Setup option and change the left and right margins to 1.2 inches.

5. Save as *EX2-1* in your name directory on your data disk. (If you do not see your directory, double click the opened file folder of your drive.)

6. Preview and print if requested by your instructor.

7. Close the file.

EXERCISE 2-2   Modifying the *INVITE* file

(Change text styles and sizes, center- and right-align lines, add/replace text)

1. Open the **INVITE** file.

2. Select the first two lines, change the font and increase its point size to 18. Use bold and italic for the name of the store. Bold the date of the sale. Center both lines.

3. Right-align your name after the last sentence, leaving one blank line between the sentence and your name.

4. Save as *EX2-2* in your name directory on your data disk.

5. Preview and print if requested by your instructor.

6. Close the file.

EXERCISE 2-3   Creating and formatting an announcement

1. Open the **ANNOUNCE** file and change it to create an announcement to open your own store.

2. Include your name and the current date in the announcement.

3. Change the name of the store and use as many style options as you wish to make the announcement attractive.

4. Center the announcement.

5. Save as *EX2-3* in your name directory on your data disk.

6. Print if requested by your instructor.

Word Processing 2

OBJECTIVES

When you finish this chapter you will be able to

- *use the ruler and the scroll bars*
- *adjust left, right, and first line indent markers*
- *place the current date in a document*
- *understand the toolbar*
- *stylize a letterhead*
- *find and change text throughout a document*
- *print a document using the Print Preview screen*
- *create a new file*
- *create hanging paragraphs*
- *count words in a document*
- *add headers and footers*

SETTING THE SCENE

PROJECT 1   The Contest Letter

The Fun Factory has decided to sponsor a contest for local elementary school students. The contest will offer a fifty-dollar gift certificate to three students—one each from grades four through six—for the best essay on the topic "How Toys Help Students Learn."

GETTING STARTED

A first draft of a letter to the school principal is stored on your data disk. This letter must be changed before it is ready to mail. As you work through the activities for this project, you will make those changes. Figure 3-1 displays the completed letter.

IT'S YOUR TURN

1. Launch *WORKS 3.0* and open the word processing file, *LETTER.WPS* from the data disk.

   Your screen will resemble the one shown in Figure 3-2.

Before editing your letter, you will check to see if the Wrap for Window command is on. This command, like many other commands, stays on or off unless changed by the user. If this command is off, you may not always

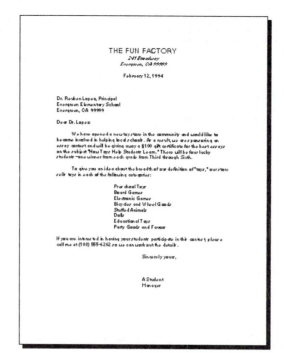

FIGURE 3-1

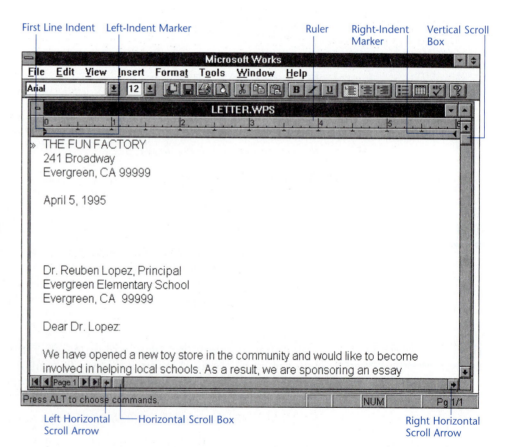

First Line Indent   Left-Indent Marker   Ruler   Right-Indent Marker   Vertical Scroll Box

FIGURE 3-2

Left Horizontal Scroll Arrow   Horizontal Scroll Box   Right Horizontal Scroll Arrow

see the ending of each line in your document. The Wrap for Window command in the VIEW menu allows you to control this situation.

2. Open the VIEW menu and click Wrap for Window if it is not already selected (a checkmark indicates this command is on as shown in Figure 3-3).

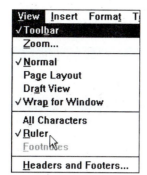

FIGURE 3-3

When this command is on, text in a word processing document will fit within your window, regardless of the location of the right-indent marker. However, when you print, the lines will wrap at the right margin. (The Print Preview window will also show the actual line endings.) You will probably find it convenient to always leave this command on.

USING THE RULER AND SCROLL BARS

Before you begin to make changes in the letter you must be able to scroll through the entire document and use the ruler.

IT'S YOUR TURN

1. Click anywhere in the horizontal scroll bar to the right of the scroll box. (Check Figure 3-2 for the placement of the scroll bar and box.)

   Your screen is blank or almost blank. But, look at the top of the screen where the ruler is located. Note that the measurements on the ruler have changed.

To see how many inches the ruler measures,

2. Click the right horizontal scroll arrow (shown in Figure 3-2) several times until the ruler reaches 21" and refuses to advance anymore.

   This shows you that you could compose a document occupying 21 inches of horizontal space.

To return to the left side of the document quickly,

3. Drag the horizontal scroll box (see Figure 3-2 to find it) from the far right of the horizontal scroll bar back to the farthest left position on the horizontal scroll bar.

   Your screen should look like Figure 3-2 again.

To experiment with the vertical scroll bar, box, and arrows,

4. Drag the vertical scroll box to the middle of the vertical scroll bar.

   Your screen will change to look similar to Figure 3-4. The scroll boxes mark the relative position of text within the file. Because you moved the vertical scroll box to the middle of the vertical scroll bar, the middle of the letter is displayed. In step 2 above, when you dragged the horizontal scroll box all the way to the left, the left side of the document was displayed.

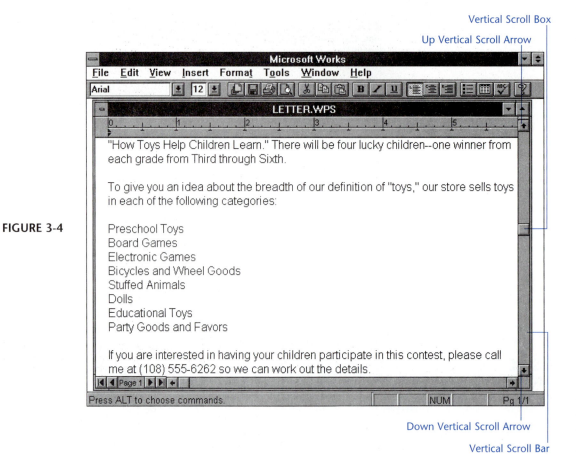

FIGURE 3-4

5. Move the mouse to point to the down vertical scroll arrow and either click several times or hold down the mouse button.

   The text will scroll by rapidly, appearing to move up the screen as you scroll down through the document.

Now, to try it in the other direction,

6. Move the mouse to the up vertical scroll arrow and hold down the mouse button as you scroll the document. Note the text scrolling down. Stop when you have reached the beginning of the document.

   Your screen should look like the one in Figure 3-2 again. Notice that the ruler is showing at the top of the *LETTER* window; you will now learn how to hide the ruler to leave more space for text.

7. Choose Ruler from the VIEW menu, as shown in Figure 3-5.

   The ruler disappears and the check mark disappears from the Ruler command in the VIEW menu.

8. Choose Ruler from the VIEW menu.

   Now the ruler is back again. You can use the ruler to set indents, and tab stops in inches, centimeters, picas, points, or millimeters. The ruler measurement unit is changed through the Options command in the TOOLS menu. The default measurement unit is in inches, the measurement unit used in this text.

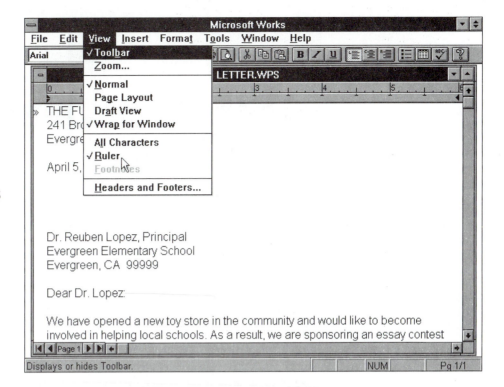

FIGURE 3-5

CHANGING THE INDENT MARKERS ON THE RULER

It is time to use the ruler. The ruler contains icons on the left and right side that allow you to quickly change the indentation of any paragraph or the entire document. The two triangles you see on the left of the ruler are the ***first line indent*** and the ***left-indent markers.*** The single triangle on the right side of the ruler is the ***right-indent marker.*** An ***indent*** is the amount of space an item is separated from the margin (the first line of a paragraph, for example). Margins are set through the Page Setup dialog box and are the same for the entire document. You will learn to manipulate the left and right page margins later in the chapter. Indents can be set either separately for selected paragraphs or for the entire document by selecting all of it before changing the indents. Indents are measured from the page margins.

The *LETTER* document was saved with left and right page margins of 1.25 inches each. That leaves six inches of space for text on standard 8.5-inch wide paper. The text space is the space delineated by the ruler. The zero position on the ruler corresponds to the left margin of the text and, in the *LETTER* file, the six-inch position on the ruler corresponds to the right margin of the text. Figure 3-6 shows the completed letter with margins and indents.

You will now use the indent markers to change the appearance of your letter. However, before you do, you will take a quick look at what the letter would look like if it were printed now.

IT'S YOUR TURN

1. Choose Print Preview from the FILE menu.

   The Print Preview screen shown in Figure 3-7 appears.

This is a miniature picture of what your letter would look like if it were printed now. Although it looks nice and neat, there is a lot you can do to add to its appearance. To return to the document,

2. Click the CANCEL button on the right of the Print Preview screen.

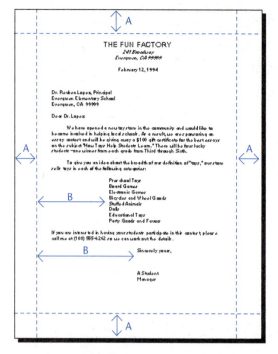

FIGURE 3-6

A: Default left, right, top,
& bottom Margins

B: Left Indents

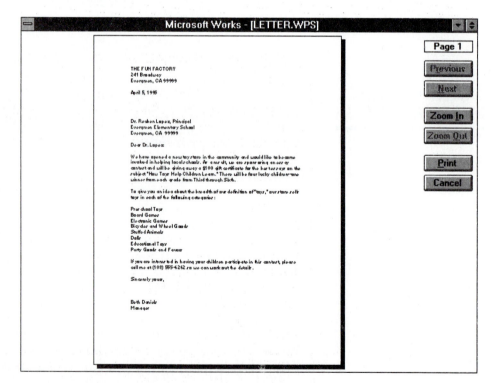

FIGURE 3-7

| HINT | Pressing the [ESC] key is another way of cancelling. |

You are returned to the document, as shown in Figure 3-2.

3. Choose Select All from the EDIT menu.

   Even if you cannot see it all, the entire document will become high-lighted to show it is selected.

4. Drag the right-indent marker (see Figure 3-2) from its current position of 6 inches to the 5-inch mark.

If your screen does not display the right-indent marker, click on the Right Scroll arrow until it does.

When you release the right-indent marker, notice that the right side of each paragraph has been reset and the text reformatted.

5. Use the vertical scroll bar to scroll to the end of the letter so you can see the effect of the right-indent change. You can click and hold on the down arrow until the end of the letter comes into view; you can drag the scroll box (the box in the scroll bar that indicates your approximate position in the file) all the way to the bottom of the scroll bar; or you can click in the bar below the scroll box to move the scroll box to the end of the letter.

Notice that only long paragraphs that take more than one line are affected by moving the right indent.

To return to the beginning of the letter in preparation for the next activity,

6. Use the vertical scroll bar to scroll to the beginning of the letter.

When the scroll box is all the way at either end of the vertical scroll bar, you are at either the beginning or the end of the file.

7. Look at the ruler again. (See Figure 3-8.)

FIGURE 3-8

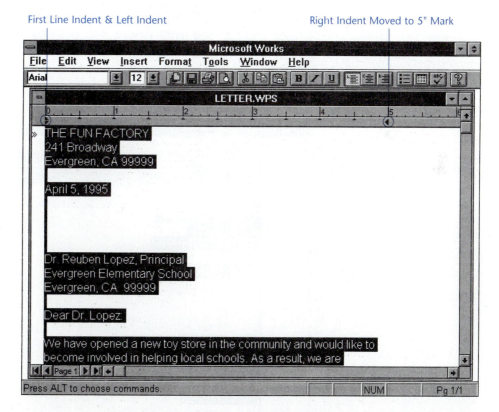

Even though there is no visual indication that the right margin is set at the six-inch mark, you will not be able to move the right-indent marker beyond the position that *WORKS* initially sets as the default line length for every document. Since standard paper size is 8.5 inches wide, *WORKS* subtracts the 2.5 inches needed for left and right margins and automatically sets the right indent at the maximum line length of six inches. You cannot exceed that mark unless you change the margins, as you will do later in this chapter.

The entire document should still be selected. To see what happens when you try to exceed the maximum,

8. Drag the right indent to the right, just beyond the six-inch mark. **You may have to use the scroll bar to bring the six-inch mark on the ruler into view.**

   As you can see, *WORKS* returns the right indent to its previous setting; it will not let you move *beyond* the margin presently set for this document.

To return to that maximum setting for the right indent,

9. Drag the right indent to the right and leave it at the six-inch mark.

Now you will practice manipulating the left indent. The entire document should remain selected until you finish step 15.

10. Point the mouse to the top half of the triangle on the left side of the ruler (first line indent), and drag it to the ½-inch marker on the ruler.

    Notice that the bottom half of the triangle (the left-indent marker) stayed in place and was not affected by dragging the top half.

11. Release the mouse button when you reach the ½-inch mark and note the appearance of the text on the screen.

    As you can see from Figure 3-9, the first line of every paragraph has been indented, and the line endings have been readjusted accordingly.

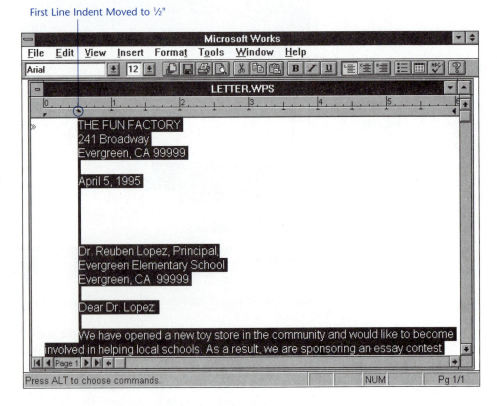

FIGURE 3-9

12. Point to the left-indent marker (the small bottom triangle on the left edge of the ruler) and drag it to the ½-inch mark.

Note that the first line indent moves with it. This is worth remembering. The first line indent will move with the left-indent marker unless the [SHIFT] key is also held down.

To see how that works,

13. Hold down the [SHIFT] key while you drag the left indent (small bottom triangle) to the one-inch mark.

14. Release the [SHIFT] key and the mouse button.

The lines on the left will move to the one-inch mark, and the first line indent will again be on top of the left-indent mark, creating the double triangle.

15. Drag the left-indent marker (the first line indent will follow) back to the zero mark.

16. Click anywhere in the document to deselect the text.

The left side of your screen should again resemble Figure 3-2.

Now you will use your newly learned skills to indent the first line of each paragraph as well as the list of toys and the closing lines.

17. Beginning with the first paragraph in the letter, drag down to select all three paragraphs, including the list of toys between the second and third paragraphs (move the cursor into the left margin where it changes to the pointer before beginning to drag down).

18. Move the first line indent (the top triangle) to the ½-inch mark on the ruler.

The first line of each paragraph, including the list of toys, has been indented. Remember, a paragraph is created whenever the [ENTER] key is pressed, so each line in the list of toys is considered a paragraph. The list of toys would look better if it were indented even further.

19. Click anywhere to deselect the paragraphs.

20. If necessary, scroll to view the complete list of toys, then drag to select the list.

21. Move the first line indent to two inches.

As you can see, the indents for the entire document need not be the same.

22. Scroll down until the last three lines of the letter are in view, then select the last three lines (starting with "Sincerely Yours").

23. Drag the first line indent to three inches.

To personalize the letter,

24. Select the line containing Beth Daniels' name at the end of the letter.

25. Type your own name.

It will replace Beth's name.

If your name and the title, Manager, run together, press [ENTER] to separate them. This could happen if you clicked in the left margin to select the line, because the ¶ symbol following the last character of that line was also selected and was, consequently, deleted.

26. Click the up vertical scroll arrow (shown in Figure 3-4) to return to the beginning of the letter (or drag the vertical scroll box).

27. Select the line containing the date (April 5, 1995, in the original draft).

28. Choose Special Character from the INSERT menu.

The dialog box shown in Figure 3-10 will appear.

FIGURE 3-10

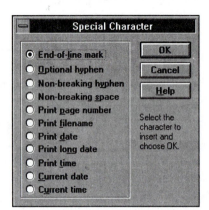

29. Click the Print Long Date option and then click the OK button.

You will be returned to the document with the old date replaced by a *placeholder* that reads *longdate*. This placeholder tells the system to insert the current date into the letter whenever it is printed in the future. If the date is a one-digit number, a zero is inserted (e.g., January 09, 1994).

 CAUTION | This date placeholder should not be used for documents where the date must remain constant.

To see the effect of the placeholder,

30. Choose Print Preview from the FILE menu.

When the print preview screen appears,

31. Move the mouse until the Zoom glass is over the date line and click.

The screen will be magnified so you can easily read the date.

32. Click the CANCEL button to return to the document.

33. Choose Save As from the FILE menu and save the file as *LETTER2* in your name directory on your data disk.

UNDERSTANDING THE TOOLBAR

The toolbar provides mouse users with shortcuts for various tasks. It is located under the Menu bar. The buttons and icons contained in the toolbar control some very powerful tools that help you work with your document. You don't even have to worry about memorizing what each button represents. Whenever you move the mouse pointer to any of the buttons, a title box pops up to remind you of the button's intended use. The toolbar presented in this text contains the preset default buttons. You can change or customize the *WORKS* toolbar so that it contains buttons for the commands and tasks you use most often. If you do not wish to work with the toolbar, you can put it away by choosing the Toolbar command in the VIEW menu. When that command has a check mark beside it, the toolbar is being displayed. To hide it, simply choose the command again; the check mark will disappear, and so will the toolbar.

Here are the buttons you will find on the preset Word Processing toolbar.

Arial ⤓ 12	The first two items on the left side of the toolbar are the Font and Font size drop-down lists. Use these drop-down lists to quickly change fonts and sizes for selected text. The list headers always show the font and size applicable to the selected text or to the paragraph containing the insertion point. If the selected text contains more than one font or size, the list headers will be blank.
STARTUP	Displays the Startup dialog box, which allows you to locate and open a file.
SAVE	Saves the active document with its current name. If you have not yet named the document, *WORKS* displays the Save As dialog box.
PRINT	Prints all pages of the active document using the current print settings.
PRINT PREVIEW	Displays the Print Preview screen for the current document.
CUT	Removes highlighted text or selected graphics from the document and stores them on the clipboard.
COPY	Copies highlighted text or selected graphics and stores them on the clipboard.
PASTE	Inserts clipboard contents at the insertion point.
BOLD, ITALICS, UNDERLINE	Applies bold style, italic style, or underline style to selected text.
LEFT, CENTER, RIGHT	This icon group is used to specify the alignment of text relative to the margins. Your choices are left alignment, center alignment, and right alignment.
BULLETS	Places a bullet in front of each highlighted paragraph.
SPREADSHEET	Displays a dialog box that allows you to insert a spreadsheet into the active word processor document.

![ABC check]	SPELL CHECK	Starts the spelling checker.
![help]	HELP	Displays the Learning Works dialog box where you can access on-line Help, the Help library, *WORKS* Tutorials, *WORKS* Wizards, and Cue Cards.

CHANGING TEXT STYLE AND SIZE

The letterhead (the top three lines of the letter containing the name of the company and its address) and the date line would look better if they were centered and made more distinctive.

IT'S YOUR TURN

1. Drag to select the letterhead and the date lines.

2. Click the Center Alignment icon on the toolbar.

3. Click anywhere in the white space to deselect.

4. Select THE FUN FACTORY.

5. Click the arrow to drop down the Font Size list on the toolbar and choose font size 18 (or larger if you wish).

6. Click the BOLD button on the toolbar.

7. Select the address lines of the letterhead.

8. Click the ITALICS button on the toolbar.

9. Click anywhere on the screen to deselect the text.

Your screen should resemble the one shown in Figure 3-11.

FIGURE 3-11

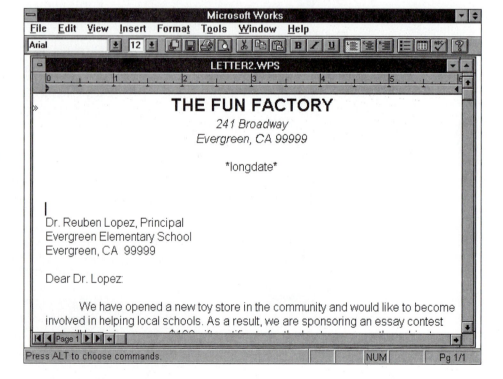

CHANGING TEXT THROUGHOUT A DOCUMENT

One of the advantages of using a word processor as opposed to a typewriter is that you can make revisions and changes quickly and easily, without having to retype the entire document. For example, you can change the references to "children" in our letter to "students" in order to avoid the appearance of talking down to them.

WORKS includes a very useful feature that will find any text string you specify and will allow you to replace it with any other text string. The Replace command is found in the EDIT menu.

IT'S YOUR TURN

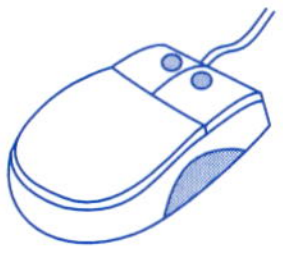

1. Choose Replace from the EDIT menu.

This menu contains certain commands that you can use to find words or pages. The Find command simply finds a word or phrase; Replace searches for the specified word or phrase and changes it to another specified word or phrase; and Go To jumps to the page number you specify.

The Replace dialog box shown in Figure 3-12 appears with the insertion point blinking in the Find What box.

FIGURE 3-12

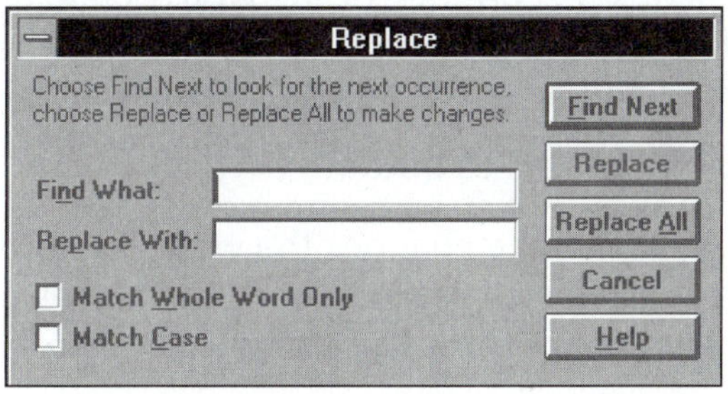

Replace

Choose Find Next to look for the next occurrence, choose Replace or Replace All to make changes.

Find What: [   ]

Replace With: [   ]

☐ Match Whole Word Only
☐ Match Case

[Find Next]
[Replace]
[Replace All]
[Cancel]
[Help]

WORKS can find a specific word, phrase, or special character and replace it with new text. You can selectively replace occurrences of the text or have *WORKS* replace all occurrences in the document. You can limit *WORKS'* searches by clicking Match Whole Word Only (useful when searching for strings such as "the," which can appear within words or as a word by itself) and Match Case (which would find "You" only when the first letter is capitalized). You can use the wildcard character "?" in the search string. For example, the search string "the??" would find all five letter words that begin with the characters "the." You can also find and replace special characters by using the following codes.

To Represent This Special Character	Use This Code
Tab Mark	^t
Paragraph Mark	^p
End of line Mark	^n
Page break	^d
Question mark	^?
Caret	^^
White Space	^w

You can combine these special characters with text to form a search pattern. For example the search string "^pWith" will find all paragraphs that begin with the letters "With."

WORKS begins the search at the current position of the insertion point and searches forward until the end of the document is reached. At that time you are asked if you want to continue searching from the beginning of the document.

To search for "children" and replace it with "students," the insertion point should be blinking in the Find What text box of the Replace dialog box.

2. Type: children

3. Press the [TAB] key to move to the Replace With box.

4. Type: students

5. If necessary, click Match Whole Word Only and Match Case to turn off both options.

6. Click the FIND NEXT button.

   The first occurrence of the word "children" will be located and high-lighted on the page. If you cannot see the highlighted word, drag on the title bar of the Replace dialog box to move it out of the way.

7. Click the REPLACE button.

Notice that Replace changes the word "children" to "students" and maintains the proper capitalization. It then goes ahead to the next instance. Since you do not want to change each word individually,

8. Click Replace All to automatically change all the remaining occurrences.

9. If you get a message box asking if you want to continue searching from the beginning of the document, click the YES button the first time to complete the search. Click NO the next time the message appears.

   WORKS will make the other replacements and will display a message in the Status bar at the bottom of the screen telling you that two occurrences of "children" have been replaced with "students."

10. Click the CLOSE button to put away the Replace dialog box.

FINISHING UP PROJECT 1

You have now changed the letter so that it presents a very professional appearance. Since you have already saved it under a new name, you can use the toolbar to save the rest of your work, preview what it will look like when printed, and print the document.

IT'S YOUR TURN

To save the work you have completed so far,

1. Click the SAVE button in the toolbar.

To see what your printed letter will look like now,

2. Click the PRINT PREVIEW button in the toolbar. Use the Zoom glass to enlarge the letter if you wish.

3. Turn on the printer and ensure that it is ready to print.

4. Click the PRINT button on the right side of the Print Preview screen.

The Print Notification dialog box will appear, and your letter should soon appear on your printer.

Since you have already saved your work,

5. Double click the CONTROL MENU box in the upper left corner of the *LETTER2* window to close the file.

The Startup dialog box will appear once again.

SETTING THE SCENE

PROJECT 2   The Want Ad

Business at The Fun Factory has been increasing so much that you need more cashiers and stock personnel. You decide to create a flyer to advertise those position openings. Your finished ad will resemble the one shown in Figure 3-13.

FIGURE 3-13

HELP WANTED

The Fun Factory is looking for several persons to fill the following positions:

Cashier   Friendly, detail-oriented, good
                                 with numbers. Previous
                                 experience and knowledge of
                                 cash register are plusses.

Stock Person   Organized, strong (able to lift 30-
                                 40 pound boxes on a regular
                                 basis. Inventory experience a
                                 plus.

Send resumes to:

A Student
The Fun Factory
241 Broadway
Evergreen, CA 99999

GETTING STARTED

You will be typing your flyer from scratch, so you will open a new word processing file. Think of this activity as reaching into your desk drawer and pulling out a fresh sheet of paper.

IT'S YOUR TURN

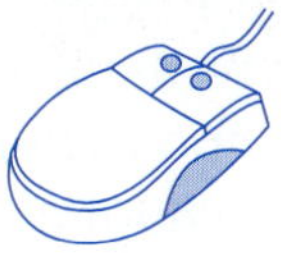

If the Startup dialog box is *not* on the screen,

1. Choose Create New File from the FILE menu.

With the Startup dialog box on the screen,

2. Click the Word Processor icon.

A new word processor window will open. You will type the text for your advertisement in this window. Most word processing programs automatically move a word to the next line if there is insufficient space for it on the current line; this feature is called **wordwrap**. The user does not press [ENTER] unless it is time for a new paragraph. *WORKS 3.0* uses wordwrap to fit text on the screen as you type it.

As mentioned at the beginning of Project 1 of this chapter, it is recommended that the Wrap for Window command be left on. If you do have this command on, you will note that the text will wrap at the right edge of the window, ignoring the right margin and right indent. When the document is printed, however, the lines will wrap correctly. You can use the Print Preview screen to verify line endings, if necessary.

3.   Change font to Arial.

INDENTS AND MARGINS

You will be using the left indent and the first line indent to create the hanging paragraphs shown in Figure 3-13. In **hanging paragraphs**, the first line of the paragraph begins at the left edge, and the rest of the lines begin further to the right. They are commonly used for typing enumerated items, such as questions on tests. In fact, this usage is so common that *WORKS* includes a shortcut method for achieving them, which will be discussed in Chapter 5.

Note that the default line length for your blank document window is six inches. As previously explained, *WORKS* automatically sets left and right margins at 1.25 inches each, which leaves six inches for the line on standard 8.5-inch wide paper. The letter you worked with earlier was typed using the default margin settings. This time you will use the Page Setup dialog box to set your own margins before you start typing any text. You are going to change the margin width on the Page Setup screen and observe the change in line length on the document window.

IT'S YOUR TURN

1.   Choose Page Setup from the FILE menu.

The Page Setup dialog box shown in Figure 3-14 will appear.

FIGURE 3-14

Page Setup		
Margins	Source, Size and Orientation	Other Options

Top margin: 1"

Bottom margin: 1"

Left margin: 1.25"

Right margin: 1.25"

Header margin: 0.5"

Footer margin: 0.75"

Sample

OK

Cancel

Help

Reset

Choose Reset to revert to default page settings.

This dialog box contains three cards with index tabs. The card marked Margins allows you to change the size of all margins. The Source, Size and Orientation card allows you to change those attributes, and the Other Options card allows you to start numbering the pages of your document with something other than the number one, as well as control printing of footnotes and endnotes.

To change both side margins to two inches instead of the default one inch, the Margins card should be active.

2.   Click the Margins tab if necessary to display the Margins card.

3.   Press [TAB] until the left margin text box is highlighted.

CAUTION

If you accidentally go too far, hold down the [SHIFT] key while pressing the [TAB] key; the previous selection will again be highlighted.

4. Type: 2

5. Press [TAB] until the right margin text box is highlighted.

6. Type: 2

7. Click the OK button or press [ENTER].

You are returned to the blank document window shown in Figure 3-15.

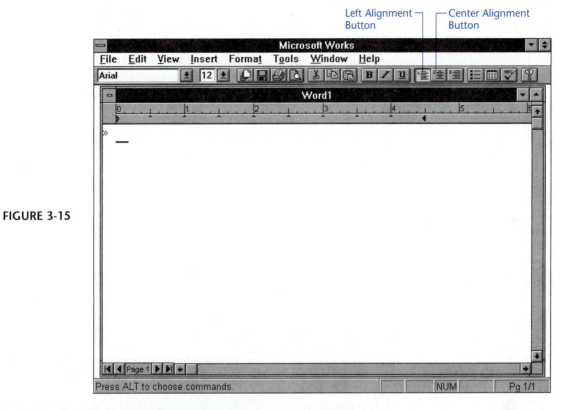

FIGURE 3-15

Notice that *WORKS 3.0* has changed your line length to 4.5 inches—calculated by subtracting the four inches in the margins from the paper width of 8.5 inches.

**TYPING AND
FORMATTING
THE DOCUMENT**

Now that the page has been prepared with appropriate margins, you are ready to type and format the advertisement. You will use the ruler to format each section before typing it. You should be aware that formatting changes take effect on highlighted material or, if no text is highlighted, the changes take effect on text typed at the cursor point until another change in formatting is made.

You will use the toolbar whenever possible.

IT'S YOUR TURN

1. Click on the center alignment icon (see Figure 3-15) on the toolbar.

The blinking insertion point will move to the center of the first line.

2. Press [CAPS LOCK].

Note the letters CAP in the Status bar at the bottom right.

3. Type: HELP WANTED

4. Press [CAPS LOCK].

5. Press [ENTER] twice.

6. Click on the left alignment icon (see Figure 3-15) on the toolbar. The insertion point moves back to the left.

7. Type the following, but do not press [ENTER] while typing:

   The Fun Factory is looking for several persons to fill the following positions:

8. Press [ENTER] twice.

   If Wrap for Window is turned on and your window is wider than 4.5 inches, the text will continue past the right-margin marker and will not wrap unless it exceeds the window width.

If your screen is in this situation,

9. Choose Wrap for Window from the VIEW menu to turn it off.

   The wrap point will now be at the right margin.

   The listing of the positions (see Figure 3-13) is to be typed as hanging paragraphs. The first line indent marks the beginning of the job titles. You will set the left indent, which will also act as a tab stop, for the beginning of the second line of the position descriptions.

10. Hold down the [SHIFT] key and drag the left indent marker (the bottom triangle) to the two-inch mark (see Figure 3-16).

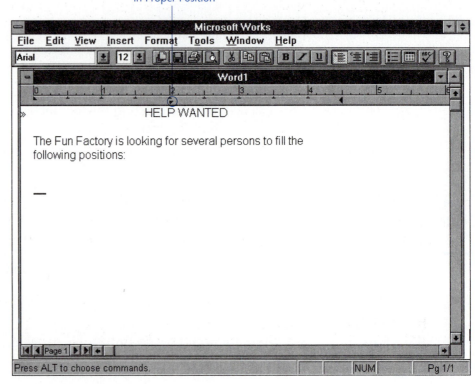

FIGURE 3-16

11. Type: Cashier

12. Press [TAB].

13. Type the following, but do not press [ENTER] while typing:

Friendly, detail-oriented, good with numbers. Previous experience and knowledge of cash register are pluses.

14. Press [ENTER] twice.

15. Type: Stock Person

16. Press [TAB].

17. Type:

Organized, strong (able to lift 30-40 pound boxes on a regular basis). Inventory experience a plus.

18. Press [ENTER] twice.

19. Type: Send resumes to:

20. Press [ENTER] three times.

21. Click on the center alignment icon on the toolbar.

22. Type: Your name [ENTER]

23. Type: The Fun Factory [ENTER]

24. Type: 241 Broadway [ENTER]

25. Type: Evergreen, CA 99999

USING WORD COUNT

WORKS 3.0 includes an option that can quickly count the number of words in all, or a portion of, a word processor document. If you want the count for the entire document, simply use the word count command without selecting any part of the document. If you want the word count for only part of the document, highlight the part you want counted before invoking the word count command.

This feature is useful for you to now count the words in your advertisement, because you will be charged for each word.

IT'S YOUR TURN

1. Choose Word Count from the TOOLS menu.

The count will begin. When finished, a box will appear, displaying the number of words in the want ad document. There should be 61 words. After you have examined the information in the box,

2. Click the OK button.

USING HEADERS AND FOOTERS

A *header* is text that automatically appears in the margin area at the tops of pages; a *footer* is text that appears in the margin area at the bottoms of pages. *WORKS 3.0* has two types of headers and footers—Paragraph and Standard. Paragraph headers and footers can have one or more lines and can include drawings or other objects. They are typed into a special section of the Word Processor screen. Standard headers and footers have only one line of text, and they cannot contain anything but text. They are typed into the Header & Footer dialog box available from the VIEW menu.

IT'S YOUR TURN

To insert a standard footer on your ad,

1. Choose Headers & Footers from the VIEW menu.

    A dialog box similar to the one shown in Figure 3-17 will appear.

FIGURE 3-17

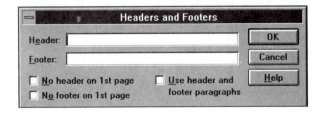

The insertion point is blinking at the left edge of the Header text box. To move to the Footer text box,

2. Press [TAB] or click in the Footer text box.

3. Type: &LWantad&C&D&RThe Fun Factory

The above line carries special codes that tell *WORKS* how to format the footer. The following codes can be used in headers and footers. The codes can be typed either in upper case or lower case.

Use This Code	To Achieve This Purpose
&L	Left align the characters that follow
&R	Right align the characters that follow
&C	Center the characters that follow
&P	Print the page number
&F	Print the filename
&D	Print the date
&N	Print the date in long format
&T	Print the time
&&	Print a single ampersand

4. Click the OK button or press [ENTER].

    The dialog box disappears, and there is apparently no change in the want ad document. You have to use Print Preview to see the footer.

5. Click the PRINT PREVIEW button on the toolbar.

    The footer appears at the bottom of the screen.

6. If desired, use the Zoom glass to zoom in on the footer so you can examine it more closely.

When you are ready to return to the want ad document,

7. Click the CANCEL button.

FINISHING UP PROJECT 2

Remember that when you quit *WORKS 3.0,* the file in the computer's memory disappears, but the files stored on the disk (either floppy or hard) are not lost. Since your want ad has not yet been saved, it still carries a generic name assigned to it by *WORKS.* You will now save it with a more descriptive name.

IT'S YOUR TURN

1. Choose Save As from the FILE menu and save this file in your directory on your data disk with the name *WANTAD.*

WORKS automatically appends the .WPS to the name.

2. Click the PRINTER button on the toolbar to print a copy of the advertisement.

3. Exit *WORKS* as previously directed at the end of Chapter 2.

SUMMARY

With your knowledge of the *WORKS 3.0* word processing module, you can now create documents (files), print them, and save them. You have learned how to create a footer, center lines, and set up hanging paragraphs. You can retrieve documents and easily edit them by inserting and deleting text, moving blocks, and finding and replacing groups of characters with corrected text. You can change the appearance of documents by changing indents, font styles and sizes, and centering lines. In the next two chapters, you will learn how to use some of the more advanced features of *WORKS'* word processing module.

REVIEW QUESTIONS

True/False

1. When wordwrapping occurs in a paragraph, the beginning of the second and remaining lines of that paragraph align with the left indent marker.

2. A document with 1 inch left and right margins would show the right indent marker at 6.5 inches.

3. Moving within a dialog box can be accomplished by using the [TAB] key.

4. You should use the Find command if you want to replace a selected word with another word.

5. You can change the margins of a file by using the Page Setup dialog box.

6. The default left and right margins are set at one inch.

7. A footer is text appearing in the margin area at the bottom of a printed page.

8. All word processing files are identified in the directory with the letters WPS.

9. Double clicking the CONTROL menu button will close a file.

10. To select an entire file for formatting, click once in the left margin of that file.

EXERCISES

EXERCISE 3-1   Modifying the *LETTER* file

(Change text styles and sizes, replace text, move first line indent, add footer)

1.   Open the *LETTER* file from your data disk.

2.   Change the date to the current date using the long form (i.e., spell out the month and type the day and year in full).

3.   Replace the name of the school, city, and state with your own.

4.   Increase the type size of the store name to the next larger point size.

5.   Select the list of toys and set the first line indent at 2.5 inches.

6.   Center the letterhead and date.

7.   Start the three closing lines at three inches.

8.   Add a footer with your name on the left and the date on the right.

9.   Save as *EX3-1* in your folder on your data disk.

10.   Print, if requested by your instructor.

EXERCISE 3-2   Creating a memo with a footer

1.   Type the following memo using single spacing for the paragraphs with double spacing between paragraphs. When you get to the dates, you may center them or set a new left indent. Your line endings will differ from our illustration.

TO ALL STORE MANAGERS

(Press [ENTER] three times)

We have received quite a few entries for our essay contest and must now decide

on the winners. Can you assist me in determining who the three lucky students

will be? *(Press [ENTER] two times)*

I would like to arrange a meeting time that is convenient for most of you. Please

mark your first and second choices from the dates below. *(Press [ENTER] two times)*

September 2

September 3

September 4

2. Type a footer with your name at the left and the date at the right.

3. Save as *EX3-2* in your name directory on your data disk.

4. Print, if requested to do so by your instructor.

EXERCISE 3-3   Creating a letter from scratch

1. Create your own letter to the first-prize winner. Mention that the award will be made at his or her school by one of the managers of The Fun Factory. Add your own comments to embellish the letter. Include the current date, and use your name as the owner.

2. Save the letter as *EX3-3* in your name directory on your data disk.

CHAPTER

4

Word Processing 3

OBJECTIVES

When you finish this chapter, you will be able to

- ▪ *use tab stops*
- ▪ *use the spelling checker*
- ▪ *use the thesaurus*
- ▪ *change margins after creating a document*

SETTING THE SCENE

As part of your sales promotion for The Fun Factory, you sponsor a Birthday Club. Each Birthday Club member receives a free, inexpensive toy during the month of his or her birthday. In this chapter, you will create two documents that will be used for the Birthday Club. The first is a membership application form, and the second is a form letter to be mailed to eligible Birthday Club members with each month's gift certificates.

GETTING STARTED

PROJECT 1 The Membership Application Form

Since you will create your own documents for this chapter in their entirety, there is less directed activity. When you finish, your membership application form should resemble the one shown in Figure 4-1.

FIGURE 4-1

```
┌─────────────────────────────────────────────┐
│              THE FUN FACTORY                  │
│           MEMBERSHIP APPLICATION              │
│                                               │
│   LAST NAME:        _____  │
│   FIRST NAME:       _____  │
│   ADDRESS:          _____  │
│                     _____  │
│                     _____  │
│   FAVORITE COLOR:   _____  │
│   BIRTHDAY:         _____  │
│                                               │
└─────────────────────────────────────────────┘
```

There is no file stored on the data disk for you, so you must first open a blank word processor document, as you did for the want ad in the previous chapter.

IT'S YOUR TURN

1. Launch *WORKS* and open a new word processor file.

   An empty screen, as shown in Figure 4-2, is now available for creating a new document. When you open a new file, you should see the ruler you worked with in Chapter 3 at the top of the screen.

Preset Tab Stops

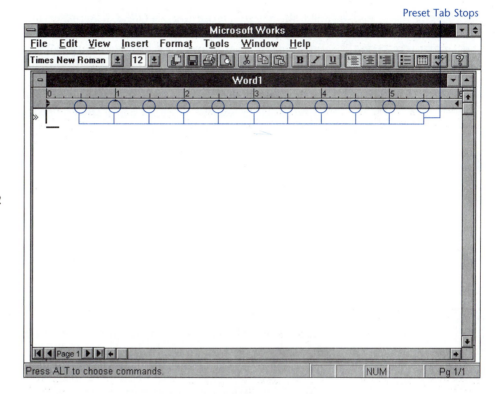

FIGURE 4-2

2. If the ruler and toolbar are not displayed at the top of the screen, choose them from the VIEW menu.

   The insertion point will be blinking on the first line at the far left of the screen.

3. Change the font to Arial and the point size to 12.

   The filename "Word1" located in the middle of the title bar is the default filename assigned by *WORKS* (see Figure 4-2). When you complete your membership application form, you will save it with a more descriptive filename.

   The application form shown in Figure 4-1 is not very long, but its appearance depends on the use of tab stops. The fill-in lines start with a left tab and end with a right tab, which keeps them evenly aligned. The fill-in lines are created by using a *leader* with the right tab.

To set the margins for the application,

4. Choose Page Setup from the FILE menu.

When the dialog box appears,

5. Set both the left and right margins to two inches.

To put away the dialog box,

6. Click the OK button or press [ENTER].

USE TABS TO FORMAT THE APPLICATION

As shown in Figure 4-2, *WORKS* has preset tabs every half inch across the ruler. When you create your own tab stops, all preset tab stops to the left of the newly created one will be deleted; preset tabs to the right stay the same. Tab stops created through the Tabs dialog box will be represented on the ruler by a left tab symbol (L), a right tab symbol (⌐), or a center tab symbol (↑).

You are now ready to type the heading for the application form. The two-line heading will be centered using the toolbar.

IT'S YOUR TURN

1. Click the Center alignment button on the toolbar.

2. Press [CAPS LOCK].

3. Type: THE FUN FACTORY

4. Press [ENTER].

5. Type: MEMBERSHIP APPLICATION

6. Press [ENTER] twice.

7. Click the Left alignment button on the toolbar.

Now you will set tab stops for the rest of the form.

8. Choose Tabs from the FORMAT menu.

The Tabs dialog box shown in Figure 4-3 appears. This dialog box is used to set, move, and delete tab stops. Tab stops are used instead of spaces (inserted by depressing the space bar) to quickly and precisely position text in columns or tables. This dialog box also allows you to insert leader lines with tab stops. Tab stops are set for selected paragraphs; if no paragraph has been selected, the tab stop takes effect on the line on which you are typing.

FIGURE 4-3

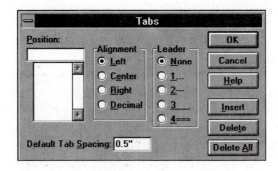

The insertion point should be blinking in the Position text box.

The header lines will be typed at the left margin. A left tab stop is then inserted to begin the fill-in line. Finally, a right tab stop with underscore leaders is inserted to finish the fill-in line.

The left side of the fill-in line should start at 1.75 inches, so you will set a left tab at that position.

9. Type: 1.75

10. Select Left from the Alignment group, if necessary.

11. Select None from the Leader group, if necessary.

12. Click the INSERT button.

   1.75" now appears in the Position list box. Note also that the Position text box has become highlighted so that anything you type will replace its current contents.

Since you want the fill-in line to end at the right margin, you will set a right tab at that piont.

13. Type: 4.5

14. Select Right from the Alignment group.

To have the right tab preceded by underscores, thus forming the fill-in line,

15. Select 3 from the Leader group.

16. Click the INSERT button.

To put away the dialog box,

17. Click the OK button or press [ENTER].

   Your screen should now resemble the one shown in Figure 4-4. Note the left tab icon at the 1.75-inch mark and the right tab icon superimposed over the right-indent marker at the 4.5-inch mark on the ruler.

FIGURE 4-4

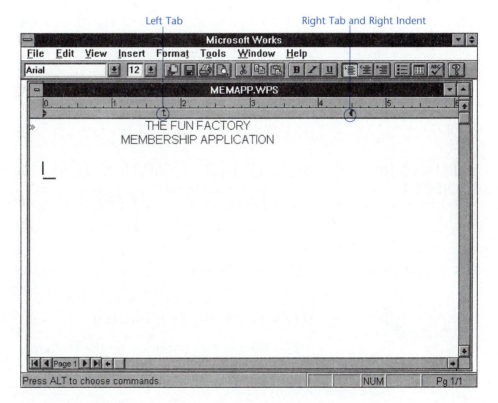

Now you are ready to type the rest of the application form.

18. Type: LAST NAME:

19. Press [TAB].

The insertion point moves to the 1.75-inch tab stop.

20. Press [TAB].

This time the insertion point moves to the 4.5-inch tab stop, but underscore leaders are inserted ahead of the tab stop, thus creating the fill-in line we want to see.

To move to the next line,

21. Press [ENTER].

To complete the second line,

22. Type: FIRST NAME:

23. Press [TAB] twice.

24. Press [ENTER].

To complete the three address lines,

25. Type: ADDRESS:

26. Press [TAB] [TAB] [ENTER].

27. Press [TAB] [TAB] [ENTER].

28. Press [TAB] [TAB] [ENTER].

To complete the last two lines,

29. Type: FAVORITE COLOR:

30. Press [TAB] [TAB] [ENTER].

31. Type: BIRTHDAY:

32. Press [TAB] [TAB] [ENTER].

FINISHING UP PROJECT 1

The membership application is designed for printing on postcard-size stock, but you can print it onto regular paper to check its accuracy and placement. Before printing, however, it is time to save your document.

IT'S YOUR TURN

1. Choose Save As from the FILE menu and save the file in your name directory on your data disk. Use the filename *MEMAPP*.

To print a copy of the application,

2. Click the PRINTER button on the toolbar.

To put away the file,

3. Choose Close from the FILE menu or double click the CONTROL MENU button in the upper left corner of the document window.

The Startup dialog box will appear, and you are now ready to start your next project.

GETTING STARTED

PROJECT 2 The Birthday Club letter.

As mentioned earlier, The Fun Factory sends out form letters each month to members of the Birthday Club whose birthdays fall in the coming month. The completed letter is shown in Figure 4-5.

FIGURE 4-5

February 14, 1994

Dear Birthday Club Member:

HAPPY BIRTHDAY!

To help celebrate your special day next month, we are enclosing a coupon that can be exchanged for one free toy from our special Birthday Club collection.

Our feature toy this month is a Nerf football, but naturally you may pick any of the wonderful toys and games in the collection.

We are looking forward to seeing you on your birthday!

Yours truly,

THE FUN FACTORY

A Student, Manager

Enclosure

P.S. Please tell your friends about our Birthday Club. Just have them drop by The Fun Factory and pick up an application form.

You are now ready to type the text of the letter. If you need to correct errors, simply press [BACKSPACE] after making the error and type the correct character(s).

IT'S YOUR TURN

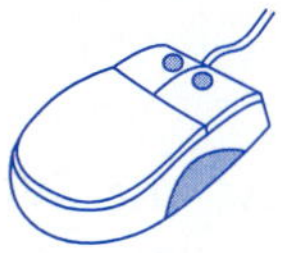

The Startup dialog box should be showing on your screen. To get a new word processing window,

1. Click the Word Processor icon.

TYPING THE LETTER

In your short letter, you want to encourage birthday celebrants to come in for their toys. You will copy the letter shown in Figure 4-6; be sure to follow the spacing directions given in that figure. Remember to use [ENTER] only when you want to leave blank lines or start a new paragraph; *WORKS* will automatically move words to the next line when you reach the end of a line. Also, to conform to desktop publishing rules, you should leave only one space after a period. As your letter gets longer, use the vertical scroll bar to view parts of your letter not displayed on the screen. It is important that you copy the first five lines of the letter exactly, for the other activities in this chapter are based on the letter, as shown in Figure 4-6.

IT'S YOUR TURN

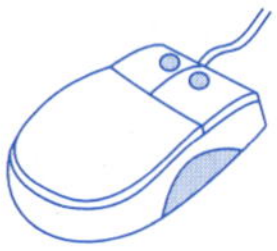

1. Turn on Wrap for Window from the VIEW menu if your word processing window is less than six inches wide.

2. Use the toolbar to change the font to Arial.

3. Type the letter shown in Figure 4-6, following the directions given in the figure; be sure to type your name as manager.

4. You can ignore any typing errors you might make after the first five lines.

FIGURE 4-6

(Type current date)

———————————————————— Press [ENTER] 5 times

Dear Birthday Club Member:

HAPPY BIRTHDAY! ————— Press [ENTER] 2 times

To help celebrate your special day next month, we are enclosing a coupon that can be exchanged for one free toy from our special Birthday Club collection.
———————————————————— Press [ENTER] 2 times
Our feature toy this month is a Nerf football, but of course you may choose any of the wonderful toys and games in the collection.
———————————————————— Press [ENTER] 2 times
We are looking forward to seeing you on your birthday!

Yours truly, ————— Press [ENTER] 2 times

THE FUN FACTORY

———————————————————— Press [ENTER] 4 times

(Type your name), Manager

Enclosure ————— Press [ENTER] 2 times

P.S. Please tell your friends about our Birthday Club. Just have them drop by The Fun Factory and pick up an application form.

In the next section you will use the built-in spelling checker to proofread your letter and correct typing and spelling mistakes.

USING THE SPELLING CHECKER

Your letter may have some misspelled words. You will use the *WORKS* spelling checker to find and correct these words. The spelling checker has a large dictionary and verifies every word in a document against it. It stops and displays a word it does not recognize and offers alternatives to the word. The spelling checker also detects repeated words. Before you start using the spelling checker, it is important that your letter contains the same misspelled word as our example.

IT'S YOUR TURN

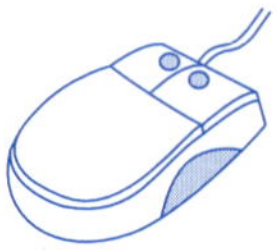

1. If necessary, change the word "celebrate" in the first line of your letter to "celabrate."

2. Click to place the insertion point at the beginning of the date line.

3. Click the SPELLING CHECKER button on the toolbar (or choose Spelling from the TOOLS menu).

A screen similar to the one shown in Figure 4-7 will appear. The spelling checker begins checking with the word in which the cursor was positioned when the spelling checker was activated, and it has correctly identified the misspelled word "celabrate."

FIGURE 4-7

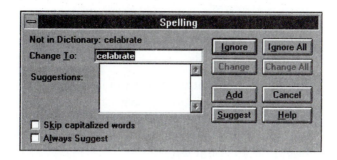

4. Click the SUGGEST button.

The correct spelling of the word appears in the suggestion box and in the Change To text box.

To accept this spelling and continue checking,

5. Click the CHANGE button.

The word will be changed in your document and the spelling checker will highlight the next word that is not in its dictionary. In our document, the next highlighted word is "Nerf," a trademark word, which we do not want to change. In your document, you may encounter other misspelled words before reaching "Nerf."

The *WORKS* spelling checker uses a 113,664 word dictionary when scanning a document. If *WORKS* finds a word that it does not recognize, and you have verified that the word is spelled correctly, you can add it to the dictionary. The word will not be questioned in subsequent spelling checks. If you are working on a network, you may not be able to add words to the dictionary. You can also use the *WORKS* spelling checker to check for repeated words, such as "the the."

WORKS' spelling checker will check the entire document or only the text you have selected. If no misspelling is found, *WORKS* displays a message to that effect. You can return to your document by choosing the OK button. If a misspelling is found, *WORKS* opens the Spelling dialog box shown in Figure 4-7 and displays the questionable word. After you respond to the first word, *WORKS* displays the next word it doesn't recognize, then continues in this fashion until no misspelled words are found and the spelling check is finished. At that time, the appropriate message is displayed and you can return to your document.

Before you make any further changes, you will explore the dialog box a little. Look at the buttons on the right-hand side of the dialog box.

IGNORE	Skips only the specfic challenged word
IGNORE ALL	Skips all instances of the challenged word

CHANGE	Changes only the specific challenged word
CHANGE ALL	Changes all instances of the challenged word
ADD	Adds the challenged word to the dictionary
CANCEL	Leaves the spelling checker
SUGGEST	Displays a suggested replacement; to see another suggestion, click this button again
HELP	Displays the on-line HELP section that describes the dialog box

When the Always Suggest option in the lower left corner of the dialog box is activated, the dictionary will always give a suggestion for each questionable word. The Skip Capitalized Words option causes the program to ignore not only capitalized words, but acronyms and other words containing only capital letters.

6. Make spelling corrections until "Nerf" is encountered.

With "Nerf" as the subject word,

7. Click the ADD button (if your system does not allow that activity, click the IGNORE button).

    The word will be added to the dictionary. The spelling checker will continue to check your document and present alternative spellings for each word it cannot find in its dictionary.

8. Choose the appropriate action for each word presented to you.

When spelling checking is complete, the program will display a dialog box informing you that it is finished. When that happens, to return to your document,

9. Click the OK button.

HINT If you wish to quickly check only a portion of the document (for example, the spelling of the word you just typed), simply highlight that word and click the SPELLING CHECK button on the toolbar. If text is selected when Spelling is chosen, only the selected text will be checked.

USING THE THESAURUS

You can add precision and variety to your writing by using the thesaurus to find synonyms for words and simple phrases, such as "of course," "a few times," or "every day." Synonyms are words that have the same meaning as the selected word or phrase.

IT'S YOUR TURN

1. Select the word "choose" in the second paragraph of your letter.

HINT You can select a word either by dragging the mouse across it or by double clicking on the word.

2.   Choose Thesaurus from the TOOLS menu.

The Thesaurus dialog box is shown in Figure 4-8.

FIGURE 4-8

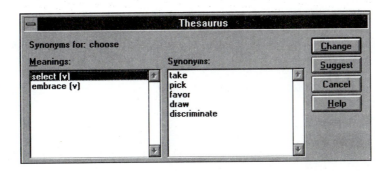

The selected word is shown at the top of the box as the word for which synonyms are displayed. The Synonyms list box on the right-hand side displays all the synonyms that *WORKS* found for the word shown in the top line of the dialog box. The Meanings list box on the left-hand side contains a list of meanings for the selected word. One of the meanings will be highlighted, and the synonyms in the Synonym box refer to the meaning of the selected word. If you highlight a different word in the Meanings box, the list of synonyms will change to reflect the new meaning. If *WORKS* doesn't find the selected word or phrase, it will display a list of words that are alphabetically close to the selection.

Since the meaning, "select," is highlighted in the Meanings box, and this is the meaning you wish to convey,

3.   Click the word "pick" in the Synonyms list.

That word will become highlighted.

4.   Click the CHANGE button in the upper right corner of the dialog box.

You will be returned to your document, but now the word "pick" has been inserted in place of the original word "choose." Other buttons and options in the Thesaurus dialog box allow you to browse through the thesaurus.

CHANGE	Replaces the word shown in the Synonyms For line with the highlighted synonym in the Synonyms list box; if no synonym is highlighted, the replacement word is the highlighted Meanings word.
SUGGEST	Replaces the word shown in the Synonyms For line with the highlighted word from the Meanings list box or the Synonyms list box. It then creates a new Meanings list and Synonyms list for the new word and can cause you to lose the original word.
CANCEL	Puts away the Thesaurus dialog box and returns to the original document with no changes.
HELP	Displays the on-line HELP section for this dialog box.

5.   Select the phrase "of course" in the second paragraph of the Birthday Club letter.

6.   Choose Thesaurus from the TOOLS menu.

The Thesaurus dialog box appears again, but this time it displays synonyms for the phrase, as shown in Figure 4-9.

FIGURE 4-9

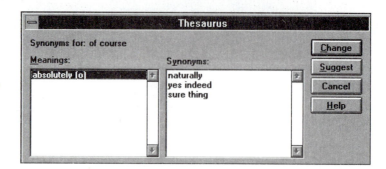

Before you finally choose a synonym for "of course," you will experiment a little with the dialog box. With "absolutely" highlighted in the Meanings list box,

7.   Click the SUGGEST button.

Lists of meanings and synonyms for "absolutely" will be displayed, and "absolutely" is now displayed in the line above the Meanings box. Note that one of the meanings is "of course."

8.   Click "of course" in the Meanings list box.

9.   Click the SUGGEST button.

The dialog box will revert to its original contents.

10.   Double click "naturally" in the synonyms box.

This is a shortcut for clicking a word and then clicking the CHANGE button. The phrase "of course" in your letter will be replaced by the word "naturally," which will continue to be selected, and the Thesaurus dialog box will go away.

11.   Click anywhere on the document to deselect the word.

ANOTHER LOOK AT PAGE SETUP

In previous exercises, you used Page Setup to change the default margin settings before creating a file. In this exercise you will change page margins after typing the file to improve the appearance of your letter on the printed page.

IT'S YOUR TURN

To see what your letter currently looks like,

1.   Click the PRINT PREVIEW button on the toolbar.

As you can see from Figure 4-10, the letter is skewed to the top of the page. You will increase the size of the top margin and side margins so that this short letter will be better centered on the printed page.

To return to your document,

2.   Click the CANCEL button.

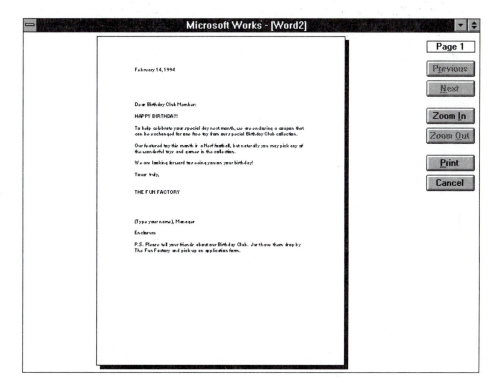

FIGURE 4-10

3. Choose Page Setup from the FILE menu.

The Page Setup dialog box will be displayed on your screen. As expected, the default margins in effect are one inch for the top and bottom margins and 1.25 inches for the left and right margins.

4. Use the techniques learned in previous chapters to set the top margin to two inches and side margins to 1.5 inches. Leave the bottom margin at one inch.

To put away the dialog box and return to your document,

5. Click the OK button.

Notice that the right-margin marker on the ruler has moved in to the 5.5-inch mark to reflect the new side margins. If Wrap for Window is turned on, the text will probably extend beyond the right-margin marker to fill the window.

To examine the letter with its new margins,

6. Click the PRINT PREVIEW button on the toolbar.

The letter looks much better when centered on the page.

When you have finished admiring your letter and want to return to your document,

7. Click the CANCEL button.

FINISHING UP PROJECT 2

Now that you have your letter typed correctly and formatted properly, it's time to save it so you can use it again. You will use the filename *BIRTHDAY*.

IT'S YOUR TURN

1. Choose Save As from the FILE menu.

When the Save As dialog box appears,

2. Save the letter in your name directory on your data disk. Use the file-name *BIRTHDAY.*

3. Print a copy of the letter, if directed to do so.

4. Close the file and quit *WORKS,* as directed at the end of Chapter 2.

SUMMARY

You have experimented with more of the word processing features of *WORKS 3.0.* You have learned to set tab stops and have used the spelling checker, the thesaurus, and the Page Setup dialog boxes. These are powerful tools available in the Word Processing module, and you should practice with them until you are comfortable with what they can do. Don't forget to also use Help to find out more about these tools.

REVIEW QUESTIONS

True/False

1. To create a new document, click on the Open button.

2. It is usual to use the default filename for a new document since it is descriptive enough.

3. The spelling checker in *WORKS* is found in the WINDOW menu.

4. The default side margins in the Page Setup dialog box are one inch.

5. The *WORKS* thesaurus allows you to choose antonyms as well as synonyms.

6. Page Setup settings are automatically saved when you save the file.

7. Preset tab stops and user-created tab stops look alike.

8. It is possible to add words to the *WORKS* dictionary.

9. The *WORKS* spelling checker will also check for grammatical errors.

10. If the spelling checker questions the spelling of a word, it is obvious that the spelling is wrong.

EXERCISES

EXERCISE 4-1   Creating a letter from scratch

(Use the spelling checker and thesaurus)

1. Create a letter to a friend about a topic of your own choice. Be creative and use as many of *WORKS'* features as you can to make your letter as attractive as possible.

    Use the thesaurus to improve your word selection and the spelling checker to proof your spelling. Use the Print Preview option to check the letter placement and, if necessary, use Page Setup to change margins to improve placement.

2. Save as *EX4-1* in your name directory on your data disk.

3. Print, if instructed to do so.

EXERCISE 4-2   Creating a memo using tab stops

1. Open a new word processing document.

2. Type the following title: MEMORANDUM

    a. Center the title, change it to bold, increase the font size to 16, and change the font to Arial.

    b. Press [ENTER] twice after the title and return to left alignment before typing the side headings.

    c. Turn off the bold style and change the font size back to 12.

3. Set a left tab at 1.5 on the ruler.

4. Type the following, using the Tab key after each heading. Fill in requested information.

    TO: All Store Managers

    FROM: (Type your name)

    DATE: (Type current date)

    SUBJECT: Birthday Club **(Press [ENTER] twice)**

    Congratulations! Our Birthday Club membership drive is coming along quite nicely. Keep up the good work. Listed below are the first week's totals for some of our branches. **(Press [ENTER] twice.)**

5. Set the following tab stops using the Tabs dialog box: a left tab at two and a right tab with a dotted leader at 3.5. (Be sure to remove any previous tab stops.)

6. Type the following using the tab settings:

    San Jose 20

    Campbell 9

    Cupertino 15

7. Type a footer with your name at the left and the date on the right.

8. Save as *EX4-2* in your name directory on your data disk.

9. Print, if instructed to do so.

EXERCISE 4-3

Create your own letter and incorporate text using tab stops.

CHAPTER 5

Word Processing 4

OBJECTIVES

When you finish this chapter, you will be able to

- *use keyboard shortcuts*
- *use Quick Formats to indent paragraphs*
- *use automatic hanging and nested paragraph indents*
- *create a WORKS word processing template*
- *change default fonts and sizes*
- *copy and paste character styles and paragraph formats*
- *insert and delete page breaks*
- *number multipage documents*
- *insert footnotes*

SETTING THE SCENE

Now that you can produce simple documents, you are ready to learn some keyboard shortcuts and a few more advanced techniques. This chapter gives you the opportunity to explore the *WORKS* word processing application in more depth. Remember to use the Help feature frequently.

You will notice that some of the instructions in this chapter are less detailed and leave more to your imagination. That is because we want to encourage you to explore the application on your own.

GETTING STARTED

You will use the word processing document titled "*BICYCLE.WPS*" to try out the shortcuts and to use as a basis for the other exercises in this chapter.

- Launch *WORKS 3.0* and open *BICYCLE.WPS* from the main directory of your data disk.

USING KEYBOARD SHORTCUTS

You can invoke all of the menu options from the keyboard instead of using the mouse to pull down a menu and select an option. The [ALT] key must be pressed to activate the Menu bar, then press the underlined letter to cause the desired menu to drop down and finally, press the underlined letter for the desired command. For example, you can choose Save from the FILE menu by pressing [ALT] [F] [S]. The keys do not have to be pressed simultaneously. All menu commands can be selected in this manner as an alternative to using the mouse. If you have not begun to use these shortcuts, make it a point to try them out while you work on the various segments of this chapter. In some instances, you may find that you like using the keyboard better than using the mouse.

In addition, some menu commands are used so frequently that special shortcut key combinations are assigned to them. If such a shortcut exists, you can sometimes find it in each menu to the right of the options. You can browse through the menus to view some of the options that have keyboard commands. To invoke an option from the keyboard, simply press the designated key or keys. If more than one key is listed with a plus sign between them, you must hold down the first key while you press the remaining key or keys for that particular option. Some of the word processing shortcuts are listed in the following tables; try as many as you wish.

Keys for Highlighting Word Processor Information

When you highlight, the background behind the selection changes color. You can then change the selection. Use the following keyboard shortcuts to highlight text.

To	Press
Extend a selection	[F8] [ARROW KEYS]
Quit extending	[ESC]

To highlight	Press
A word	[F8] twice
A sentence	[F8] three times
A paragraph	[F8] four times
To the beginning of line	[SHIFT] + [HOME]
To the end of line	[SHIFT] + [END]
To the beginning of document	[CTRL] + [SHIFT] + [HOME]
To the end of document	[CTRL] + [SHIFT] + [END]

Keys for Changing Information

Use the following shortcut keys to make changes to highlighted information in a word processor document.

To	Press
Copy selection	[CTRL] + [C]
Paste selection	[CTRL] + [V]
Cut selection	[CTRL] + [X]

To	Press
Delete selection	[DEL] or [BACKSPACE]
Delete character to left of insertion point	[BACKSPACE]
Delete character to right of insertion point	[DEL]
Undo last command or action	[CTRL] + [Z]
Repeat search	[F7]
Paginate document	[F9]

Keys for Changing the Appearance of Text

Use the following keyboard shortcuts to change the appearance of high-lighted text in a document.

To	Press
Make text bold	[CTRL] + [B]
Make text italic	[CTRL] + [I]
Make text subscript	[CTRL] + [=] (equal sign)
Make text superscript	[CTRL] + [SHIFT] [=] (equal sign)
Underline text	[CTRL] + [U]
Remove all font styles	[CTRL] + [SPACEBAR]
Repeat format	[SHIFT] + [F7]

Keys for Choosing Menus and Commands

Use the following keyboard shortcuts to choose menus and commands.

To	Press
Save a document	[CTRL] + [S]
Get Help	[F1]
Activate the menu bar	[F10] or [ALT]
Choose the Tutorial	[SHIFT] + [F1]
Print a document	[CTRL] + [P]
Close any open menu	[ESC]
Open the Font box on the toolbar	[CTRL] + [F]

To	Press
Open the Font Size box on the toolbar	[CTRL] + [K]
Quit *WORKS*	[ALT] + [F4]

Keys for Indenting Word Processor Information

Use the following keyboard shortcuts to add or change indents of highlighted paragraphs in a document.

To	Press
Add hanging indent	[CTRL] + [H]
Undo hanging indent	[CTRL] + [G]
Add nested indent	[CTRL] + [N]
Undo nested indent	[CTRL] + [M]

Keys for Inserting Information

Use the following keyboard shortcuts to insert line breaks, page breaks, hyphens, or tab marks.

To Insert	Press
A page break (in the word processor)	[CTRL] + [ENTER]
The current date	[CTRL] + [;] (semicolon)
The current time	[CTRL] + [SHIFT] + [;] (semicolon)
The filename (when printed)	[CTRL] + [A]
The date (when printed)	[CTRL] + [D]
The time (when printed)	[CTRL] + [T]
A nonbreaking hyphen	[CTRL] + [SHIFT] + [-] (hyphen)
A nonbreaking space	[CTRL] + [SHIFT] + [SPACEBAR]

Keys for Line and Paragraph Spacing

Use the following keyboard shortcuts to change the spacing of highlighted lines or paragraphs in a word processor document.

To	Press
Single space lines	[CTRL] + [1]
Double space lines	[CTRL] + [2]

To	Press
Space lines 1.5 lines apart	[CTRL] + [5]
Reduce space before paragraph	[CTRL] + [0] (zero)
Add space before paragraph	[CTRL] + [O] (letter O)

Keys for Moving Around in a Dialog Box

This section reviews basic Windows shortcuts for moving a dialog box. You can also choose a dialog box option by pressing the [ALT] key and the underlined letter in the option name.

To	Press
Move forward through options	[TAB]
Move backward through options	[SHIFT] + [TAB]
Open a list box	[DOWN ARROW]
Confirm an option or carry it out	[ENTER]
Cancel the changes and close the dialog box	[ESC]

Keys for Moving Around in a Word Processor Document

Use the following keyboard shortcuts to move the insertion point within a word processor document.

To Move	Press
To the beginning of line	[HOME]
To the end of line	[END]
To the beginning of document	[CTRL] + [HOME]
To the end of document	[CTRL] + [END]

Keys for Aligning Text

Use the following keyboard shortcuts to change the alignment of highlighted paragraphs in a document.

To	Press
Center text	[CTRL] + [E]
Justify text	[CTRL] + [J]
Left align text	[CTRL] + [L]

To	Press
Right align text	[CTRL] + [R]
Remove paragraph styles	[CTRL] + [Q]

INDENTING PARAGRAPHS

You can use indents to offset text or to create numbered lists and outlines. *WORKS* also offers several "Quick Formats" with which you can apply indents to create commonly used paragraph styles. For example, you can use the Quick Format options to:

- Indent the first line of the paragraph.
- Create a bulleted list.
- Create hanging indents—useful for formatting numbered lists and bibliographies. (You used hanging indents when you did the want ad document.)
- Format quotations so that they are set apart from the rest of the document. The Quotation format is useful for academic papers and reports.This type of indent is often called a "nested indent."

Applying "Quick Format" Paragraph Styles

1. Highlight the paragraphs you want to change.
2. Choose the Paragraph command from the FORMAT menu, click the Quick Formats tab, and then choose the options you want.

 HINT   You can quickly display the Paragraph dialog box by double clicking either indent marker on the ruler.

3. Click the OK button.

Manually Setting an Indent

1. Highlight each paragraph you want to indent.
2. On the ruler, drag an indent marker (first line, left, or right) to the position you want.

Automatically Setting a Hanging Indent

1. Highlight each paragraph you want to indent.
2. Press [CTRL] + [H].

Automatically Setting Nested Indents

1. Highlight each paragraph you want to indent.
2. Press [CTRL] + [N] once for each level of indent you want.

Precisely Setting Any or All Indents at One Time

1. Highlight each paragraph you want to indent.
2. Choose Paragraph from the FORMAT menu, then click the Indents And Alignment tab.

3. In the Left Indent, Right Indent, or First Line Indent boxes, type the measurements you want. You can type measurements in inches (0.5"), centimeters (1.26cm), picas (3pi), points (36pt), or millimeters (12.7mm).

4. Click the OK button.

CREATING A TEMPLATE DOCUMENT

Whenever a certain document format is used over and over again, it is useful to create a template that includes the text, margin settings, font selection, line spacing, etc. that are always required in that type of document. Once the template is created and saved, the user can simply open that template document and proceed to fill in whatever new text is required before printing. Figure 5-1 illustrates a possible template document.

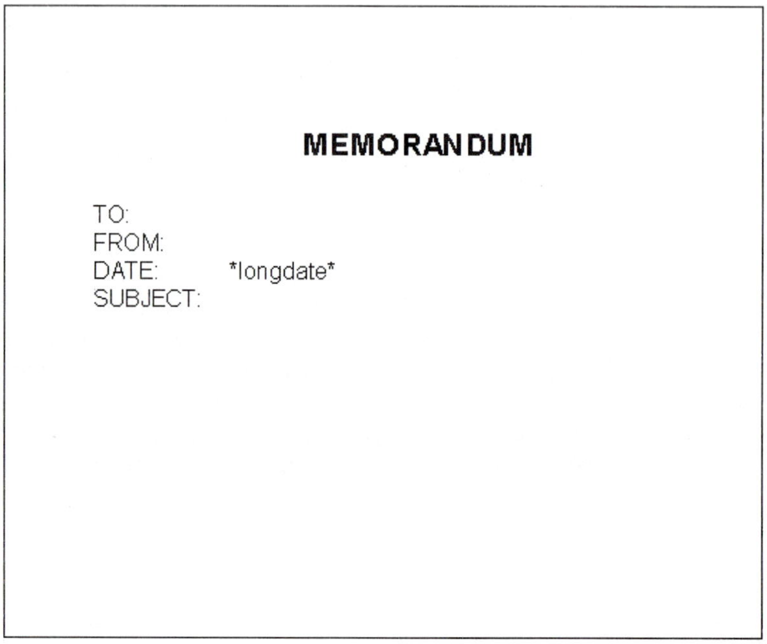

FIGURE 5-1

MEMORANDUM

TO:
FROM:
DATE: *longdate*
SUBJECT:

Take special note of the appearance of the date; if you insert the *longdate* or *date* special character, the current date will always display whenever the template document is used.

To create a template document, simply type the document as you would like it to appear in a new word processing window. Use the Save As command to save the document, and click the TEMPLATE button in the Save As dialog box. The Save As Template dialog box will appear for you to type a template name. Choose an appropriate name (such as *MEMO* for the example), and click the OK button to complete the save.

When you want to use the template, choose Templates from the FILE menu to display the Use A Template section of the Startup dialog box; choose the Custom Template group, Custom Category, and Memo template. Then click the OK button to open the template document. A copy of the blank memorandum will open, leaving the original document unchanged.

When you investigate the Use A Template section of the Startup dialog box, you will see that *WORKS* also includes many predefined templates. You may want to explore these, as some of them may be helpful to you in increasing your own productivity.

Note that the Use A Template section of the Startup dialog box is also the place where you can delete templates you no longer want to keep.

CAUTION   *WORKS* stores templates in a special section of the system files. If you are working in a network situation, you may not be able to access this special section.

CHANGING DEFAULT FONTS AND SIZES

When you are working on your *own* computer system and wish to change the font and size defaults used by the *WORKS* tools, you can do so at any time by choosing Font and Style from the FORMAT menu. Font, size, color, position, and style options will be displayed and can be changed by clicking the desired choices. After making your choices, click the SET DEFAULT button in the dialog box. Then whenever you create a new word processor document, the font attributes you have chosen will be used. You should not change any default settings in a school laboratory.

ANOTHER LOOK AT TAB STOPS

It is easy to move tab stops even after they have been set. To move a tab stop, simply click in the paragraph containing the tab, point to the tab marker on the ruler and drag it to the left or right. To delete the tab, drag the marker down and off the ruler into the text area and then release the mouse button. When you release the mouse button, the tab marker disappears. To bring up the Tabs dialog box, simply double click anywhere in the ruler area.

COPYING CHARACTER STYLES AND PARAGRAPH FORMATS

To save time and create a uniform appearance, you can copy formatting from one paragraph to another. *WORKS* copies formats, including alignment, indents, tabs, and line spacing. To copy the format for a paragraph so it can be used elsewhere, highlight the text from which you want to copy a style or format and choose Copy from the EDIT menu. To paste those formats, highlight the characters or paragraphs needing the formatting and choose Paste Special from the EDIT menu. *WORKS* will display the Paste Special dialog box from which you can choose either the Character Style or Paragraph Format option (but not both at the same time).

INSERTING AND DELETING PAGE BREAKS

As you enter text in a new file, *WORKS* automatically inserts page breaks according to the page length and margin settings established in the Page Setup dialog box. The default is set for 8.5 by 11-inch paper. When you insert or delete text, *WORKS* automatically adjusts the page breaks. Automatic page breaks are identified by the small chevron symbol (>>) in the left margin in normal view. Sometimes you may want to insert a manual page break. Manual page breaks are useful when you want to keep a table or a paragraph from being broken between two pages. If you insert a manual page break, *WORKS* will readjust the automatic page breaks that follow. On your screen, manual page breaks are indicated by a dotted line (.......) across the document window.

To insert a manual page break, you must first move the insertion point to the beginning of the line where you want the page to begin and press [CTRL] + [ENTER] to make the insertion. To delete a manual page break, move the insertion point to the line immediately below the manual page break, and press [BACKSPACE]. Once again, *WORKS* readjusts any automatic page breaks that follow the deleted manual one, and of course any following manual page breaks stay as they have been set.

IT'S YOUR TURN

You should still have your Bicycle Trivia file open.

1. Choose *BICYCLE.WPS* from the WINDOW menu if it does not display.

2. Scroll down to the end of the document.

You will insert a page break so that the Bibliography starts on a separate page.

3. Click the I-beam to set the insertion point at the beginning of the word "Bibliography."

4. Select Page Break from the INSERT menu (or press [CTRL] + ENTER]).

   A dotted line will appear across the document to indicate the manual page break.

To number the pages of this multi-page document in the upper right corner of each page,

5. Choose Headers & Footers from the VIEW menu.

   Since the insertion point is already in the header box,

6. Type: &rPage &p

   To eliminate the page number on page 1,

7. Click the No Header on 1st Page option and close the dialog box by clicking the OK button.

8. Use Save As, name this document *BICYCLE2,* and save it in your name directory on your data disk. Do not close this file yet, as you will use it once more in the footnote section.

CREATING FOOTNOTES

WORKS 3.0 has a fairly extensive capability for creating and manipulating footnotes and endnotes. Footnotes are numbered reference notes that occur at the bottom of a page, while endnotes (also numbered) occur at the end of the entire document. Footnotes and endnotes are used to provide additional information or to cite references. *WORKS* automatically marks and numbers the notes and opens a window in which you type the text for the notes. Both kinds of notes can be numbered sequentially throughout the document. If you wish, you can choose a distinctive character to denote a footnote. You cannot, however, mix footnotes and endnotes in a document. The distinction as to whether you are using footnotes or endnotes is made through the Other Options section of the Page Setup dialog box. Henceforth, we will use footnotes to mean both footnotes and endnotes, unless a specific distinction must be made.

Footnotes consist of two parts: a reference number (which is assigned sequentially by *WORKS*) or a special marker (which is chosen by you) in the body of the text, and the footnote text (which is placed either at the end of the page or at the end of the document). You can edit footnote text in a special footnote window. You can edit, delete, cut, copy, and paste footnote reference numbers in the main document window; *WORKS* automatically moves footnote text with the reference number and adjusts other numbers appropriately.

There are two ways to create footnotes using *WORKS 3.0.* You can either type and format the footnote yourself, or you can use a WorksWizard. When you use the WorksWizard, you are presented with a special form into which you type the necessary information, and *WORKS* does all the formatting for you. In the exercise that follows, both methods are presented.

IT'S YOUR TURN

You will now use WorksWizard to insert a footnote in the Bicycle file.

1. Choose Page Setup from the FILE menu.

2. Click the Other Options tab to bring that section of the Page Setup dialog box into view.

Figure 5-2 shows the Other Options section of the Page Setup dialog box. Note the option to print footnotes at the end of the document on the left-hand side. That option should be turned off, because you want the footnotes to be printed on each page.

FIGURE 5-2

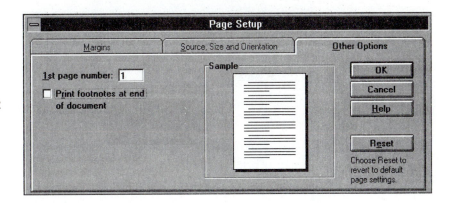

3. If it is not already turned off, click the Print Footnotes At End of Document option to remove the "x" from the box so that footnotes will be printed at the end of the page containing the footnote reference number.

    You would leave the End of Document option turned on if you wanted *WORKS* to print endnotes at the end of the document.

To return to the document,

4. Click the OK button or press [ENTER].

To create a numbered footnote regarding the motorcycle reference,

5. Choose Find from the EDIT menu, type "motorcycle" in the Find What box, and click FIND NEXT or press [ENTER].

6. Click YES if the Continue Searching from the Beginning of the Document dialog box appears.

    The word "motorcycle" is highlighted.

7. Click CANCEL to close the Find dialog box.

8. Press [RIGHT ARROW] twice to move the insertion point after the period, as shown in Figure 5-3.

9. Choose Footnote from the INSERT menu.

    The Footnote dialog box shown in Figure 5-4 will appear.

10. Click the "Numbered" option in the Footnote Type box if it is not already selected.

11. Click the USE WORKSWIZARD button.

    The Footnote WorksWizard screen shown in Figure 5-5 will appear. As shown in that figure, "Book" should already be selected as the kind of source you want to cite.

12. If "Book" is not selected, click it to select it.

To advance to the next screen in this WorksWizard,

Place Insertion Point Here

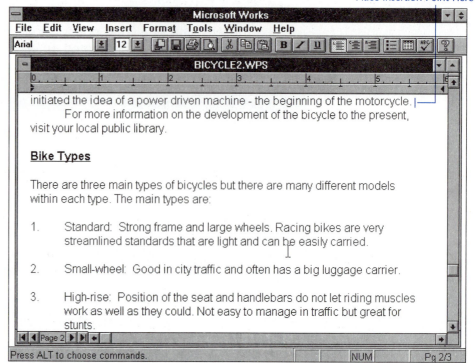

FIGURE 5-3

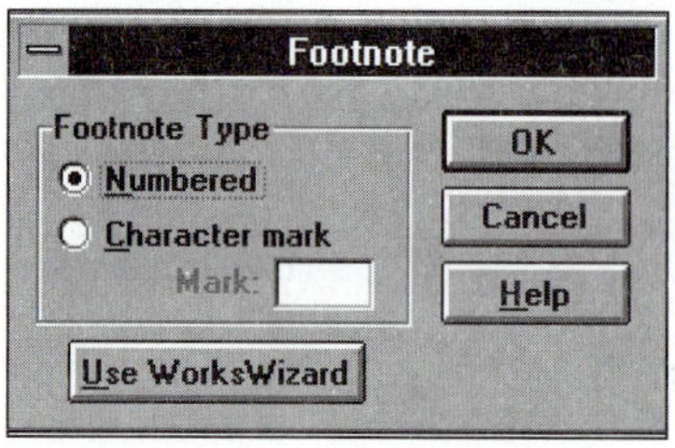

FIGURE 5-4

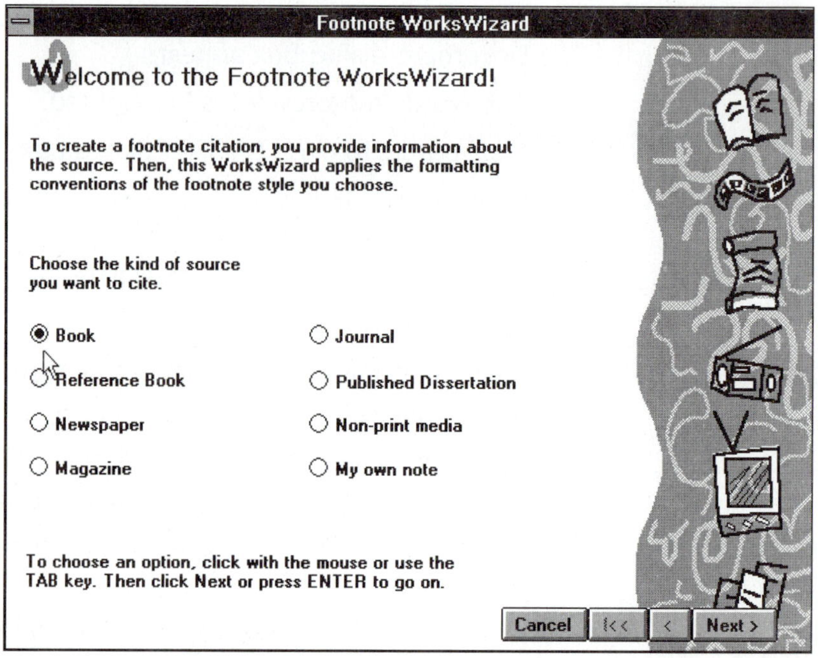

FIGURE 5-5

13. Click the NEXT button in the bottom right-hand corner of the screen.

    The Book screen of the Footnote WorksWizard will appear, as shown in Figure 5-6.

FIGURE 5-6

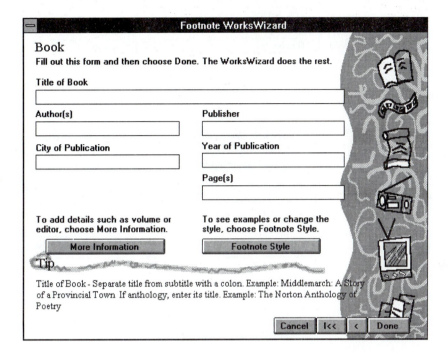

The insertion point should be blinking in the Title of Book text box.

14. **Type:** Two Hundred Years of Bicycles

To move to the Author box,

15. Press [TAB].
16. **Type:** Murphy, Jim
17. Press [TAB].

    You are now in the Publisher text box.

18. **Type:** J. B. Lippincott

To move to the City of Publication box,

19. Press [TAB].
20. **Type:** New York
21. Press [TAB].

To fill in the Year of Publication,

22. **Type:** 1983

    You are almost finished. Simply move to the Pages box and type in the page numbers used for this citation, as follows:

23. Press [TAB].
24. **Type:** 1-52

    Your screen should now look like the one shown in Figure 5-7.

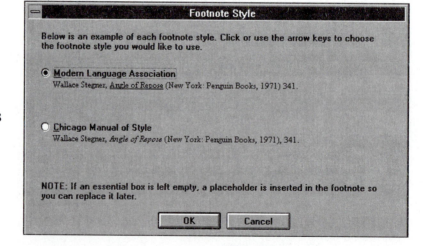

FIGURE 5-7

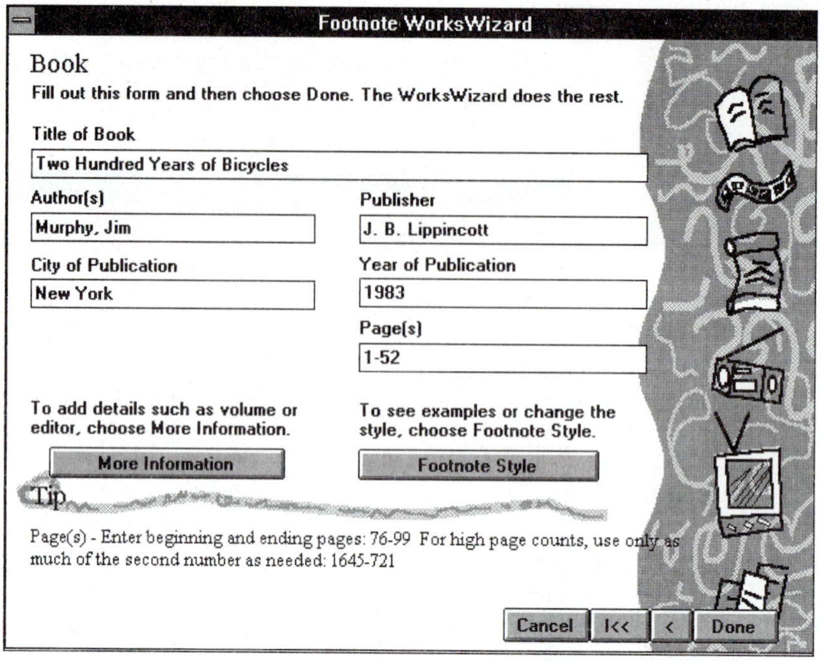

25. Make any necessary corrections, until your screen is identical to the one shown in Figure 5-7. Use [TAB] to move from one text box to another, and use standard text editing techniques to make changes within the text boxes.

When your screen is completed,

26. Click the FOOTNOTE STYLE button.

The Footnote Style dialog box shown in Figure 5-8 will appear.

FIGURE 5-8

27. Click "Modern Language Association" to choose that style, if it is not already selected.

28. Click the OK button or press [ENTER].

You will be returned to the Book screen, as shown in Figure 5-7.

Since you are finished entering all the information,

29. Click the DONE button.

Lots of things happen now. The properly formatted footnote is entered into a footnote pane at the bottom of your screen, a small superscript number one appears in the document at the position of the insertion point, and the original Footnote dialog box disappears. The footnote is complete. Your screen should now resemble the one shown in Figure 5-9.

FIGURE 5-9

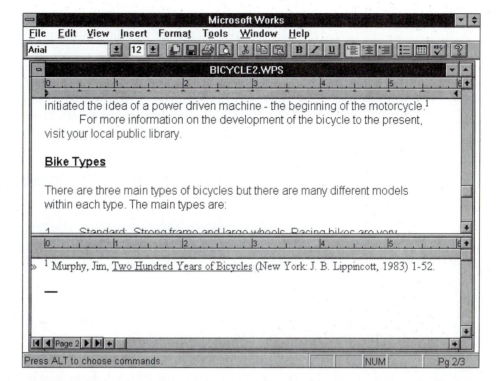

As you examine the footnote, you may notice that it is not the same font style as the main document. That is because footnotes use the default font attributes. If your system defaults have not been changed, the footnotes will appear in 12 point Times New Roman. To change the footnote to match the font style of the rest of the document, but in a slightly smaller size,

30. Double click in the left margin of the footnote to select the entire footnote paragraph.

31. Choose Arial from the drop-down Font Style box on the toolbar.

32. Choose 10 from the drop-down Font Size box on the toolbar.

If changes in the footnote are still necessary,

33. Edit the footnote as you would any text.

CAUTION
You can add, change, or delete footnote text in the footnote pane; but to delete a footnote entirely, select the footnote number in the document itself and then press [BACKSPACE].

34. Click the VIEW menu and note that the Footnotes command is checked.

To hide the footnote pane,

35. **Click the Footnotes command to remove the checkmark.**

The VIEW menu closes and the footnote pane at the bottom of the screen goes away. You can make the footnote pane reappear at any time by choosing Footnotes from the VIEW menu.

You will now insert another footnote without using WorksWizard.

36. **Place the insertion point at the end of the document on page two (after the word "stunts") as illustrated in Figure 5-10.**

HINT

Using the scroll bar is one way to advance through a document. Another way is to move one or more pages by clicking the page control buttons in the lower left corner of the screen. (See Figure 5-10.)

FIGURE 5-10

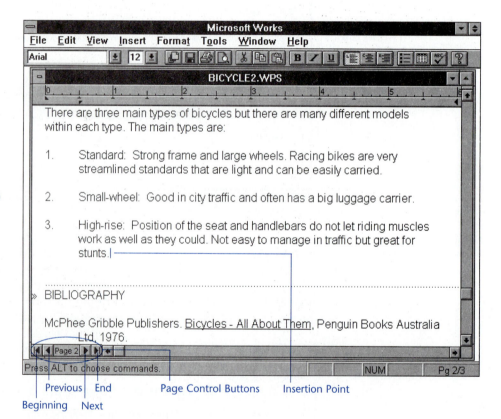

37. **Choose Footnote from the INSERT menu.**

Once again the Footnote dialog box appears. Remember, this time you are not going to use the WorksWizard.

38. **If necessary, select Numbered in the Footnote Type box, then click OK or press [ENTER].**

A small superscript number two appears in the text at the insertion point position, and the footnote pane opens, with the insertion point blinking in it immediately following another small superscript number two.

39. Type the following for the second footnote:

McPhee Gribble Publishers, <u>Bicycles—All About Them</u> (Australia: Penguin Books, 1976) 3-4.

40. Select Footnote two and change the font style and size to 10 point Arial.

As you add footnotes, the text of the most recent one is displayed in the Footnote pane. You can use the vertical scroll bar and arrows to scroll through all the footnotes.

To hide the footnote pane again,

41. Choose Footnotes from the VIEW menu.

To see how the footnotes will look when printed,

42. Click the PRINT PREVIEW button on the toolbar or choose Print Preview from the FILE menu.

43. Click the NEXT and PREVIOUS buttons to page through the Bicycle document.

The document has three pages. You will be able to see the effect of the page breaks, as well as the footnotes you created at the bottom of page two.

44. When you have finished viewing the Print Preview screen, print if directed to do so, then click the CANCEL button to return to your document.

FINISHING UP

You are now finished with the *BICYCLE2* file, so it is time to put it away and leave *WORKS*.

IT'S YOUR TURN

1. Choose Close from the FILE menu and click the YES button when asked if you want to save changes to your *BICYCLE2* file.

2. Quit *WORKS,* as directed at the end of Chapter 2.

SUMMARY

Congratulations! You have now completed the word processing chapters, although a few more features will be introduced in the advanced chapters at the end of this text. You now know about using keyboard shortcuts, templates, and how to change the default font size and style. You have inserted page breaks and created footnotes. There is still a lot more to learn about the word processing module, so remember to use the Help feature or refer to the *WORKS 3.0* manual.

REVIEW QUESTIONS

True/False

1. There is more than one way of selecting text.

2. You open a template file from the Page Setup dialog box.

3. The Paragraph dialog box (FORMAT menu) allows you to set a hanging indent.

4. You can format text in only one style at a time; e.g., if text is in bold, you cannot italicize it.

5. To remove a tab stop, you double click it.

6. There is no visible difference between a manual page break and an automatic page break.

7. The words "footer" and "footnote" are synonymous.

8. When a manual page break is inserted, all page breaks (manual and automatic) are automatically readjusted.

9. Footnote numbering need not start with the number one.

EXERCISE

Create a word processing document of your own choice, perhaps a report or research paper for another class or a letter to the editor of a newspaper.

CHAPTER 6

Spreadsheet 1

OBJECTIVES

When you finish this chapter you will be able to

- *identify rows, columns, and cells in a spreadsheet file*
- *explain the difference between text and values*
- *view all parts of the spreadsheet*
- *select part of a spreadsheet*
- *insert rows and columns*
- *enter and edit cell content*
- *understand formulas and functions*
- *delete and clear rows and columns*
- *format values*
- *play "What If"*
- *save and print a spreadsheet*

WHAT ARE SPREADSHEET PROGRAMS?

Spreadsheet programs are immensely popular because of how quickly and accurately they create professional, quality documents containing calculations. In fact, one in four computer owners buys a spreadsheet program. Two well known spreadsheet programs are Lotus 1-2-3™ and Excel™. As you complete Chapters 6, 7, 8, and 9, you will discover why so many people from so many different backgrounds find spreadsheet programs useful for business or for personal projects.

What is a *spreadsheet?* A paper spreadsheet is a tool normally used for financial analysis. It is a page divided into vertical columns and horizontal rows. An electronic spreadsheet displays the same structure on a computer screen but with some significant differences. For example, a paper spreadsheet is limited by the size of the paper, but an electronic spreadsheet can be hundreds of columns wide and thousands of rows long. Figure 6-1 displays a section of a blank electronic spreadsheet.

With a paper spreadsheet, a *cell* (block located at the intersection of a row and a column) holds only text (words) or numbers; but a cell in an electronic spreadsheet can hold text, a number, another cell's address, a mathematical formula, or a logical instruction. If a cell holds a second cell's address, the program will display the content of that second cell. If a cell holds a formula, the cell will display the number resulting from the application of the formula. The program will show the formula itself in another section of the screen. The

95

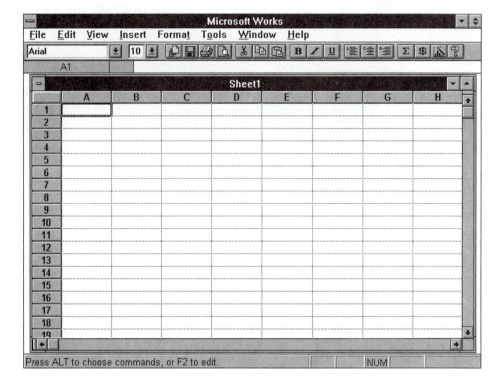

FIGURE 6-1

formula can be as complex as a trigonometric equation or a logical comparison, or it can be as simple as a two-number addition.

An electronic spreadsheet program creates in memory an enormous grid of rows and columns, a very small portion of which can be seen on the screen at any one time. Some people create spreadsheets that take many pages to print.

Although many spreadsheet programs are available, there is much similarity between them. As a result, if you learn one program, such as the spreadsheet tool in *WORKS,* you can easily adapt to another.

SETTING THE SCENE

In order to discover seasonal trends in the sales of various toy products, a spreadsheet has been created to itemize sales by category for each month of the year. The spreadsheet contains formulas that will compute total sales, sales taxes collected, and total receipts.

GETTING STARTED

You will modify the existing spreadsheet by deleting one category and adding one month's data. Figure 6-2 shows the spreadsheet and indicates the changes to be made.

IT'S YOUR TURN

1. Launch *WORKS 3.0.*

2. Open the *MONSAL.WKS* file from your data disk.

Your screen should resemble the one shown in Figure 6-3.

IDENTIFYING ROWS, COLUMNS, AND CELLS

Figure 6-3 displays the spreadsheet with some of the parts labeled. Especially note the areas labeled Formula bar, Select All box, Row Headers, and Column Headers.

Look at your screen. Note that the menus are somewhat like those in word processing, but the rest of the screen is quite different. Here the screen area is

Delete This Column

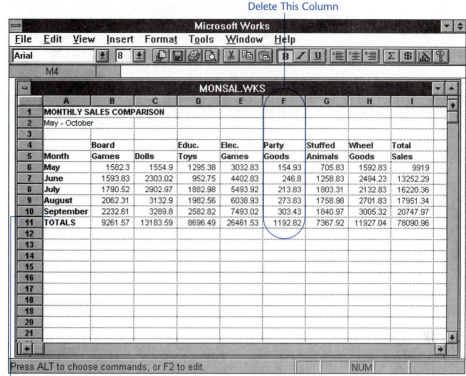

FIGURE 6-2

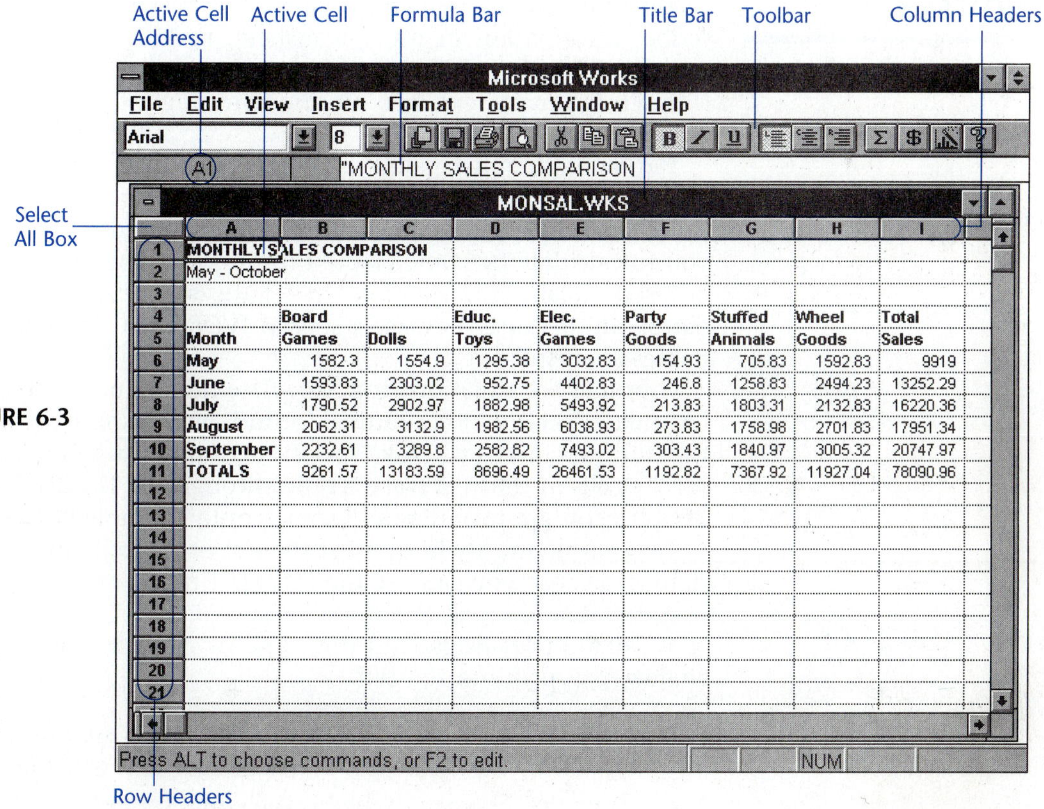

Insert October Figures

Active Cell   Active Cell   Formula Bar   Title Bar   Toolbar   Column Headers
Address

Select
All Box

FIGURE 6-3

Row Headers

labeled across the top by letters and down the left side by numbers. The letters label the vertical *columns* and the numbers label the horizontal *rows*. A column and row intersect to form a cell.

To refer to a cell, you use its *address*. This includes the letter of its column and the number of its row. For example, in Figure 6-3, cell B6 (column B, row 6) gives the May sales of board games.

When you use the mouse to click in a cell, the border around that cell becomes darkened to remind you that it is the ***active cell***. The active cell is the one with which the spreadsheet program is ready to work. If you want to work with a different cell, you have to change the selection.

You can also identify which cell is the active cell by looking at the cell address displayed in the extreme left side of the Formula bar located immediately above the Title bar in Figure 6-3. (Under some configurations, when the spreadsheet window has been maximized, the Formula bar will be located immediately above the window's column headers.) In Figure 6-3, the Formula bar displays A1, because that is the cell that is currently active.

IT'S YOUR TURN

To change the active cell,

1. Move the pointer to cell B6.

2. Click once to select the cell.

To return to cell A1 as the active cell,

3. Click on cell A1.

IDENTIFYING VALUES, FORMULAS, AND TEXT

A spreadsheet cell can hold three types of information: text, values, or formulas.

Text can include headings, labels, notes, and explanatory text. Text describes information in the spreadsheet, making the numbers and formulas easier to understand. Column A of the Monthly Sales spreadsheet and rows 1 through 5 contain text. You can use letters, numbers, or a combination of letters and numbers in text.

Values are numbers you type into a spreadsheet cell and can include numbers, dates, or times. Dates and times are special kinds of values. Dates and times can be placed in spreadsheet cells and used in formulas, thus allowing you to calculate the time elapsed from one event to another. Dates can also be used to label information. In Figure 6-3, cells A6 through A10 contain dates; but, because they use a special *WORKS* date format, only the months' names are displayed.

Formulas are equations that calculate new values from existing values and formulas. A cell that contains a formula will display the value calculated by that formula unless you take specific action to cause it to display the formula. All the cells in the area from cell B6 through cell I11 display values, but some of them contain formulas and some contain simple values.

Text automatically lines up at the left of the cell, and values line up at the right. However, you can use the FORMAT menu or the toolbar to left, center, or right align any cell.

WORKS 3.0 distinguishes one type of cell content from another by the characters typed into the cell.

- If the first and succeeding characters typed are numeric characters (0, 1, 2 . . . 9), *WORKS 3.0* treats the cell content as a numeric value.

- If the first character typed is the equal symbol (=), *WORKS 3.0* treats the cell content as a formula (and the formula must conform to the syntax, or rules, for formulas).

- If the first character typed is a letter or the double quotation mark (") or some other special character that is not used for anything else, *WORKS* treats the cell content as text.

CAUTION   Do not use the lowercase letter L for the number one. The number one is a value which can be used in calculations; the letter L cannot be used in calculations. A clue that a mistake has been made is that a number containing a letter L will align on the left side of a cell instead of the right.

MOVING AROUND THE SPREADSHEET

A *WORKS 3.0* spreadsheet can be enormous (up to 16,384 rows and 256 columns). Obviously, you cannot see all of a large spreadsheet at one time. To move to cells not displayed, you will first use the scroll arrows at the ends of the scroll bars shown in Figure 6-4.

FIGURE 6-4

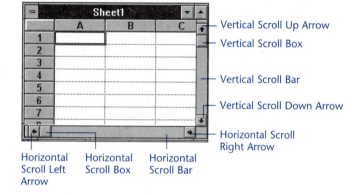

IT'S YOUR TURN

To move around the spreadsheet,

1. Move the pointer to the right horizontal scroll arrow in the lower right corner of your screen and click the mouse until you can see an area where the cells are empty.

   Note that the spreadsheet scrolls one column every time you click the mouse and that the column letters at the top of the screen advance as you move to the right. Also note that the active cell does not change when you scroll the spreadsheet using the scroll arrow. The Formula bar still contains the A1 notation, indicating that is the active cell.

2. Move the pointer to the left horizontal scroll arrow in the lower left corner of your screen and click the mouse (or hold down the mouse button) until you have moved back to where you can see cell A1.

3. Move the pointer to the down scroll arrow in the lower right corner of your screen and click the mouse (or hold down the mouse button) until you can see only empty cells.

   Note that the spreadsheet scrolls down one row every time you click the arrow and that the row numbers at the left of the screen increase as you move down the spreadsheet. Once again, note that the active cell is still cell A1.

4. Move the pointer to the up scroll arrow in the upper right corner of your screen and click the mouse until you have moved back to the area where you can see cell A1.

   As you have probably noticed, using the arrows is a rather slow way of moving long distances. You would not want to move to the bottom of a large spreadsheet full of data using the scroll arrows! Luckily, you don't have to. To move long distances in the same row or same column, you can use the scroll boxes at the bottom and at the right of the screen. These boxes are also shown in Figure 6-4. For example, to move quickly down the columns,

5. Move the pointer to the scroll box in the vertical scroll bar on the right of your screen.

6. Drag the scroll box to the bottom of the scroll bar (hold down the mouse button while you drag the scroll box to the bottom of the scroll bar, then release the mouse button).

    Once again, note that the row numbers increase but the column labels do not change. Do you know how to move back quickly to the top of the spreadsheet?

7. Move the pointer to the scroll box at the bottom of the vertical scroll bar and drag it back up to the top.

8. Move the pointer to the scroll box at the bottom left of the screen in the horizontal scroll bar.

9. Drag the box to the far right.

To return to the beginning (left side) of the file,

10. Drag the box back to the far left of the scroll bar.

USING THE GO TO CELL OPTION

It is important that you remember that none of the above methods of viewing other parts of the spreadsheet changed the active cell. You can move quickly to a distant cell and select it at the same time by using the Go To option from the EDIT menu. Follow the steps in the next section to select cell Z1000.

IT'S YOUR TURN

1. Choose Go To from the EDIT menu or press [F5].

The Go To dialog box shown in Figure 6-5 will appear with the cursor blinking in the Go To text box.

FIGURE 6-5

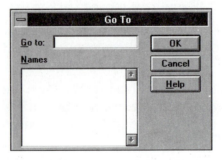

You can use this box to find a specific cell by its location, so

2. Type: Z1000

    Always use the zeros located on the top row of the keyboard (or on the numeric keypad if NUM displays in the Status Bar); if you type the letter "O," it may look the same, but it will cause an error message to be generated when you complete the next step.

3. Click the OK button (or press [ENTER]).

    The screen displays an empty portion of the document with cell Z1000 highlighted in the lower right corner, making it the active cell. Look at the left side of the Formula bar; cell Z1000 is listed as the active cell.

    Now you will use the Find option to find a cell that contains the value $9,919. When typing amounts in spreadsheets, it is important to note that the dollar sign and commas are not typed. They are inserted when the cells are formatted.

4. Choose Find from the EDIT menu

    When the Find dialog box appears,

5. Type: 9919

6. Click the OK button (or press [ENTER]).

    The highlighting moves to cell I6, which contains the value 9919. If several cells contained the value 9919 and the program did not find the proper cell, you could perform step 4 again.

See if you can return to the upper left corner of the spreadsheet again so you can view the entire file. If you need help, take the following steps.

7. Choose Go To from the EDIT menu ([F5]).

8. Type: A1

    (That's the number one.)

9. Click the OK button (or press [ENTER]).

    Cell A1 is now selected and visible on your screen.

    There are also special shortcut keys that are helpful for moving around in the spreadsheet. These keys will be included in Chapter 9, the final chapter on spreadsheets.

SELECTING PARTS OF A SPREADSHEET

In order to work with a cell or a group of cells, you must select (highlight) it. To select a single cell, you simply click on that cell; for example, to select cell F4 where the column title "Party" was typed,

IT'S YOUR TURN

1. Move the pointer to cell F4 and click.

    The boldly outlined border of cell F4 indicates that it is the active cell.

To select the cell to the right (cell G4),

2. Press [TAB] or [RIGHT ARROW].

    The other arrow keys will also select adjoining cells.

To select a block (or range) of cells, such as the sales amounts by category for each month,

3. Move the pointer to cell B6 in the upper left corner of the block (see Figure 6-6).

Start Dragging Here

FIGURE 6-6

	Microsoft Works								
<u>F</u>ile <u>E</u>dit <u>V</u>iew Insert Format T<u>o</u>ols <u>W</u>indow <u>H</u>elp									

Arial   8   B / U   Σ $?

B6:H10   1582.3

MONSAL.WKS

	A	B	C	D	E	F	G	H	I
1	MONTHLY SALES COMPARISON								
2	May - October								
3									
4		Board		Educ.	Elec.	Party	Stuffed	Wheel	Total
5	Month	Games	Dolls	Toys	Games	Goods	Animals	Goods	Sales
6	May	1582.3	1554.9	1295.38	3032.83	154.93	705.83	1592.83	9919
7	June	1593.83	2303.02	952.75	4402.83	246.8	1258.83	2494.23	13252.29
8	July	1790.52	2902.97	1882.98	5493.92	213.83	1803.31	2132.83	16220.36
9	August	2062.31	3132.9	1982.56	6038.93	273.83	1758.98	2701.83	17951.34
10	September	2232.61	3289.8	2582.82	7493.02	303.43	1840.97	3005.32	20747.97
11	TOTALS	9261.57	13183.59	8696.49	26461.53	1192.82	7367.92	11927.04	78090.96
12									
13									
14									
15									
16									
17									
18									
19									
20									
21									

Press ALT to choose commands, or F2 to edit.   NUM

End Dragging Here

4. Drag diagonally to cell H10 in the opposite corner (see Figure 6-6).

HINT

To drag, press down on the mouse button and hold it down until you reach the opposite corner, then release the button.

When you have selected a range of cells, the Formula bar displays the range together with the content of the first cell selected in the range.

To extend (or reduce) the selected area, you can hold down [SHIFT] while dragging an edge of the selected area. For example, to extend the selection to include the Total Sales column,

5. Move the pointer back to cell H10, where you stopped your block selection.

6. Hold down [SHIFT] while dragging the mouse to cell I10.

Frequently you will want to select entire rows or columns in order to format or delete them. There is an easy way to do this. For example, to select row 6,

7. Move the pointer to the row header 6 on the far left of the spreadsheet and click.

The entire row is selected, as indicated by the boldly outlined border of the first cell in the row and the darkened cells in the rest of the row (see Figure 6-7). You also can tell that the selection includes the entire row because the range A6:IV6 is displayed in the Formula bar.

To select a single column, such as column D,

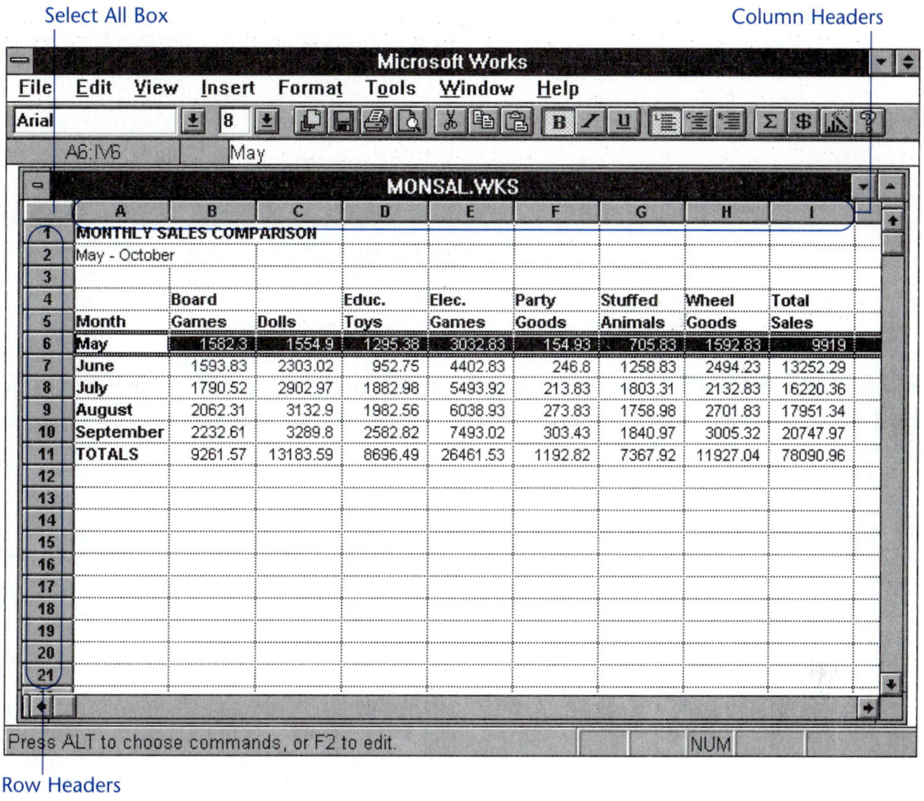

Select All Box   Column Headers

FIGURE 6-7

Row Headers

8.   Move the pointer to the column header D at the top of the spread-sheet and click.

Look at the range displayed in the Formula bar this time. This column contains 16,384 cells.

To select columns B through I,

9.   Move the pointer to the column header B and drag to include column I.

To quickly select all cells in the spreadsheet,

10.   Click on the Select All box to the left of the column headings (see Figure 6-7 for its location) or choose Select All from the EDIT menu.

Every cell in the spreadsheet is now selected, whether or not it contains any information.

You can verify this by looking at the range displayed in the Formula bar, or

11.   Click the horizontal scroll bar anywhere on the right side of the horizontal scroll box.

The scroll box jumps to the far right end of the scroll bar and you can see all the empty cells that have been selected.

To return to the data in your spreadsheet,

12.   Click the horizontal scroll bar anywhere on the left side of the scroll box.

The scroll box jumps back to the left, and your spreadsheet data is back in view.

To deselect,

13. Click anywhere in the spreadsheet.

Chapter 9 contains a table giving keyboard shortcuts for selecting cells and ranges of cells in a spreadsheet.

INSERTING ROWS AND COLUMNS

You will frequently need to make changes to your spreadsheets. In this particular case, October data have just become available so you will add the data to this file. First you must select the row where the October data will appear.

IT'S YOUR TURN

1. Click on the row header 11 for the TOTALS line.

The entire line becomes highlighted. Don't worry that the row already has entries. When you insert a row, the program will move the present content of the selected row down to the next row.

2. Choose Row/Column from the INSERT menu.

A new line is inserted at row 11 for your October data, and the remaining lines are moved down. *WORKS* knew that you wanted to insert a row (and not a column), because you had the row selected.

Columns are inserted in the same way as rows. Simply select the column in which you want the blank column to appear and choose Row/Column from the INSERT menu. A blank column will appear in that position and all the succeeding columns will be shifted to the right.

TYPING CHARACTERS INTO CELLS

The most common way of entering values and text into a spreadsheet is by selecting a cell and typing. The characters typed will appear in that cell.

IT'S YOUR TURN

1. Click on cell A1.

Notice that the title for this report overflows into column B. However, only cell A1 is considered occupied (see the Formula bar). When a cell containing text is not wide enough to show all the characters it contains, *WORKS* displays the characters until it encounters an occupied cell. Since the other cells on row 1 are not occupied, the entire line is available for displaying the label stored in cell A1.

To verify that cell B1 is empty,

2. Click on cell B1.

As you can see from the Formula bar, cell B1 is empty. If it contained anything, the continuation of the title from cell A1 would not be displayed in this cell.

Dates and times are values in *WORKS*; therefore, they are confined to one cell and will not overflow into the next. There may be times when you want to display a date as text, and in that event, simply precede it with a quotation mark ("). The quotation mark will appear in the Formula bar but will not appear on the spreadsheet.

To enter the new month,

3.   Move the pointer to cell A11 and click to select that cell.

4.   Type: October

Your screen should resemble the one shown in Figure 6-8.

FIGURE 6-8

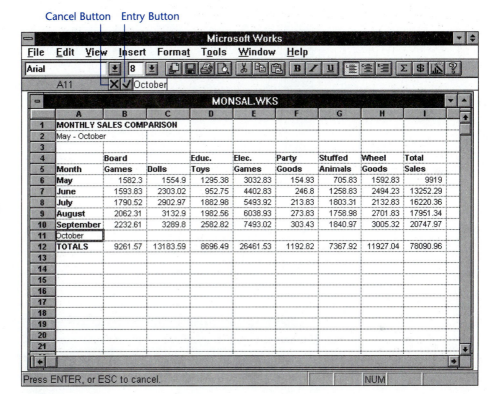

As you can see, the information you typed appears both in the Formula bar and on the spreadsheet. However, it has not yet been officially confirmed and accepted. You may have noticed the appearance of two new items in the Formula bar. These are the CANCEL button (marked by an "X") and the ENTER button (marked by a checkmark). Look at Figure 6-8 and find the locations of these new items on your screen.

By clicking the CANCEL button, you can cancel the entry. By clicking the ENTRY button, you can confirm that the information contained in the Formula bar is correct and can enter the typing into the spreadsheet. These boxes are very useful when you are using the mouse to enter data. But if you are already using the keyboard (as you have been by typing "October"), you will normally press [ENTER], [TAB], or one of the arrow keys to enter data into cells. You will press [ENTER] in this instance, in order to remain in the same cell.

5.   Press [ENTER].

Your screen should now resemble the one shown in Figure 6-9.

Note that the CANCEL and ENTER buttons have now disappeared from the Formula bar.

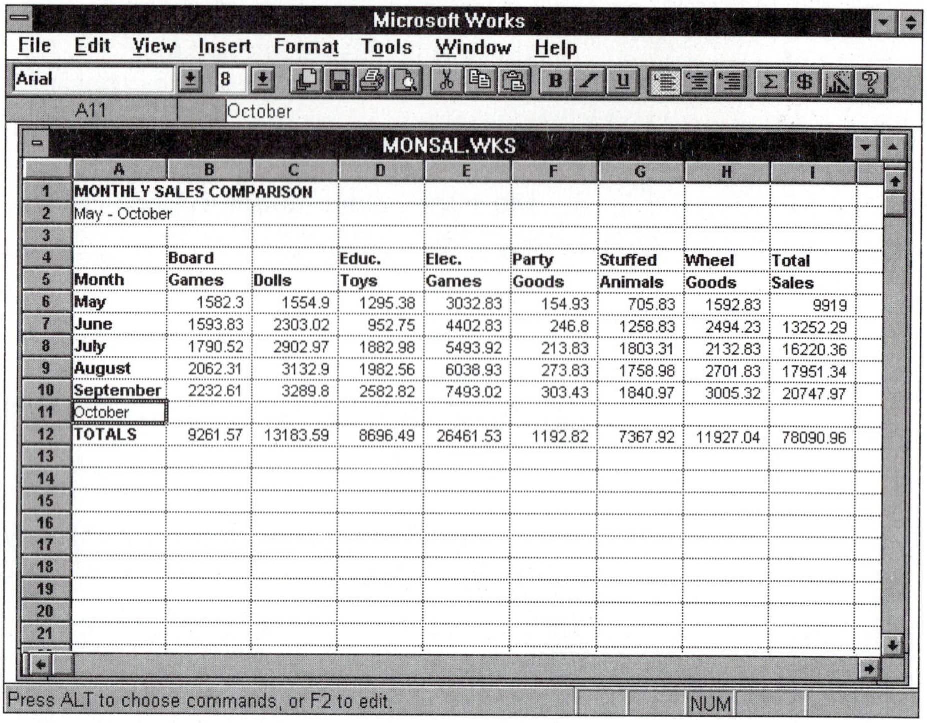

FIGURE 6-9

	A	B	C	D	E	F	G	H	I
1	MONTHLY SALES COMPARISON								
2	May - October								
3									
4		Board		Educ.	Elec.	Party	Stuffed	Wheel	Total
5	Month	Games	Dolls	Toys	Games	Goods	Animals	Goods	Sales
6	May	1582.3	1554.9	1295.38	3032.83	154.93	705.83	1592.83	9919
7	June	1593.83	2303.02	952.75	4402.83	246.8	1258.83	2494.23	13252.29
8	July	1790.52	2902.97	1882.98	5493.92	213.83	1803.31	2132.83	16220.36
9	August	2062.31	3132.9	1982.56	6038.93	273.83	1758.98	2701.83	17951.34
10	September	2232.61	3289.8	2582.82	7493.02	303.43	1840.97	3005.32	20747.97
11	October								
12	TOTALS	9261.57	13183.59	8696.49	26461.53	1192.82	7367.92	11927.04	78090.96
13									
14									
15									
16									
17									
18									
19									
20									
21									

6. Click on cell A11, if it is not already selected.

7. Choose Number from the FORMAT menu.

    The Number dialog box shown in Figure 6-10 should appear.

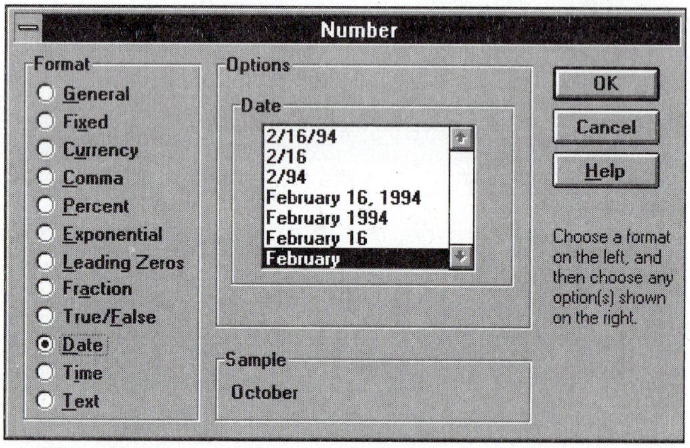

FIGURE 6-10

The Number dialog box allows you to select from many different options for displaying the contents of a cell of the spreadsheet. In this particular dialog box, *WORKS* has correctly guessed that you want to display the contents of cell A11 in date format and that you want to display only the name of the month. *WORKS* made that deduction from the format applied to other cells in this column. As you can see from the Date list box, there are other options you could use for displaying the date. However, you want to use the names of the months as labels for the rows, so you will leave the dialog box as it is. To put away the dialog box without making any changes,

8. Click the CANCEL button.

When you are returned to the spreadsheet, notice that "October" does not have the same appearance as the other months, all of which are displayed in bold type.

To display cell A11 in bold type, be sure that it is still selected, and

9.   Click the BOLD button on the toolbar.

October now appears in bold type.

To move to the next cell,

10.   Press [TAB].

The highlight moves to cell B11.

Now to enter the sales for the month,

11.   Type the numbers given below, pressing [TAB] after each to move to the next column.

HINT ▶   If you make a mistake, remember to simply press [BACKSPACE] and retype.

---

12.   With cell B11 selected, type: 2582.89 [TAB]

Cell C11 is now selected.

13.   Type: 3081.38 [TAB]

2783.93 [TAB]

7632.87 [TAB]

282.43 [TAB]

1938.29 [TAB]

2818.93 [TAB]

Notice that since they are numeric values, your entries display against the right side of the cells.

ERASING, DELETING, AND CLEARING CELLS

Suppose you want to erase a cell that contains data. For example, suppose you are concerned that the October value for wheel goods may be incorrect, and you decide to leave that cell blank until you check on its accuracy. Follow the instructions below to erase its contents.

IT'S YOUR TURN

1.   Select cell H11.

This is the cell you want to erase.

2.   Press [BACKSPACE].

Notice that the number disappears from both the Formula bar and cell A11, but the CANCEL and ENTRY buttons are still showing in the Formula bar.

To enter the correction,

3.   Press [ENTER] or click the ENTRY button.

The correction is entered and the cell is empty.

Assume that the original amount for wheel goods was correct. Do you remember how to reverse the previous action?

4. Choose Undo Entry from the EDIT menu or press [CTRL] + [Z].

If you had done anything between clearing the cell and choosing Undo, the program could not reverse the action. If that should happen, simply retype the amount, 2818.93, and press [ENTER].

CAUTION

Pressing [DELETE] or [BACKSPACE] and [ENTER] erases the content of a cell, but if the cell was specially formatted (e.g., bold, decimal places), the format would remain. To eliminate the format as well as the content, choose Cut from the EDIT menu.

USING FORMULAS

You now need to calculate the sum of sales from all departments and display total sales for October in column I. A *formula* is another kind of value used in spreadsheets. Formulas may consist of operands (values and/or cell addresses), together with arithmetic and/or logical operators. The arithmetic operators are:

- + for add
- – for subtract
- * for multiply
- / for divide

You enter a formula in a cell, and it tells *WORKS* how to calculate the numeric value to be displayed in the spreadsheet. *WORKS* accepts two kinds of formulas. These are sometimes called user-defined formulas and *functions*. Functions are simply predefined (or built-in) formulas. First you will create a user-defined formula.

IT'S YOUR TURN

1. Click on cell I11, if it is not already selected.

Can you create a formula to calculate total sales for October? You could type in each sales amount with a plus sign between each (e.g., 2582.89+ 3081.38+2783.93, etc.) but then the sum would not change if one of the department's sales figures changed. In addition, this would be tedious; a calculator could perform that function as well as the computer. The formula you will use first will insert the cell address of each sales amount with a plus sign between each. This may also sound tedious, but *WORKS 3.0* makes it easy using the "point and click" method described in the next steps. To signal *WORKS* that a formula follows,

2. Type: =

3. Click on cell B11, the first cell to be added.

Notice that *WORKS* has inserted the cell address into the formula in the Formula bar as well as into cell I11.

4. Type: +

WORKS accepts the B11 and inserts the plus immediately following it in the Formula bar and in cell I11. To enter the next cell address in the formula,

5. Click on cell C11, the second cell to be added.

   Cell C11 is inserted into the formula.

6. Type: +

7. Click on each of the remaining cells from cell D11 through G11, typing a plus after clicking on each cell.

   To insert the final cell address and complete the formula,

8. Click on cell H11.

9. Click the ENTRY button or press [ENTER].

   Your screen should resemble Figure 6-11.

FIGURE 6-11

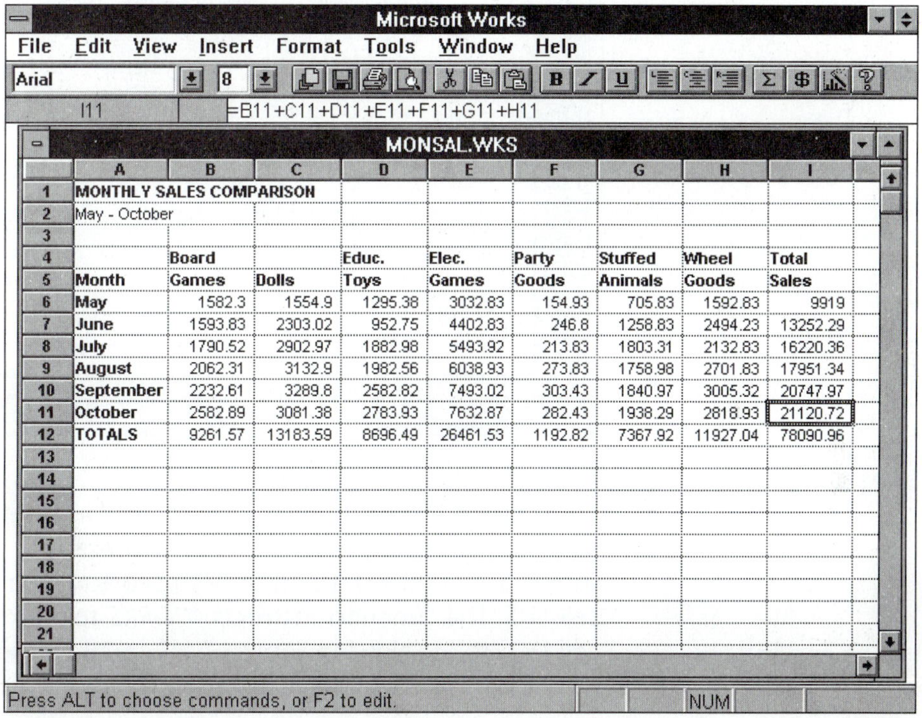

Note that, unlike most of the cells you have worked with previously, the value displayed in the spreadsheet looks far different from the contents displayed in the Formula bar. If the value of any cell addressed in the formula were to change, the displayed value would also change. *WORKS 3.0* makes the calculations as directed in the formula and displays the resulting value in the spreadsheet.

Although creating the addition formula was relatively easy, there is an even easier way described in the next section.

USING A FUNCTION

Some formulas (such as the previous summing formula) are used so often that spreadsheet programs include them as built-in formulas, requiring only that you provide the necessary values (arguments) for the calculations. Such predefined formulas are called ***functions***, and one is used in Column I to compute the total sales for each month.

IT'S YOUR TURN

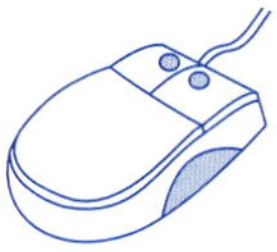

1. Click on cell I10. (That's the letter I and the number 10.)

   Your Formula bar should look like the one displayed in Figure 6-12.

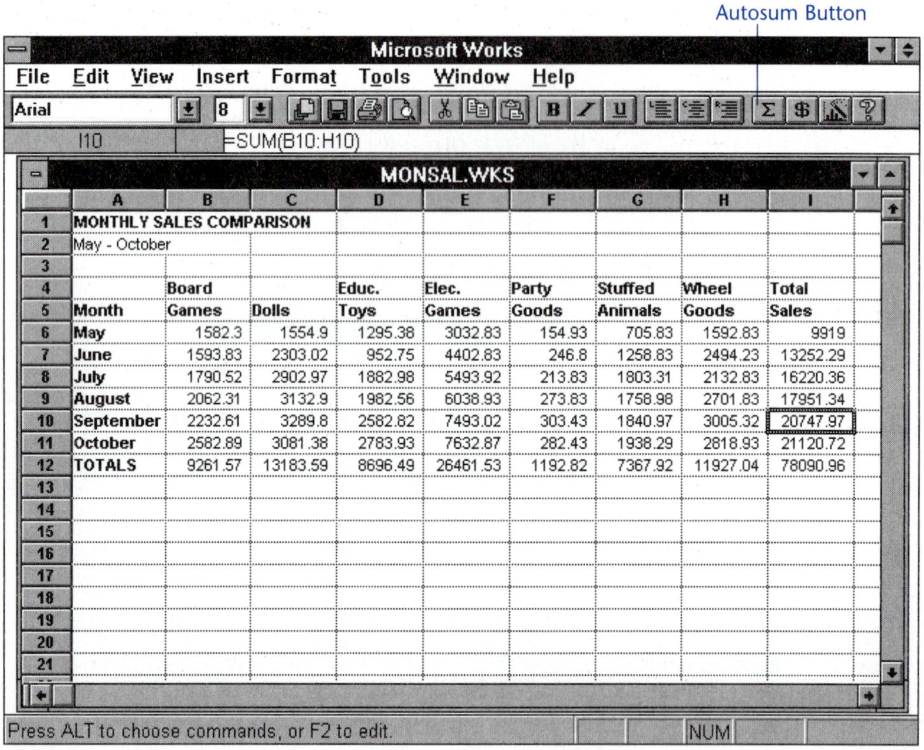
Autosum Button
Microsoft Works
File Edit View Insert Format Tools Window Help
Arial 8
I10 =SUM(B10:H10)
MONSAL.WKS
Press ALT to choose commands, or F2 to edit.
NUM

	A	B	C	D	E	F	G	H	I
1	MONTHLY SALES COMPARISON								
2	May - October								
3									
4		Board		Educ.	Elec.	Party	Stuffed	Wheel	Total
5	Month	Games	Dolls	Toys	Games	Goods	Animals	Goods	Sales
6	May	1582.3	1554.9	1295.38	3032.83	154.93	705.83	1592.83	9919
7	June	1593.83	2303.02	952.75	4402.83	246.8	1258.83	2494.23	13252.29
8	July	1790.52	2902.97	1882.98	5493.92	213.83	1803.31	2132.83	16220.36
9	August	2062.31	3132.9	1982.56	6038.93	273.83	1758.98	2701.83	17951.34
10	September	2232.61	3289.8	2582.82	7493.02	303.43	1840.97	3005.32	20747.97
11	October	2582.89	3081.38	2783.93	7632.87	282.43	1938.29	2818.93	21120.72
12	TOTALS	9261.57	13183.59	8696.49	26461.53	1192.82	7367.92	11927.04	78090.96

FIGURE 6-12

Compare the value displayed in cell I10 with the content stored in the Formula bar. As you can see, the two are very different. The Formula bar shows a function (named SUM) used to calculate the value displayed in cell I10. The function instructs *WORKS* to make the amount displayed in cell I10 (total sales for September) equal to the sum of all cells from B10 through H10. Each element of the function has a special meaning.

=	Equal sign signifies that one or more formulas or functions follow
SUM	Name of a predefined formula (function); it adds the contents of a range of cells
( )	Parentheses surround the arguments (values required by the function) with which the function will work
B10	Cell B10 is the first cell in the range to be added
:	Colon separates the first cell from the last cell in the range of cells to be added
H10	Cell H10 is the last cell in the range to be added

Many other functions are available. (For a comprehensive listing of functions and an explanation of each, see the *WORKS 3.0* manual or use the on-screen Help system.) There are four types of functions:

- mathematical functions, such as random numbers
- statistical functions, such as average value
- logical functions, such as if-then-else
- financial functions, such as present value

Can you use the SUM function instead of the addition formula to calculate the total sales for October? If you need help, follow the next steps.

2. Move the pointer to cell I11 and click to select that cell.

   You will be replacing the lengthy formula you created with a function that will provide the same answer.

3. Type: =SUM(B11:H11)

   Although it may appear that you are through, you have not yet entered the function.

4. Press [ENTER].

   Notice that the total displayed has remained the same, because the formula and the function do the same thing.

An even easier way of creating the SUM function is to use the AUTOSUM button in the toolbar. It is shown in Figure 6-12. To achieve the same results with far less effort, you still have cell I11 selected, so

5. Click the AUTOSUM button (see the Sigma button on Figure 6-12) on the toolbar.

   Look at the Formula bar. *WORKS* has correctly assumed that you want to sum the values in row 11 and has entered the correct range in the sum formula. However, the range is highlighted, so if you want to change it, all you have to do is type a new range. To accept the formula as presented,

6. Click the ENTRY button or press [ENTER].

DELETING AND CLEARING COLUMNS AND ROWS

The Party Goods department has not been very popular, because a large gift shop has opened nearby with an extensive offering of this type of merchandise. As a result, you will close the Party Goods department and delete the Party Goods column on this sales comparison spreadsheet.

You must select (highlight) cells before you tell *WORKS 3.0* to perform actions on those cells. Therefore, you will first select the entire column.

IT'S YOUR TURN

1. Move the pointer to the header F at the top of the Party Goods column and click once.

   The entire column will be selected (see Figure 6-13).

2. Choose Delete Row/Column from the INSERT menu.

   The old column F is eliminated, and the columns on the right move to the left to fill in the vacated space. *WORKS* adjusts all formulas to reflect the change in position of the columns to the right of the Party Goods column.

FIGURE 6-13

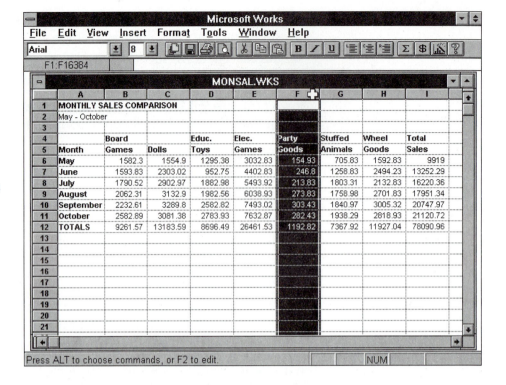

3. Click anywhere on the spreadsheet to remove the highlighting.

Rows are cleared and deleted in the same way as columns. You would click on the desired row header (one of the numbers at the far left of the screen) to select the row marked for deletion and then choose Delete Row/Column from the INSERT menu.

CHECKING AND ADJUSTING FORMULAS

You may have noticed when you were inserting the numbers for October that the values on the TOTALS line did not change. To understand this anomaly, you need to look at the formulas in question.

IT'S YOUR TURN

1. Click cell B12.

The formula from the original spreadsheet (before you added the extra row) is still showing in that cell. As you can see, it calculates the sum of the range from cell B6 through cell B10. But, when you added the row to the end of the range, the new row went into row 11 which is outside the range that is being summed in the formula. Therefore, the new numbers are not included in the TOTALS line. If you had added a row somewhere in the middle of the range, the new row would have been included and the total would have changed.

Cell B12 should still be selected. To correct the formulas,

2. Click the AUTOSUM button on the toolbar.

A formula appears in the Formula bar. See Figure 6-14.
The program correctly assumes you want to sum the values in the range of cells from B6 to B11.

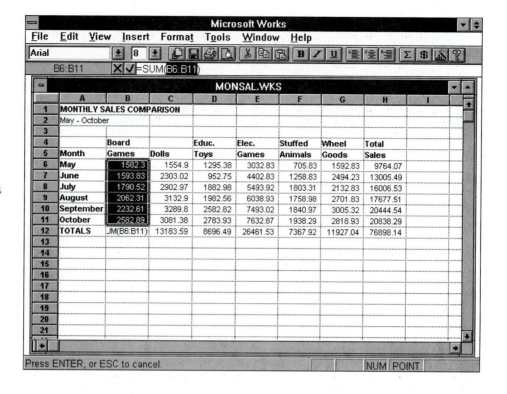

FIGURE 6-14

To accept the formula,

3.   Click the ENTRY button or press [ENTER].

A new total (11844.46) appears in cell B12.

You will use the Autosum feature to change the other formulas on the TOTALS line. In Chapter 7, you will be using another method to copy formulas and/or cell contents that simplifies steps 4–7; however, for now you will use Autosum to acquaint yourself with this command.

4.   Select cell C12.

5.   Click the AUTOSUM button on the toolbar.

WORKS presents the proposed formula for cell C12 in the Formula bar with the correct range, C6:C11.

To accept the formula,

6.   Click the ENTRY button or press [ENTER].

7.   Continue selecting the cells in row 12 and clicking the AUTOSUM button to create the formula, then click the ENTRY button or press [EN-TER] to accept the proposed formulas until you finish with cell H12. If you need help,

a.   Select cell D12.

b.   Click the AUTOSUM button, then click the ENTRY button or press [ENTER].

c.   Select cell E12.

d.   Click the AUTOSUM button, then click the ENTRY button or press [ENTER].

    e. Select cell F12.

    f. Click the AUTOSUM button, then click the ENTRY button or press [ENTER].

    g. Select cell G12.

    h. Click the AUTOSUM button, then click the ENTRY button or press [ENTER].

    i. Select cell H12.

    j. Click the AUTOSUM button, then click the ENTRY button or press [ENTER].

8. Click in cell H6.

Note that the formula in cell H6 correctly sums the range from cell B6 to cell G6. If you use the [DOWN ARROW] key to move down column H, you will see that all the formulas are correct, even though you deleted one column earlier. *WORKS* is able to change the formulas properly when a column or row is deleted or if a column or row is inserted in the middle of a range, but inserting a column or row at either end of a range creates an ambiguous situation that *WORKS* cannot deal with appropriately.

FORMATTING NUMERIC VALUES

Although the Monthly Sales Comparison report is complete, it is difficult to read the amounts and to compare numbers, because they are not all aligned on the decimal point. In fact, some numbers contain one decimal place, while others have two. In this section, you will learn to change cell formats.

IT'S YOUR TURN

1. Move the pointer to cell B6, hold down the mouse button, drag to cell H12, and release the mouse button.

All numeric cells are selected (highlighted).

2. Choose Number from the FORMAT menu.

The Number dialog box appears on your screen, providing you with many Formats from which to choose. The General format displays a number as accurately as possible, given the width of each cell. This is the default setting presently used for this file. The next option, Fixed, displays decimal places but no commas. The next option, Currency, displays dollar signs, decimals, and commas. The fourth option, Comma, is one of the most popular formats, providing commas and decimals. Other options listed are used in special situations. You can learn more about them by clicking the HELP button in the dialog box.

The Currency format may seem like the logical format for these cells, but the dollar signs can be distracting when used for a large block of cells. Financial worksheets are often formatted to display numbers with commas and two decimal places. Dollar signs are often used for the first and last items in tables, however.

3. Click on the Comma option.

Because you selected a format with decimal places, the Number of Decimals box becomes active. Since the purpose of this spreadsheet is to quickly compare sales by department, you will suppress printing of cent values, which would add little meaning to the report. *WORKS* will round the values and display them according to the decimal places you indicate. The Number of Decimals box should be highlighted, indicating that whatever you type will replace its current contents.

4. Type the number "0."

    The Sample box at the bottom of the dialog box changes from 1,582.30 to 1,582, reflecting the suppression of the cent values.

5. Click the OK button or press [ENTER].

6. Click in one of the blank cells to deselect the block.

    Each number is now displayed rounded to the nearest whole number. Your spreadsheet should look like the one shown in Figure 6-15.

FIGURE 6-15

	A	B	C	D	E	F	G	H	I
1	MONTHLY SALES COMPARISON								
2	May - October								
3									
4		Board		Educ.	Elec.	Stuffed	Wheel	Total	
5	Month	Games	Dolls	Toys	Games	Animals	Goods	Sales	
6	May	1,582	1,555	1,295	3,033	706	1,593	9,764	
7	June	1,594	2,303	953	4,403	1,259	2,494	13,005	
8	July	1,791	2,903	1,883	5,494	1,803	2,133	16,007	
9	August	2,062	3,133	1,983	6,039	1,759	2,702	17,678	
10	September	2,233	3,290	2,583	7,493	1,841	3,005	20,445	
11	October	2,583	3,081	2,784	7,633	1,938	2,819	20,838	
12	TOTALS	11,844	16,265	11,480	34,094	9,306	14,746	97,736	

PLAYING "WHAT IF"

Now that you have worked with a spreadsheet, you are probably wondering if you would really save any time by using a spreadsheet rather than pencil and paper. If you use the model you develop only once, then the answer may be no. But if you use the model over and over again, the answer is probably yes. One reason is that error correction is much easier with the electronic spreadsheet. For example, suppose there was a transposition error in the October sales for dolls; the amount should be $3,801.38, not $3,081.38.

If you were using pencil and paper to correct the Monthly Sales comparison, you would have to correct cell C11 and recalculate the following three items:

1. Total October sales in cell H11
2. Total doll sales in cell C12
3. Total sales in cell H12

However, to correct the electronic spreadsheet you simply take the following steps.

IT'S YOUR TURN

1. Click on cell C11.

   Notice that, although the spreadsheet itself displays the rounded figure 3,081, the Formula bar shows 3,081.38 as the value stored in that cell. If the cell should ever be reformatted to display cents, the complete amount would then display. Therefore, even though the cents will not display in the spreadsheet, you should type the entire amount.

2. Type: 3801.38

   As you press [ENTER] in the next step, try to watch cells H11, C12, and H12 as they are updated.

3. Press [ENTER].

   The changes occurred so quickly that you were lucky if you observed one change. *WORKS 3.0* automatically updated the other cells, because those cells contain formulas that refer directly or indirectly to cell C11. So, if you wanted to play "What If," you could change any of the daily sales amounts and watch the totals change. Thus, the model becomes a handy tool for forecasting and budgeting. (For more information, see your *WORKS 3.0* manual.) Your spreadsheet should now agree with Figure 6-16.

FIGURE 6-16

Month	Board Games	Dolls	Educ. Toys	Elec. Games	Stuffed Animals	Wheel Goods	Total Sales
May	1,582	1,555	1,295	3,033	706	1,593	9,764
June	1,594	2,303	953	4,403	1,259	2,494	13,005
July	1,791	2,903	1,883	5,494	1,803	2,133	16,007
August	2,062	3,133	1,983	6,039	1,759	2,702	17,678
September	2,233	3,290	2,583	7,493	1,841	3,005	20,445
October	2,583	3,801	2,784	7,633	1,938	2,819	21,558
TOTALS	11,844	16,985	11,480	34,094	9,306	14,746	98,456

MONTHLY SALES COMPARISON / May - October (MONSAL.WKS)

FINISHING UP

You now have a complete spreadsheet that allows you to compare your monthly sales by department. Each month you can add to it. You are ready to save and print your spreadsheet.

IT'S YOUR TURN

1. Choose Save As from the FILE menu and save this file as *MONSAL2* in your name directory on your data disk.

   When using a spreadsheet, you may sometimes create situations where an extra blank page would be printed. For example, if you inadvertently entered data into a distant cell and neglected to clear it completely, the Print command would produce enough pages to include that cell. For this reason, you should always use Print Preview and only print the desired pages.

2. Click the PRINT PREVIEW button on the toolbar or choose Print Preview from the FILE menu.

The PREVIOUS and NEXT buttons on the Print Preview screen are both dimmed, indicating that this spreadsheet contains only one page.

To print from this screen,

3. Click the PRINT button.

4. Quit *WORKS*, as directed in previous chapters.

SUMMARY

Congratulations! You've covered a lot of territory in this chapter. You can now recognize spreadsheets and identify rows, columns, and cells. You can move the highlighting around the spreadsheet, distinguish text from values, enter and delete cells, insert and delete columns and rows, explain the difference between cell content and cell display, distinguish between formulas and functions, and apply formats to cells.

REVIEW QUESTIONS

1. Cell addresses are composed of two parts. What are the two parts? Which comes first in *WORKS 3.0*?

2. What menu and option allows you to change the format of a number?

3. If you want to move to a distant cell to enter data, what menu and what option would you use?

4. How can you delete the existing content of cells but keep the formatting used for those cells?

5. Values are aligned on which side of a cell—left or right?

6. If you want *WORKS 3.0* to perform a calculation in a cell, what symbol would you use to begin the formula?

7. What is the difference between a formula and a function?

8. If a cell contains the value 56.7389, what would be displayed in the cell if it were formatted in General format? In Comma format with two decimal places?

EXERCISES

EXERCISE 6-1 Cell formatting, editing, inserting text

1. Open the spreadsheet file called *MONSAL* from your data disk.

2. Make the following changes:

   a. Format cells B6 through H10 for commas and zero decimals.

   b. Format the TOTALS row 11 and Total Sales column I for Currency and zero decimals.

   c.   Change the value in cell B10 to 3000.

   d.   Type your name in cell A14.

   e.   Type the current date as text in cell A15.

3.   Save the file as *EX6-1* in your name directory on your data disk.

4.   Print the file, if directed to do so by your instructor.

EXERCISE 6-2 Inserting and deleting rows, using spreadsheet functions, formatting

1.   Open the spreadsheet file called *MONSAL* from your data disk.

2.   Make the following changes:

   a.   Insert a new row where May sales data resides. Use bold type to insert "April" immediately under "May" in the new row. Make up and enter April sales data for all departments.

   b.   Create a SUM function for adding sales for April.

   c.   Format all values for commas and zero decimals.

   d.   Check all formulas and correct them if necessary.

   e.   Type your name in cell A14.

   f.   Type the current date as text in cell A15.

3.   Save the file as *EX6-2* in your name directory on your data disk.

4.   Print the file, if directed to do so by your instructor.

EXERCISE 6-3 Additional use of formulas and functions—formatting

1.   Open the spreadsheet file called *BANKREC* from the Exercise folder on your data disk.

2.   Create the following formulas or functions:

   a.   Formula 1: SUM function to add B7, B8, and B9.

   b.   Formula 2: Formula to add C5 and C9.

   c.   Formula 3: SUM function to add B12, B13, and B14.

   d.   Formula 4: Formula to subtract C14 from C10.

   e.   Formulas 5 through 8: You're on your own!

3.   Format all numbers for currency and two decimals.

4.   Type your name in cell A1.

5.   Type the current date as text in cell G1.

6.   Save the file as *EX6-3* in your name directory on your data disk.

7.   Print the file if directed to do so by your instructor.

Spreadsheet 2

OBJECTIVES

When you finish this chapter you will be able to

■ *insert the current date*

■ *copy cells using Fill Down and Fill Right*

■ *explain absolute and relative cell references*

■ *change a formula*

■ *format text and labels to improve readability*

■ *change the width of a column*

■ *format cells using borders*

■ *display and print formulas in cells*

■ *use page Setup to print horizontally*

■ *use gridlines*

■ *insert headers and footers*

SETTING THE SCENE

In the last chapter you learned what spreadsheets are and how they can be used for creating and updating documents that include calculations. This chapter provides you with techniques for improving the appearance of your documents and helps you understand absolute and relative references in cell addresses.

The Fun Factory has a number of part-time employees, and most of them are students. One of your previous employees created a spreadsheet to keep track of the payroll, but it could use some improvement (see Figure 7-1).

The spreadsheet lists the employees alphabetically with their pay rates (columns A–C). Each week column D will be updated to include hours worked that week. Column F contains the Federal income tax deduction for each employee. Columns E, G, and H contain formulas and functions that compute each employee's gross pay, FICA (Social Security) tax deduction, and the net amount of each paycheck.

GETTING STARTED

As you can see from Figure 7-1, headings have not been aligned and the values are difficult to read because they are in General format—some are displayed with no decimal places, others with four decimal places. You will change the format of all dollar amount columns so that the amounts will be displayed accurately to two decimal points. You will insert the current date. You will also insert a column for bonuses and, to further improve the ap-

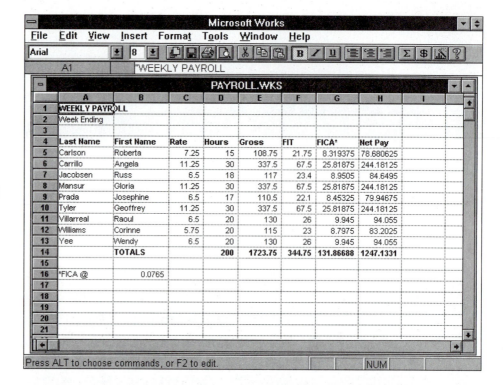

	A	B	C	D	E	F	G	H	I
1	WEEKLY PAYROLL								
2	Week Ending								
3									
4	Last Name	First Name	Rate	Hours	Gross	FIT	FICA*	Net Pay	
5	Carlson	Roberta	7.25	15	108.75	21.75	8.319375	78.680625	
6	Carrillo	Angela	11.25	30	337.5	67.5	25.81875	244.18125	
7	Jacobsen	Russ	6.5	18	117	23.4	8.9505	84.6495	
8	Mansur	Gloria	11.25	30	337.5	67.5	25.81875	244.18125	
9	Prada	Josephine	6.5	17	110.5	22.1	8.45325	79.94675	
10	Tyler	Geoffrey	11.25	30	337.5	67.5	25.81875	244.18125	
11	Villarreal	Raoul	6.5	20	130	26	9.945	94.055	
12	Williams	Corinne	5.75	20	115	23	8.7975	83.2025	
13	Yee	Wendy	6.5	20	130	26	9.945	94.055	
14		TOTALS		200	1723.75	344.75	131.86688	1247.1331	
15									
16	*FICA @	0.0765							
17									
18									
19									
20									
21									

FIGURE 7-1

	A	B	C	D	E	F	G	H	I	J
1	WEEKLY PAYROLL									
2	Week Ending	2/16/94								
3										
4	Last Name	First Name	Rate	Hours	Bonus	Gross	FIT	FICA*	Net Pay	
5	Carlson	Roberta	7.25	15	50.00	158.75	21.75	12.14	124.86	
6	Carrillo	Angela	11.25	30	50.00	387.50	67.50	29.64	290.36	
7	Jacobsen	Russ	6.50	18	50.00	167.00	23.40	12.78	130.82	
8	Mansur	Gloria	11.25	30	50.00	387.50	67.50	29.64	290.36	
9	Prada	Josephine	6.50	17	50.00	160.50	22.10	12.28	126.12	
10	Tyler	Geoffrey	11.25	30	50.00	387.50	67.50	29.64	290.36	
11	Villarreal	Raoul	6.50	20	50.00	180.00	26.00	13.77	140.23	
12	Williams	Corinne	5.75	20	50.00	165.00	23.00	12.62	129.38	
13	Yee	Wendy	6.50	20	50.00	180.00	26.00	13.77	140.23	
14		TOTALS		200	450.00	2,173.75	344.75	166.29	1,662.71	
15										
16	*FICA @	7.65%								
17										
18										
19										
20										
21										

FIGURE 7-2

pearance of the spreadsheet, you will center some of the column labels. When you finish, the spreadsheet will look like the one shown in Figure 7-2.

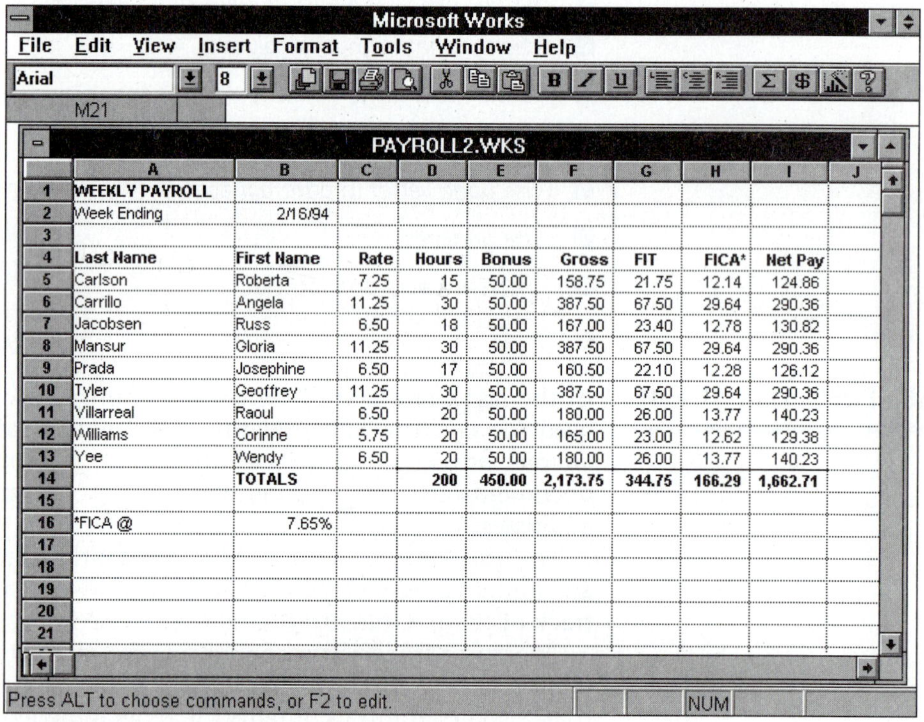

IT'S YOUR TURN

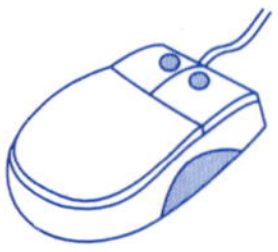

1. Launch WORKS 3.0.
2. Open the *PAYROLL* spreadsheet file from your data disk.

   You may have to scroll down the Filename list box to find it. When it is open, your screen will resemble the screen shown in Figure 7-1.

**INSERTING THE
CURRENT DATE**

Note in Figure 7-1 that cell A2 contains the label "Week Ending" but that there is no date following that label. There are several ways to insert the current date into your spreadsheet. You can

- type the date. It will be entered as a constant and will not change unless you retype it.
- use the NOW function. The current date will be entered and it will be updated every time the spreadsheet is recalculated.
- use the keyboard shortcut, [CTRL] + [;] (semicolon) to insert the current date. The current date will be entered as a constant.

Whenever you plan to use a cell to contain a date value, it is a good idea to format the cell first. Although *WORKS* tries to determine the formatting you desire from the way you type the date, the program does not have any such clues if you use the NOW function or use the keyboard shortcut.

IT'S YOUR TURN

1. Click cell B2

2. Choose Number from the FORMAT menu.

   The Number dialog box will appear, with General selected in the Format box on the left-hand side.

3. Click Date in the Format box and observe the results in the Options box and the Sample box.

   Your screen should look like the one shown in Figure 7-3, with the Date options box showing the various options for displaying the current date.

FIGURE 7-3

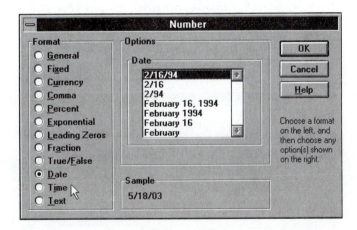

To display the short form of the date, you will leave the highlight where it is. To return to the spreadsheet,

4. Click the OK button or press [ENTER].

Now you are ready to insert the date. To insert the current date using the keyboard shortcut,

5. Hold down the [CTRL] key and press the semicolon [;] key.

   The short form date will appear aligned against the left side of the cell. The CANCEL button and the ENTRY button also appear in the Formula bar to remind you that the operation is not complete.

To complete the entry,

6. Click the ENTRY button or press [ENTER].

The date becomes aligned against the right side of the cell.

INSERTING A NEW COLUMN

You need to insert additional space into the spreadsheet for a $50 bonus you plan to give each employee. Use the following steps to insert a new column named "Bonus" between the columns named "Hours" and "Gross."

IT'S YOUR TURN

1. Move the pointer to column header E and click once.

The column labelled "Gross" is selected (highlighted). WORKS will insert a new column immediately preceding the selected one when you complete the next step.

2. Choose Row/Column from the INSERT menu.

Column E is now empty and still highlighted. The "old" column E is now in column F.

To label the new column,

3. Click once in cell E4 to select it.

This is where the label for the new column should appear. Note that the rest of the column is now deselected.

4. Type: Bonus

5. Click the ENTRY button or press [ENTER].

Before making another entry, you will decrease the width of the Bonus column.

6. Move the pointer to the line dividing column headers E and F.

The pointer becomes a two-way arrow (see Figure 7-4).

FIGURE 7-4

```
 ┌──────────────────────────────────────────────────────────────┐
 │ ─                        Microsoft Works                  ▼ ▲ │
 │ File  Edit  View  Insert  Format  Tools  Window  Help        │
 │ Arial          ▼ 8 ▼  □ 🖫 🖶 🔍  ✂ 🖺 🖺  B I U 🖹 🖹 🖹 Σ $ 🖩 ? │
 │ E4              "Bonus                                         │
 │ ┌────────────────────── PAYROLL.WKS ──────────────────── ▼ ▲ │
```

	A	B	C	D	E	F	G	H	I
1	WEEKLY PAYROLL								
2	Week Ending	2/16/94							
3									
4	Last Name	First Name	Rate	Hours	Bonus	Gross	FIT	FICA*	Net Pay
5	Carlson	Roberta	7.25	15		108.75	21.75	8.319375	78.680625
6	Carrillo	Angela	11.25	30		337.5	67.5	25.81875	244.18125
7	Jacobsen	Russ	6.5	18		117	23.4	8.9505	84.6495
8	Mansur	Gloria	11.25	30		337.5	67.5	25.81875	244.18125
9	Prada	Josephine	6.5	17		110.5	22.1	8.45325	79.94675
10	Tyler	Geoffrey	11.25	30		337.5	67.5	25.81875	244.18125
11	Villarreal	Raoul	6.5	20		130	26	9.945	94.055
12	Williams	Corinne	5.75	20		115	23	8.7975	83.2025
13	Yee	Wendy	6.5	20		130	26	9.945	94.055
14		TOTALS		200		1723.75	344.75	131.86688	1247.1331
15									
16	*FICA @	0.0765							
17									
18									
19									
20									
21									

```
 │ Press ALT to choose commands, or F2 to edit.          NUM    │
 └──────────────────────────────────────────────────────────────┘
```

Two-way Arrow Used for Changing Column Width

7. Hold down the mouse button while you drag the edge of the column to the left until it is approximately the same width as column D.

It is not necessary to be exact, for you can easily increase or decrease the column's width later if you become dissatisfied with it.

8. Release the mouse button.

COPYING BY USING FILL DOWN AND FILL RIGHT

Now you will enter and total the figures for the Bonus column. All employees will receive the same $50 bonus.

IT'S YOUR TURN

1. Move the pointer to cell E5 and click once to select it.

2. Type: 50

3. Click the ENTRY button or press [ENTER] to enter the amount.

Copying one cell through a range of adjacent cells (below or to the right) is very easy. First you identify the cell you want to copy (in our example, E5) and the range through which you want to copy it (in our example, E6 through E13) by selecting them.

4. Move the pointer to cell E5, hold down the mouse button, drag from E5 through E13, and release the button.

From here on, we will simplify this direction to "Drag to select cells E5 through E13."

You have selected all the cells from E5 through E13, as shown in Figure 7-5.

FIGURE 7-5

	A	B	C	D	E	F	G	H	I	J
1	WEEKLY PAYROLL									
2	Week Ending	2/16/94								
3										
4	Last Name	First Name	Rate	Hours	Bonus	Gross	FIT	FICA*	Net Pay	
5	Carlson	Roberta	7.25	15	50	108.75	21.75	8.319375	78.680625	
6	Carrillo	Angela	11.25	30		337.5	67.5	25.81875	244.18125	
7	Jacobsen	Russ	6.5	18		117	23.4	8.9505	84.6495	
8	Mansur	Gloria	11.25	30		337.5	67.5	25.81875	244.18125	
9	Prada	Josephine	6.5	17		110.5	22.1	8.45325	79.94675	
10	Tyler	Geoffrey	11.25	30		337.5	67.5	25.81875	244.18125	
11	Villarreal	Raoul	6.5	20		130	26	9.945	94.055	
12	Williams	Corinne	5.75	20		115	23	8.7975	83.2025	
13	Yee	Wendy	6.5	20		130	26	9.945	94.055	
14		TOTALS		200		1723.75	344.75	131.86688	1247.1331	
15										
16	*FICA @	0.0765								
17										
18										
19										
20										
21										

Microsoft Works — PAYROLL.WKS — E5:E13 — 50

Press ALT to choose commands, or F2 to edit.   NUM

Note the boldly outlined border around cell E5. This border indicates that E5 is the active cell. The program will copy it to the other selected cells.

5. **Choose Fill Down from the EDIT menu.**

   The selected range will quickly be filled with the $50 bonus for each employee.

   Notice that the EDIT menu also contains a Fill Right command. Fill Right is used to copy cell contents to adjacent cells on the right within a row. Had the range you selected been horizontal within a row, you would have chosen Fill Right.

6. **Click on any empty cell in the spreadsheet to deselect the range.**

COPYING FORMULAS USING FILL DOWN AND FILL RIGHT

The Bonus column must now be totaled. You can type your own formula or type a function or use the AUTOSUM button on the toolbar, as you did in Chapter 6, but there is another way. In the next steps, you will use the Fill Right option to copy the function used to add hours in column D so it will add the bonus values in column E.

IT'S YOUR TURN

1. **Click on cell D14.**

   As you can see, the function "=SUM(D5:D13)" appears in the Formula bar, with the total amount calculated by that formula displayed at the bottom of column D. The function sums the nine cells above the active cell. Since this is exactly what the formula in column E should do and since column E is immediately to the right of column D, you can use the Fill Right option to copy this formula to the new column.

2. **Drag to select cells D14 and E14.**

   Cells D14 and E14 are both selected. The active cell D14 contains the formula that will be copied to the right (to cell E14).

3. **Choose Fill Right from the EDIT menu.**

   The copy is quickly completed, and the total is calculated. As you can see, this would have been a much faster way of copying the Sum totals in row 12 in the previous chapter.

4. **Click any empty cell to deselect.**

   You can also use the EDIT menu to copy a cell or cells and paste them to another part of the spreadsheet. But when the cells are adjacent, as in this problem, the Fill Right and Fill Down options are much faster.

UNDERSTANDING ABSOLUTE AND RELATIVE REFERENCES

To understand more about copying formulas with cell addresses, read the next section carefully and study the spreadsheet displayed on the screen. Copy commands are time-savers and help keep errors to a minimum, so it is worth some effort to understand the cell references they contain. Let's consider the original formula in cell D14.

IT'S YOUR TURN

1. **Click on cell D14.**

   The formula displayed in the Formula bar reads "=SUM(D5:D13)."

What do you think the copy in cell E14 looks like? To compare the original formula with the copy,

2. **Click on cell E14.**

The Formula bar for the copy of the formula in cell D14 reads "= SUM(E5:E13)."

WORKS has changed the cell references to make them relative to the position of the cell that contains the formula. This is called a ***relative reference***. In other words, the formula in cell D14 adds the values appearing above it in rows 5 through 13. When you copied the formula, *WORKS* assumed that you wanted the formula in cell E14 to add the values appearing above it in rows 5 through 13—exactly the function of the formula "=SUM (E5:E13)." The column addresses changed but the row numbers did not.

But what if you don't want a cell address to change when you copy formulas? In that case you need an ***absolute reference***. An example of this is the computation of FICA taxes (column H). Here each employee's gross pay is multiplied by the current FICA rate stored in cell B16. So, even though the gross pay changes in the formula for each employee, the FICA rate should not. To understand this better, look at the FICA formula.

3. **Click on cell H5.**

Your screen will resemble the one shown in Figure 7-6.

FIGURE 7-6

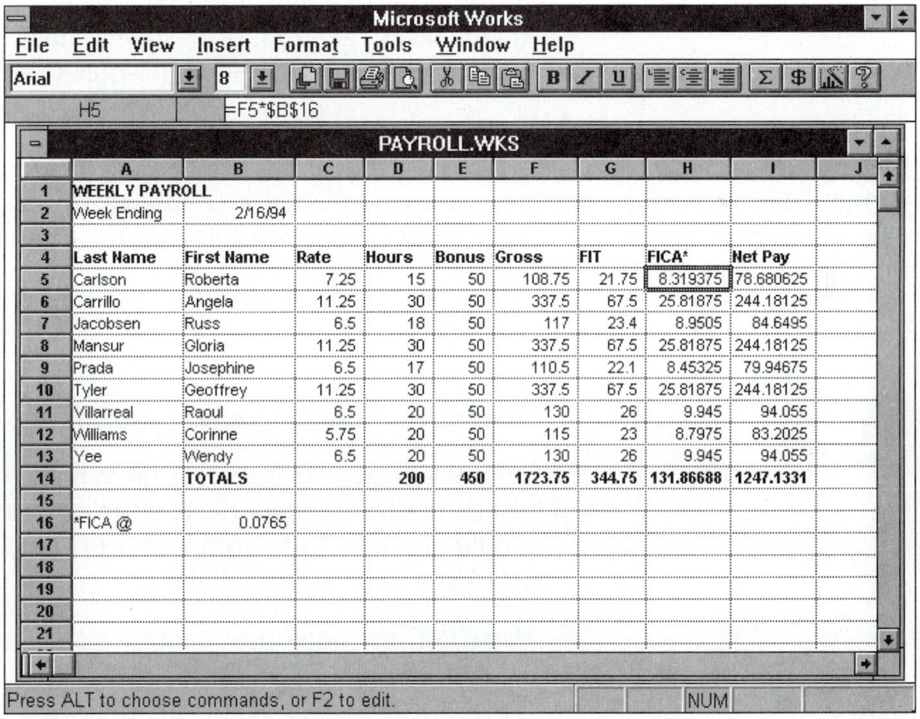

Microsoft Works — PAYROLL.WKS

H5   =F5*B16

	A	B	C	D	E	F	G	H	I	J
1	WEEKLY PAYROLL									
2	Week Ending	2/16/94								
3										
4	Last Name	First Name	Rate	Hours	Bonus	Gross	FIT	FICA*	Net Pay	
5	Carlson	Roberta	7.25	15	50	108.75	21.75	8.319375	78.680625	
6	Carrillo	Angela	11.25	30	50	337.5	67.5	25.81875	244.18125	
7	Jacobsen	Russ	6.5	18	50	117	23.4	8.9505	84.6495	
8	Mansur	Gloria	11.25	30	50	337.5	67.5	25.81875	244.18125	
9	Prada	Josephine	6.5	17	50	110.5	22.1	8.45325	79.94675	
10	Tyler	Geoffrey	11.25	30	50	337.5	67.5	25.81875	244.18125	
11	Villarreal	Raoul	6.5	20	50	130	26	9.945	94.055	
12	Williams	Corinne	5.75	20	50	115	23	8.7975	83.2025	
13	Yee	Wendy	6.5	20	50	130	26	9.945	94.055	
14		TOTALS		200	450	1723.75	344.75	131.86688	1247.1331	
15										
16	*FICA @	0.0765								
17										
18										
19										
20										
21										

Press ALT to choose commands, or F2 to edit.   NUM

This cell computes FICA taxes for Roberta Carlson. When the spreadsheet was prepared, the formula in this cell was copied to compute taxes for all the other employees. The formula "=F5*B16" is displayed in the Formula bar. The formula looks a little difficult, but it's quite simple if you look at each part individually.

=   Equal sign indicates that a formula follows.

F5   A cell reference not preceded by a dollar sign indicates the address is relative. The program will change it relative to the position of the cell to which you are copying. For example, if you copy the formula down one row, this address will change to F6; if it is copied one column to the right, it will become G5.

*   Asterisk indicates multiplication.

$B   Dollar sign indicates the program will not change the following column reference when this formula is copied, so this is an absolute reference.

$16   Dollar sign indicates the program will not change the row reference when this formula is copied, so this is also an absolute reference.

While performing the following steps, notice that the absolute reference "B16" did not change when the formula was copied to the remaining cells in column H, but the row number in the relative reference F5 was incremented by one digit each time the formula was copied to a new row.

4. Click on cell H6 and study the changes in the formula.

5. Continue selecting and studying the cells in column H.

A simple illustration may help you understand the difference between relative and absolute addresses. Joe invites Mike, a new neighbor, to a party at his home, which is just up the street from Mike's. If he tells Mike to "walk north and stop at the fourth house on the right," he is giving a relative direction that applies only to Mike. If Joe tells Mike that he lives "at 125 Ocean Street," he is giving Mike an absolute address that does not change, no matter where it is given.

CHANGING A FORMULA

Let's go back to the bonuses. Did you happen to notice that the Net Pay totals did not change when you entered the bonuses? Do you know why? Hopefully you will after you complete the following section.

IT'S YOUR TURN

1. Click on cell F5.

2. Look at the Formula bar.

Your screen should resemble the one shown in Figure 7-7.

The formula to compute Roberta's gross pay is incomplete, because it does not include the bonus amount. You still need to multiply C5 times D5, but you should also add E5 to compute gross pay.
   With F5 still selected (highlighted),

3. Press [F2] or move the pointer to the Formula bar and click to the right of the existing formula, "C5*D5."

The insertion point should now appear immediately to the right of D5.

4. Type: +

5. Click on cell E5. (If you prefer, you could type "E5.")

The formula in the Formula bar now reads "=C5*D5+E5." As you complete the next step, watch the numbers in the subsequent columns adjust to reflect the change in this formula. That's because they all contain formulas that refer to this cell.

6. Click the entry button or press [ENTER].

FIGURE 7-7

	A	B	C	D	E	F	G	H	I	J
1	WEEKLY PAYROLL									
2	Week Ending	2/16/94								
3										
4	Last Name	First Name	Rate	Hours	Bonus	Gross	FIT	FICA*	Net Pay	
5	Carlson	Roberta	7.25	15	50	108.75	21.75	8.319375	78.680625	
6	Carrillo	Angela	11.25	30	50	337.5	67.5	25.81875	244.18125	
7	Jacobsen	Russ	6.5	18	50	117	23.4	8.9505	84.6495	
8	Mansur	Gloria	11.25	30	50	337.5	67.5	25.81875	244.18125	
9	Prada	Josephine	6.5	17	50	110.5	22.1	8.45325	79.94675	
10	Tyler	Geoffrey	11.25	30	50	337.5	67.5	25.81875	244.18125	
11	Villarreal	Raoul	6.5	20	50	130	26	9.945	94.055	
12	Williams	Corinne	5.75	20	50	115	23	8.7975	83.2025	
13	Yee	Wendy	6.5	20	50	130	26	9.945	94.055	
14		TOTALS		200	450	1723.75	344.75	131.86688	1247.1331	
15										
16	*FICA @	0.0765								
17										
18										
19										
20										
21										

If you did not see the changes as they were made in step 4, try to watch more carefully in the next sequence. To copy the new formula for each employee's gross pay calculation,

7. Drag to select cells F5 through F13.

8. Choose Fill Down from the EDIT menu.

Copying is now complete, and the Net Pay column includes the bonus for all employees.

9. Click any empty cell to deselect.

FORMATTING VALUES

Although the Payroll columns are calculated accurately, the amounts are difficult to read because some numbers contain no decimals and others have from one to four decimal places. In this section, you will change the appearance of numeric values in the last five columns to two decimal places. See if you can remember how to do this from Chapter 6.

IT'S YOUR TURN

1. Format the last five columns for commas and two decimal places. If you need help,

    a. Drag from cell E5 through cell I14.

    b. Choose Number from the FORMAT menu.

    c. Click on Comma in the Format box.

    d. If the number two does not display in the Number of Decimals box, type "2" to replace the highlighted number that is there.

    e. Click OK or press [ENTER].

    f. Click any blank cell to deselect.

Your screen should now be similar to the one shown in Figure 7-8.

FIGURE 7-8

	Microsoft Works										▼ ▲
File	Edit	View	Insert	Format	Tools	Window	Help				

Arial | 8 | | | | | | B | I | U | | | Σ | $ | | ?

I2

| | | | | | | PAYROLL.WKS | | | | | | ▼ ▲ |

	A	B	C	D	E	F	G	H	I	J
1	WEEKLY PAYROLL									
2	Week Ending	2/16/94								
3										
4	Last Name	First Name	Rate	Hours	Bonus	Gross	FIT	FICA*	Net Pay	
5	Carlson	Roberta	7.25	15	50.00	158.75	21.75	12.14	124.86	
6	Carrillo	Angela	11.25	30	50.00	387.50	67.50	29.64	290.36	
7	Jacobsen	Russ	6.5	18	50.00	167.00	23.40	12.78	130.82	
8	Mansur	Gloria	11.25	30	50.00	387.50	67.50	29.64	290.36	
9	Prada	Josephine	6.5	17	50.00	160.50	22.10	12.28	126.12	
10	Tyler	Geoffrey	11.25	30	50.00	387.50	67.50	29.64	290.36	
11	Villarreal	Raoul	6.5	20	50.00	180.00	26.00	13.77	140.23	
12	Williams	Corinne	5.75	20	50.00	165.00	23.00	12.62	129.38	
13	Yee	Wendy	6.5	20	50.00	180.00	26.00	13.77	140.23	
14		TOTALS		200	450.00	2,173.75	344.75	166.29	1,662.71	
15										
16	*FICA @	0.0765								
17										
18										
19										
20										
21										

Press ALT to choose commands, or F2 to edit. | | NUM | |

2. If any cell on your screen is filled with the pound symbol (#) instead of displaying a value, the column containing that cell is not wide enough to display the value. To widen any column,

   a. Move the pointer to the right side of the column header for the column you wish to widen. When it is in the proper position, the pointer will become a two-way arrow, as it did when you were adjusting the Bonus column earlier.

   b. Drag the column header until it is the size you desire.

An alternative method of changing the width of one column or several adjacent columns is to let *WORKS* decide how wide to make the column or columns. To use this method,

3. Select (highlight) columns E through I.

4. Choose Column Width from the FORMAT menu.

When the Column Width dialog box shown in Figure 7-9 appears,

5. Click Best Fit and then click OK or press [ENTER].

FIGURE 7-9

Column Width

Width: 10

☐ Best Fit

OK

Cancel

Help

You will be returned to the spreadsheet, and each of the selected columns will be adjusted to best fit their contents.

6. Click any empty cell to deselect.

7. Use the procedures outlined in step 1 to reformat the numbers in column C using the comma option and two decimal places.

If you need help,

a. Select cells C5 through C13.

b. Choose Number from the FORMAT menu.

c. Click on Comma.

d. If necessary, type "2" in the Number of Decimals box.

e. Click OK or press [ENTER].

f. Click any empty cell to deselect.

The totals would stand out more if they were set off from the columns by a line. By attaching the line to the top of the Totals row, data may be added to the spreadsheet without affecting the placement of the dividing line. To insert such a line,

8. Drag from cell D14 through I14.

9. Choose Border from the FORMAT menu.

The Border dialog box appears as shown in Figure 7-10.

FIGURE 7-10

10. Click on the Top option box in the Border section.

11. Click the second option box from the top (the lightest colored solid line) in the Line Style section, if necessary.

12. Click OK or press [ENTER].

13. Click any empty cell to deselect.

Because this spreadsheet is set up to display the gridlines that mark off the cells, it may be difficult for you to see the border along the top of the selected cells. To remove the gridlines temporarily,

14. Choose Gridlines from the VIEW menu.

Your spreadsheet should look like the one shown in Figure 7-11.

It is easier to identify cells with the gridlines displayed, so to display the gridlines again,

15. Choose Gridlines from the VIEW menu.

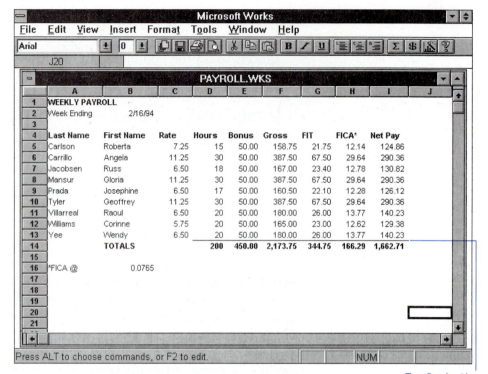

FIGURE 7-11

Top Border Line

There is one more numeric cell that needs formatting—the FICA percentage in cell B16.

16. Click cell B16 to select it.

17. Choose Number from the FORMAT menu.

When the Number dialog box appears,

18. Click Percent in the Format list box.

19. If necessary, type "2" in the Number of decimals box.

    The Sample box should contain 7.65%.

20. Click OK or press [ENTER].

FORMATTING TEXT LABELS

The spreadsheet is looking much better, but some of the column headings (especially Rate and FIT) appear out of alignment with the column contents. To format labels, you will also use the FORMAT menu.

IT'S YOUR TURN

1. Click row header 4 to select the entire row.

To see what the spreadsheet would look like with these titles centered,

2. Click the CENTER alignment button on the toolbar.

    The CENTER alignment button is the sixth button from the right on the toolbar and is pointed out in Figure 7-12.

The headings become centered and look somewhat better, but because most of the data in these columns are right aligned, you might prefer to have the headings also right aligned. Since the row is still selected, you can experiment and choose the one you like best.

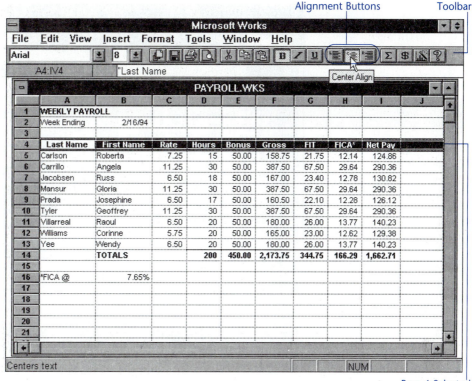

FIGURE 7-12

3. Click the RIGHT button on the toolbar.

   Of course you may format each column heading independently of the others, aligning some at the left, some at the right, and some at the center.

4. Drag to select cells A4 through B4, and click the LEFT alignment button on the toolbar.

5. Select cell G4 and click the CENTER alignment button on the toolbar.

   You will leave the other column labels formatted for right alignment.

6. Click any empty cell to deselect.

PRINTING CELL FORMULAS

It is always a good idea to keep a printout of the spreadsheets you use displaying the formulas stored in the cells. These printouts are invaluable should there be any question regarding how the spreadsheet was designed or whether it should be modified. Sometimes spreadsheets are altered inadvertently, and such a master copy would save many hours of work.

IT'S YOUR TURN

1. Click the VIEW menu.

   See Figure 7-13.

Note the checkmarks in front of Toolbar and Gridlines, which indicates that those items are to be displayed. Note that Formulas does not have a checkmark preceding it, indicating that formulas are not to be displayed. To cause the spreadsheet to display the actual content of all cells,

2. Choose Formulas from the VIEW menu.

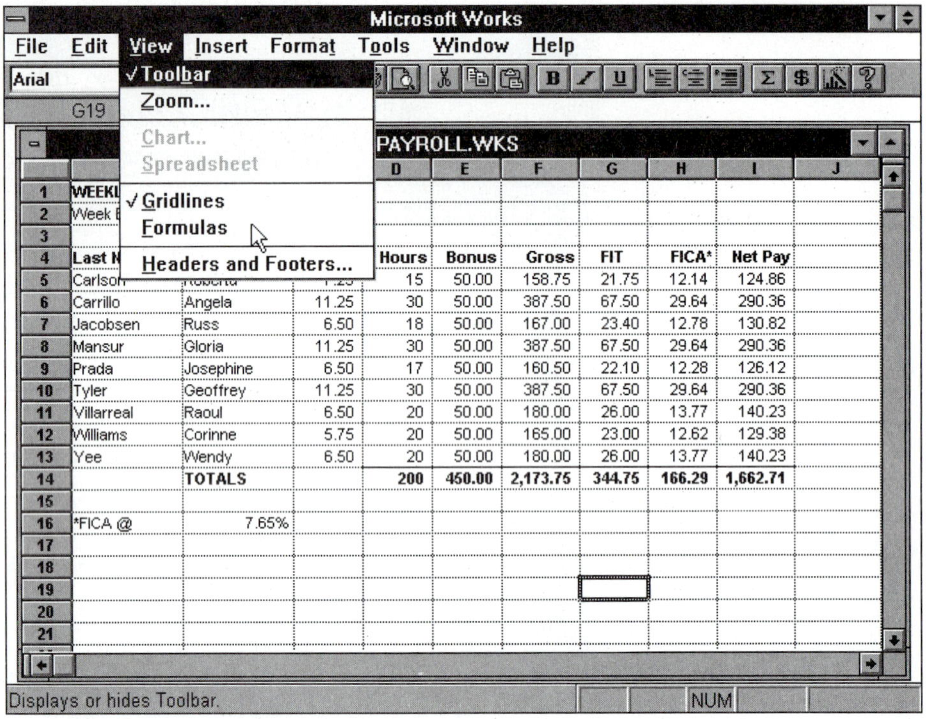

FIGURE 7-13

The cells containing formulas now display those formulas on the spreadsheet. Notice that all of the columns on the spreadsheet are considerably wider to make room for the formulas to be displayed.

3. Use the two-way arrow to adjust the width of each column to make it just wide enough to display the longest entry in the column.

If you have forgotten how to resize the columns,

a. Move the pointer to the vertical line between column headers A and B. The pointer will become a two-way arrow when it is in the right position.

b. Drag the two-way arrow to the left until column A is the proper size.

c. Repeat the preceding steps for each succeeding column.

When you reach column G or H, depending on the size of your screen, you may have to use the right horizontal scroll arrow to bring the right most columns of the spreadsheet into view. When you finish, your screen should be similar to the screen shown in Figure 7-14.

4. Click the left horizontal scroll arrow until cell A1 comes into view again.

Now your screen should look like the one shown in Figure 7-15.

Note that the heading "Weekly Payroll" no longer spills over into the unused cells in its row, and all data is left aligned. Also note that the cell B2 now contains an integer number. Both of these changes are the result of switching to Formula view. The number in cell B2 represents the day number assigned to the date that was contained in that cell. *WORKS* automatically calculates the number of days that have elapsed between January 1,

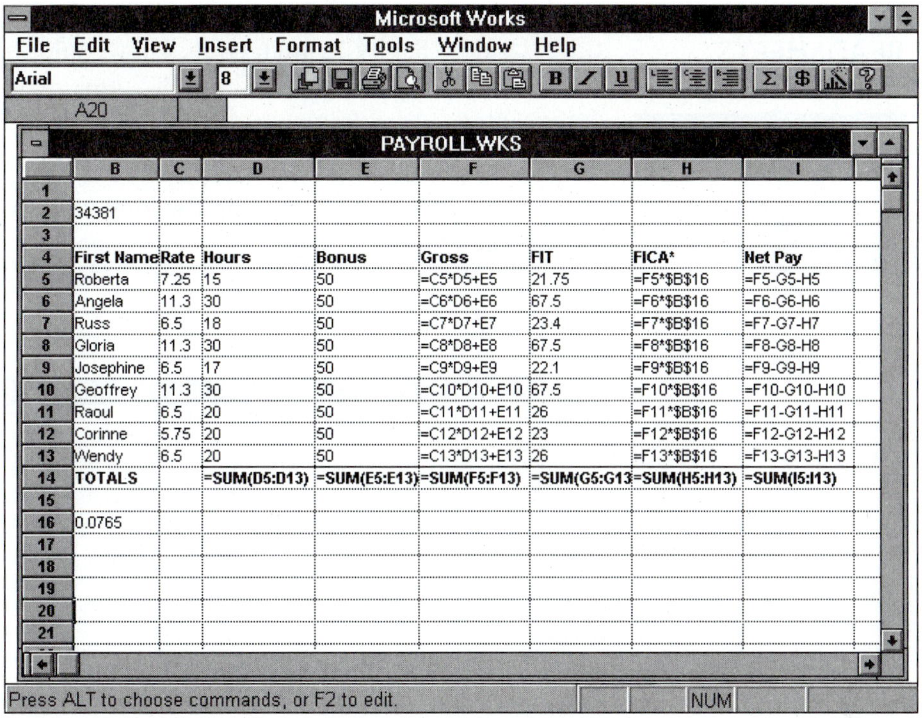

	B	C	D	E	F	G	H	I
1								
2	34381							
3								
4	First Name	Rate	Hours	Bonus	Gross	FIT	FICA*	Net Pay
5	Roberta	7.25	15	50	=C5*D5+E5	21.75	=F5*B16	=F5-G5-H5
6	Angela	11.3	30	50	=C6*D6+E6	67.5	=F6*B16	=F6-G6-H6
7	Russ	6.5	18	50	=C7*D7+E7	23.4	=F7*B16	=F7-G7-H7
8	Gloria	11.3	30	50	=C8*D8+E8	67.5	=F8*B16	=F8-G8-H8
9	Josephine	6.5	17	50	=C9*D9+E9	22.1	=F9*B16	=F9-G9-H9
10	Geoffrey	11.3	30	50	=C10*D10+E10	67.5	=F10*B16	=F10-G10-H10
11	Raoul	6.5	20	50	=C11*D11+E11	26	=F11*B16	=F11-G11-H11
12	Corinne	5.75	20	50	=C12*D12+E12	23	=F12*B16	=F12-G12-H12
13	Wendy	6.5	20	50	=C13*D13+E13	26	=F13*B16	=F13-G13-H13
14	TOTALS		=SUM(D5:D13)	=SUM(E5:E13)	=SUM(F5:F13)	=SUM(G5:G13	=SUM(H5:H13)	=SUM(I5:I13)
15								
16	0.0765							
17								
18								
19								
20								
21								

FIGURE 7-14

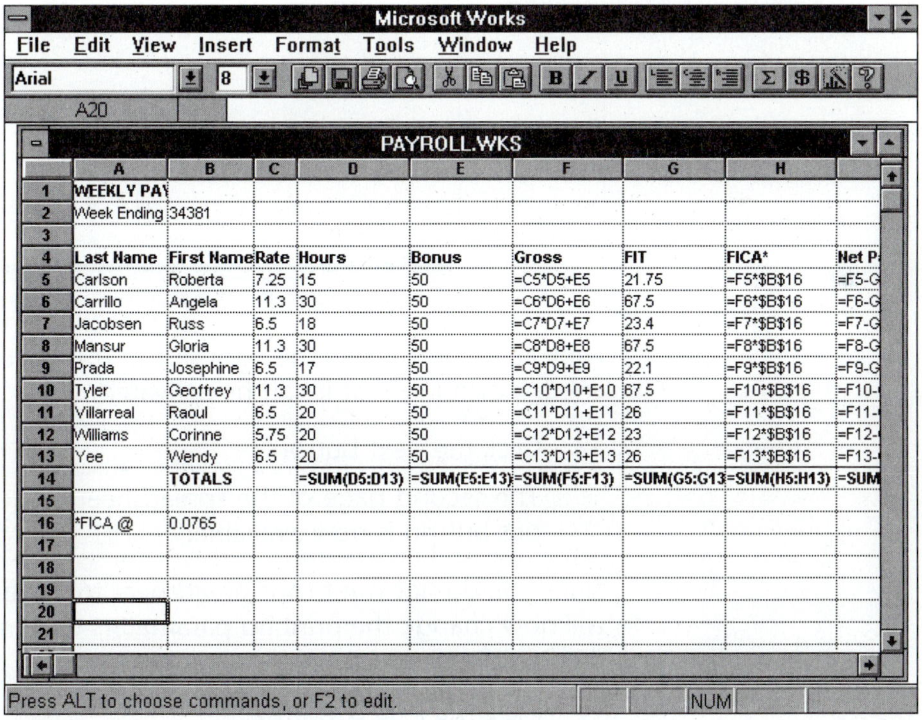

	A	B	C	D	E	F	G	H	
1	WEEKLY PA								
2	Week Ending	34381							
3									
4	Last Name	First Name	Rate	Hours	Bonus	Gross	FIT	FICA*	Net P
5	Carlson	Roberta	7.25	15	50	=C5*D5+E5	21.75	=F5*B16	=F5-G
6	Carrillo	Angela	11.3	30	50	=C6*D6+E6	67.5	=F6*B16	=F6-G
7	Jacobsen	Russ	6.5	18	50	=C7*D7+E7	23.4	=F7*B16	=F7-G
8	Mansur	Gloria	11.3	30	50	=C8*D8+E8	67.5	=F8*B16	=F8-G
9	Prada	Josephine	6.5	17	50	=C9*D9+E9	22.1	=F9*B16	=F9-G
10	Tyler	Geoffrey	11.3	30	50	=C10*D10+E10	67.5	=F10*B16	=F10-
11	Villarreal	Raoul	6.5	20	50	=C11*D11+E11	26	=F11*B16	=F11-
12	Williams	Corinne	5.75	20	50	=C12*D12+E12	23	=F12*B16	=F12-
13	Yee	Wendy	6.5	20	50	=C13*D13+E13	26	=F13*B16	=F13-
14		TOTALS		=SUM(D5:D13)	=SUM(E5:E13)	=SUM(F5:F13)	=SUM(G5:G13	=SUM(H5:H13)	=SUM
15									
16	*FICA @	0.0765							
17									
18									
19									
20									
21									

FIGURE 7-15

1900 and any date that may be used in a spreadsheet. In Formula view, the day number is displayed instead of the actual day.

You are almost ready to print this spreadsheet, but you would really like for the title to be printed. In order to have the title print,

5. Use the two-way arrow to widen column A until the entire title is visible.

PRINTING SPREADSHEETS HORIZONTALLY

Because spreadsheets are often quite wide, they frequently do not fit vertically on a standard 8½ by 11-inch page. They could, however, fit horizontally.

IT'S YOUR TURN

1. Click the PRINT PREVIEW button on the toolbar.

   A Preview screen such as the one shown in Figure 7-16 should appear.

Active Button Tells You This Spreadsheet
Requires More Than One Page to Print

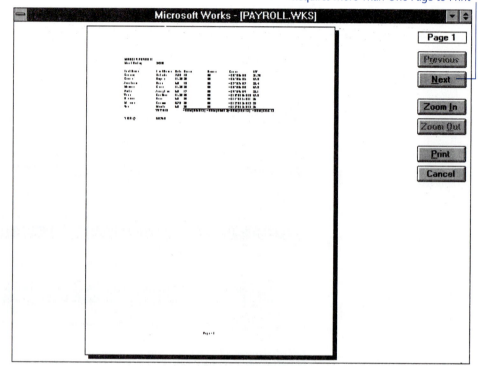

FIGURE 7-16

Look at the buttons on the right side of the screen. The NEXT button is darkened, indicating that it can be activated.

2. Click the next button.

   The second page of the spreadsheet comes into view, and the PREVIOUS button is now available.

Since you do not want this spreadsheet to use two pages for printing, you will now change the printing parameters to print it on one page. To leave the Print Preview screen,

3. Click the CANCEL button.

4. Choose Page Setup from the FILE menu.

   A Page Setup dialog box similar to the one shown in Figure 7-17 appears.

5. Click the tab labelled "Source, Size and Orientation."

   That section of the Page Setup dialog box comes into view, as shown in Figure 7-18.

6. Click on Landscape in the Orientation block.

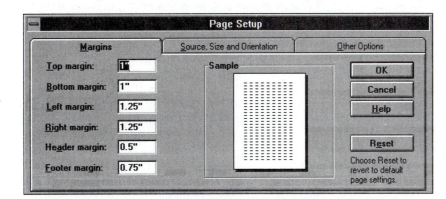

FIGURE 7-17

FIGURE 7-18

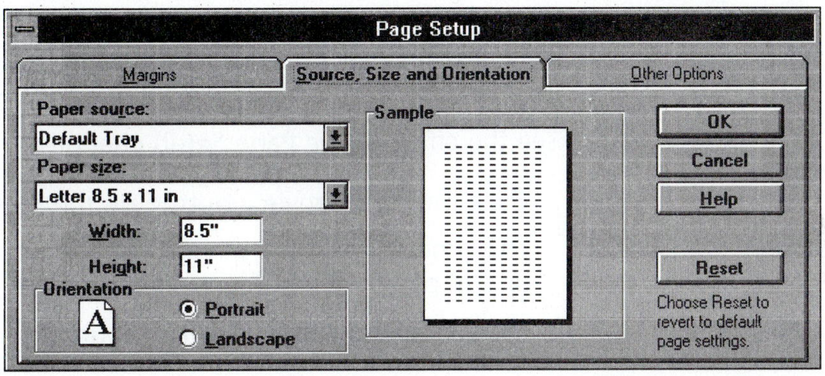

When you click the Landscape orientation option, note that the width and height boxes automatically adjust themselves and that the Sample block now contains a picture of a small page turned sideways.

7. Click the tab labelled "Other Options."

The Other Options section of the Page Setup dialog box comes into view, as shown in Figure 7-19.

FIGURE 7-19

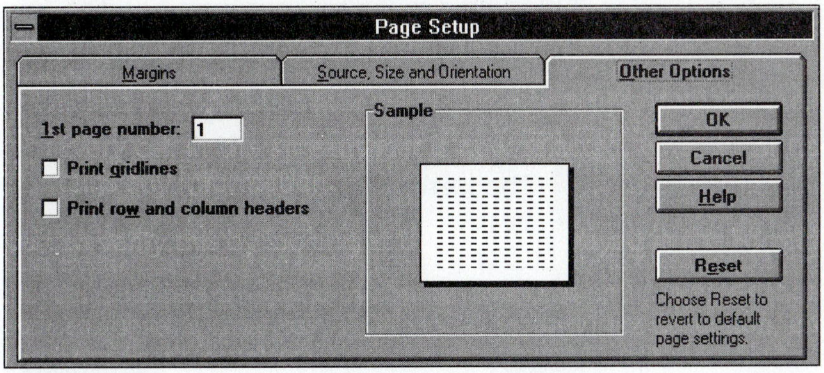

The formulas with their cell addresses will not be very valuable if the reader cannot easily find the reference for those addresses. You can use the Other Options section of the Page Setup dialog box to have the column and row headers printed.

8. Click the option labelled "Print Row and Column Headers."

Printing gridlines will make it much easier to identify the cell addresses as they are used in the formulas.

9. Click the option labelled "Print Gridlines."

Note the First Page Number option box. Changing this option would allow you to select the page number assigned to the first page of this spreadsheet. If this spreadsheet were to be included as page 15 of a larger report, for example, you could change the page number from 1 to 15. You will not need to change the first page number for the current spreadsheet.

Now that you have changed all the necessary parameters, you must return to the spreadsheet.

10. Click ok or press [ENTER].

The spreadsheet reappears, but nothing looks different about it.

To see the effect of the Page Setup changes,

11. Click the print preview button on the toolbar.

This time the preview screen shows the spreadsheet turned sideways on the paper, and you can see that it will easily fit on one page.

12. Use the zoom buttons to view your spreadsheet more closely.

When you are finished,

13. Click the cancel button to return to the spreadsheet.

USING HEADERS AND FOOTERS

WORKS 3.0 allows you to print a header (text that appears in the top margin) and a footer (text that appears in the bottom margin) on spreadsheets, just as you can on word processing documents. Spreadsheet headers and footers can contain only one line. They are specified using the same ampersand codes that are used in the word processing module for single line headers and footers.

To insert a footer on your spreadsheet to identify the file, who created it, and when it was printed, follow the next set of steps.

IT'S YOUR TURN

1. Choose Headers & Footers from the VIEW menu.

The Headers and Footers dialog box shown in Figure 7-20 will appear.

FIGURE 7-20

Headers and Footers		
H_eader: [ ]		OK
F_ooter: [Page - &p]		Cancel
☐ N_o header on 1st page ☐ _Use header and		Help
☐ N_o footer on 1st page footer paragraphs		

To highlight the Footer text box,

2. Press [TAB].

The Footer text box will become highlighted, indicating that anything you type will replace the current contents of the box.

3. Type the following sequence of characters, replacing the underlined portion with the appropriate information.

    &L<u>your name</u>&C&D&R&F

The You should recall from working with the word processing module footer that this sequence of characters will cause your name to be printed at the left margin with the date in the center of the page and the filename at the right margin.

4. Click OK or press [ENTER].

When you return to the spreadsheet,

5. Click the PRINT PREVIEW button on the toolbar, and use the ZOOM button to view the footer line on the spreadsheet.

6. CLICK THE cancel button to return to the spreadsheet from the preview screen.

FINISHING UP

As usual, save your work under a new name before closing.

IT'S YOUR TURN

1. Choose Save As from the FILE menu and save this spreadsheet in your name directory on your data disk. Use the filename *payroll2*.

2. Choose Print from the FILE menu and print with formulas displayed, if printing is required by your instructor.

3. Quit *WORKS,* as directed in previous chapters.

SUMMARY

Congratulations! While updating the Payroll spreadsheet, you have changed column widths, copied cells using the fill commands, used absolute and relative cell addresses, formatted cells, printed a spreadsheet horizontally displaying cell formulas, and inserted a footer. Now you are ready to create a new spreadsheet file in the next chapter.

REVIEW QUESTIONS

1. What menu and option would you choose to change the orientation of a spreadsheet?

2. How do you select an entire column?

3. If cell E6, containing the formula "=SUM(E2:E5)," is copied to cell F6, what would the formula stored in cell F6 be?

4. How can you distinguish an absolute reference from a relative reference in a formula?

5. Which menu and option would you use to quickly copy the contents of one cell to the ten cells immediately below it in the same column?

6. Which menu and option would you use to display the formulas in cells?

EXERCISES

EXERCISE 7-1 Inserting a column, changing width, entering data, formatting cells, adding footnotes, and changing margins

1. Open the file called *PAYROLL* from your data disk.

2. Make the following changes:

   a. Insert a column between First Name and Rate.

   b. Title the new column Emp. ID#.

   c. Decrease the width of the new column.

   d. Enter any three-digit value for each employee.

   e. Format the Rate column for Fixed format and two decimals.

   f. Format the Gross, FIT, FICA and Net Pay columns for Commas and two decimals.

   g. Adjust the widths of any columns that need it.

   h. Right align the column headings for D through I.

   i. Insert the current date in cell B2.

3. Add a footer with your name on the left and the current date on the right.

4. Save the file with the name *EX7-1* in your name directory on your data disk.

5. Print the spreadsheet, if requested by your instructor.

EXERCISE 7-2 Inserting a column, entering data, changing formulas, and copying formulas

1. Open the file called *PAYROLL* from your data disk.

2. Insert current date in B2.

3. Make the following changes:

   a. Insert a column between "Hours" and "Gross."

   b. Title the new column "Overtime."

   c. Enter dollar amounts for each person except Carrillo, Mansur, and Tyler. They are all salaried personnel and do not receive overtime.

   d. Change the Gross Pay formula in cell F5 to include the overtime pay.

   e. Use Fill Down to copy the formula down in the rest of column F.

   f. Use Fill Right to copy the formula from D14 to E14.

   g. Format the money columns for commas and two decimal places. (Don't forget column C.)

   h. Adjust the column widths as necessary.

4. Add a footer with your name on the left and the current date on the right.

5. Save the file with the name *EX7-2* in your name directory on your data disk.

6. Print the spreadsheet if requested by your instructor.

EXERCISE 7-3   Creating and displaying formulas

1. Open the *PAYROLL* file.

2. Insert a new column between "FICA" and "Net Pay" and label it "Gift Fund."

3. Use Fill Down to enter "$1" for each employee in the newly created column.

4. Use Fill Right to copy the formula on the Totals line in cell G14 to cell H14.

5. Edit the formula in the Net Pay column for Roberta (cell I5) to show that $1 has been deducted, then copy the new formula down the column for the other employees.

6. Format all dollar amounts for commas and two decimals.

7. Change page orientation to horizontal (landscape).

8. Show the formulas on the spreadsheet and adjust column width so all formulas display.

9. Add a footer to include your name on the left and the current date on the right.

10. Save the file with the name *EX7-3* in your name directory on your data disk.

11. Print the spreadsheet, if directed to do so by your instructor.

Spreadsheet 3

OBJECTIVES

When you finish this chapter you will be able to

- create a new spreadsheet file
- display labels over more than one cell
- use the Insert Function option
- determine margins
- move cell contents using copy and paste
- create an IF statement
- format blocks of cells
- protect cells

SETTING THE SCENE

PROJECT 1 The Income Statement

It's time for you to create your own new file and learn some additional techniques for enhancing the appearance of a file. Since *WORKS* makes calculations so quickly and easily, you decide to create a financial statement each month showing revenues and expenses and have the spreadsheet calculate total expenses and net income. Figure 8-1 displays the completed report.

FIGURE 8-1

```
                    THE FUN FACTORY
                    Income Statement
                 For the Month of November

    SALES                                    $30,079.00

    EXPENSES
           Cost of Goods Sold    $13,982.00
           Payroll                 6,129.44
           Depreciation            1,322.00
           Rent                    1,000.00
           Utilities                 525.00
           Insurance                 420.00
           Payroll Taxes             398.65
           Advertising               467.00
           Supplies                  369.00
           Miscellaneous             174.74
           Total                              24,787.83

    NET INCOME                                $5,291.17
```

GETTING STARTED

There is no file on your data disk to use for this activity. You will create your own new spreadsheet file and type in the needed data. A new spreadsheet file is created in much the same way as word processing files are created.

IT'S YOUR TURN

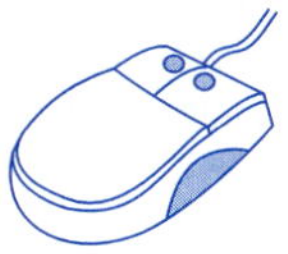

1. Launch *WORKS 3.0*.

When the Startup dialog box appears with the NEW & RECENT DOCUMENTS button highlighted,

2. Click the SPREADSHEET button.

    An empty spreadsheet is displayed. See Figure 8-2.

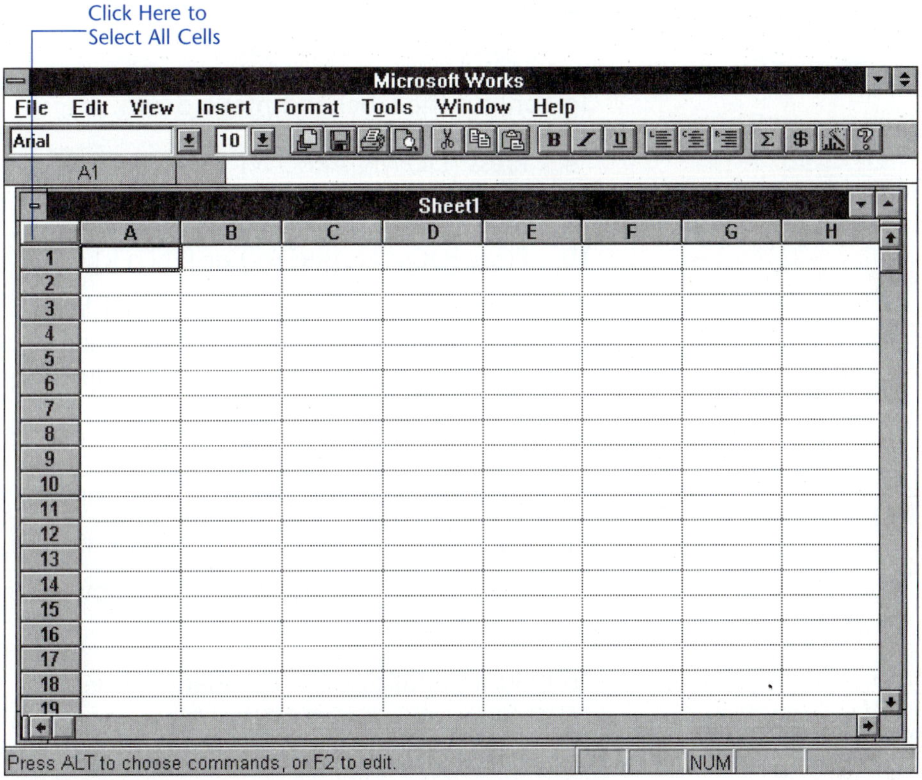

Click Here to
Select All Cells

FIGURE 8-2

3. If the toolbar does not display choose Toolbar from the VIEW menu.

**TYPING
THE HEADING**

Next you will type the main heading lines in column C. Do not worry about centering the headings yet. Before beginning to type you will reduce the font size for the entire spreadsheet.

IT'S YOUR TURN

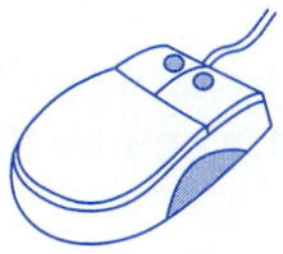

1. Click the SELECT ALL button at the intersection of the row and column headers in the upper left corner of the spreadsheet, as shown in Figure 8-2.

2. Click the arrow on the Font Size box on the toolbar.

    The Font Size box will drop down.

3. Click 8.

To deselect and to prepare to type the title,

4. Click on cell C1.

5. Type: THE FUN FACTORY

Remember, if you make a mistake before confirming, simply press [BACKSPACE] and retype.

6. Press [DOWN ARROW] to enter the label and move down to the next cell.

If you discover a mistake in a cell after you have entered it, simply select that cell, type the correct characters, and press [ENTER] or click the ENTRY button.
The highlight should now be in cell C2.

7. Type: Income Statement

To confirm the label and move down,

8. Press [DOWN ARROW]

9. Type: For the Month of November

10. Press [DOWN ARROW] or [ENTER].

Because the heading lines are all labels, they are formatted against the left edge of column C and, because columns D and E are empty, the headings overflow into the adjoining cells.

Since they would look much better if centered,

11. Drag to select the block of cells from C1 through C3.

12. Click the CENTER alignment button on the toolbar.

Notice that the labels now overflow to the blank cells on either side of column C.

To bold and italicize the company name,

13. Click on cell C1.

14. Click the BOLD button on the toolbar.

15. Click the ITALIC button on the toolbar.

TYPING THE SIDE LABELS AND AMOUNTS

You are now ready to type the report side labels and amounts. Again, don't worry about formatting; you will do that after entering all the data.
Study the following table of procedures for confirming and entering data and moving the selection from cell to cell; you will then better understand the steps that follow.

Press [TAB]	Enters data and moves the highlight to the cell to the right
Press [ENTER]	Enters data and leaves the present cell highlighted
Press an arrow key	Enters data and moves the highlight to the next cell in the direction of the arrow.
Click the entry button in the Formula bar	Enters data and leaves the present cell highlighted

| Click the CANCEL button in the Formula bar | Deletes the unconfirmed data and leaves the present cell highlighted |
| Click on a different cell | Enters data and moves the highlight to the clicked cell |

IT'S YOUR TURN

1. Click on cell A5.
2. Type: SALES
3. Press [TAB] four times to move to cell E5.
4. Type: 30079

   Reminder: Do not type dollar signs or commas when inputting values. They will be inserted later when you format the cells.

5. Click on cell A7.
6. Type: EXPENSES
7. Press [DOWN ARROW] to enter the label and move to the next row.
8. Press [TAB].

   You should now be in cell B8. Notice that we are using columns much as tabs are used in word processing to indent the various types of expenditures under the "EXPENSES" heading.

9. Type: Cost of Goods Sold [DOWN ARROW]

   To simplify your work, you will type the expenses in column B before typing the amounts in column D.

10. Type: Payroll [DOWN ARROW]

    Depreciation [DOWN ARROW]

    Rent [DOWN ARROW]

    Utilities [DOWN ARROW]

    Insurance [DOWN ARROW]

    Payroll Taxes [DOWN ARROW]

    Advertising [DOWN ARROW]

    Supplies [DOWN ARROW]

    Miscellaneous [DOWN ARROW]

    Total [DOWN ARROW]

Now you will type in the amounts for each expenditure.

11. Click on cell D8.
12. Type: 13982 [DOWN ARROW]

    6129.44 [DOWN ARROW]

    1322 [DOWN ARROW]

    1000 [DOWN ARROW]

    525 [DOWN ARROW]

    420 [DOWN ARROW]

398.65 [DOWN ARROW]

467 [DOWN ARROW]

369 [DOWN ARROW]

174.74 [DOWN ARROW]

When you are finished, your screen should resemble the screen shown in Figure 8-3.

FIGURE 8-3

	A	B	C	D	E	F	G	H	I
1		*THE FUN FACTORY*							
2		Income Statement							
3		For the Month of November							
4									
5	SALES				30079				
6									
7	EXPENSES								
8		Cost of Goods Sold		13982					
9		Payroll		6129.44					
10		Depreciation		1322					
11		Rent		1000					
12		Utilities		525					
13		Insurance		420					
14		Payroll Taxes		398.65					
15		Advertising		467					
16		Supplies		369					
17		Miscellaneous		174.74					
18		Total							
19									
20									
21									

Press ALT to choose commands, or F2 to edit.   NUM

You are now ready to create more formulas.

USING THE INSERT FUNCTION COMMAND

You now need to direct *WORKS* to total the expenses and compute net income. You have already used the SUM function but, for the purpose of this exercise, let's suppose you forgot the name of the function you wanted. *WORKS* provides some hints for you.

IT'S YOUR TURN

To move to column E, which has been reserved for summary figures,

1. Press [TAB] or click on cell E18.
2. Choose Function from the INSERT menu.

The dialog box shown in Figure 8-4 will appear.

WORKS lists function categories in the Category block on the left side of the dialog box. As you can see, Category All is already selected, and the list box on the right displays the beginning of a list that contains all 76 functions that are available in *WORKS*. If you know the category for the function you want, you can click that category name and restrict the list of functions considerably.

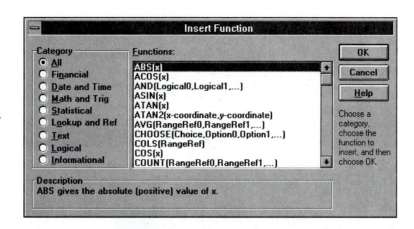

FIGURE 8-4

The Description block at the bottom of the dialog box describes the function that is currently highlighted in the Functions list box. When the dialog box is first presented, the ABS function is highlighted and the Description box tells what it does. To get an idea of the number of functions Works recognizes,

3. Click and hold the down scroll arrow on the vertical scroll bar of the Functions list box to scroll to the end of the list.

You may have seen the SUM function flash by as you scrolled, but there is an easier way to find it. SUM is in the Statistical category, so

4. Click Statistical in the Category block.

A short list of functions is now displayed in the Functions list box.

5. Click on SUM(RangeRef0,RangeRef1,...).

The Description box now describes what the selected function will do. It is interesting to note that the SUM function is much more versatile than you may have realized. The arguments enclosed within the parentheses indicate that the function can work with more than one range. Suppose you were working on a spreadsheet and needed the sum of the values in cells E4 through E8, H10 through H13 and H20. The formula "=SUM(E4:E8,H10:H13,H20)" would make the calculation for you. Your use of the SUM function in the current activity will be much less complex than this example.

To insert the SUM function into the highlighted cell of your spreadsheet,

6. Click OK or press [ENTER].

WORKS has inserted the function you selected into the Formula bar with the first dummy argument highlighted. The dummy arguments represent the values to be acted upon by the function. Anything you type or select will replace the highlighted argument. Since the cells to be added are adjacent to each other, there is a very fast way of inserting them into the function.

7. Drag from cell D8 through D17.

As you dragged, the cells became highlighted, and when you released the mouse button, the cell addresses were inserted into the formula in the Formula bar in place of the first dummy argument. Your screen should resemble the one shown in Figure 8-5.

FIGURE 8-5

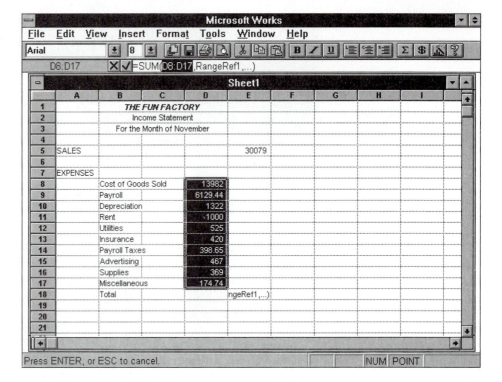

8. Type:)

9. Press the [DELETE] key until all characters to the right of the insertion point in the Formula bar have been deleted.

To confirm the formula and cause it to take effect,

10. Click the ENTRY button or press [ENTER].

Cell E18 will now contain 24787.83 The expenses have been totaled, and the Formula bar indicates that the selected range, D8:D17, has been inserted into the function.

COMPLETING THE SPREADSHEET

You are almost finished. However, you still need to input the Net Income line and complete some minor formatting.

IT'S YOUR TURN

1. Click on cell A20.

You may have to scroll down to bring row 20 into view.

2. Type: NET INCOME

3. Press [TAB] four times to enter the label and move to cell E20.

4. Type a formula that will subtract total expenses from sales.

If you need help, the formula "=E5-E18" will work. If you prefer, you could have typed the equal sign, clicked on cell E5, typed the minus, and clicked on cell E18.

5. Click the ENTRY button or press [ENTER] to record the formula.

The difference of 5291.17 is now displayed in cell E20.

Now for the finishing touches. You will format all dollar amounts for commas and two decimal places, but you will format the first number in each column and the Net Income amount for dollars. You will underline the last expense item and the total expenses, and you will double underline the net income figure. You can try to complete the formatting on your own; but if you need help, follow the directions listed below for each step.

6. Format Sales and the first expense item to dollar format.

   a. Drag from cell D5 through E8.

   b. Choose Number from the FORMAT menu.

   c. Click Currency in the Format block.

      Two decimals and commas are automatically displayed.

   d. Click OK or press [ENTER].

7. Format all other expense amounts for commas and two decimals.

   a. Drag from cell D9 through E18.

   b. Choose Number from the FORMAT menu.

   c. Click Comma in the Format block.

   d. If "2" does not display in the Number of Decimals box, type "2" to replace the current highlighted number.

   e. Click OK or press [ENTER].

8. Format cell E20 for currency with two decimal places.

   a. Click cell E20.

   b. Choose Number from the FORMAT menu.

   c. Click Currency in the Format block.

   d. Click OK or press [ENTER].

9. Underline the last expense item and the total expense figure by attaching top borders to the cells below.

   a. Click cell D18.

   b. Choose Border from the FORMAT menu.

   c. Click the box labled "Top" in the Borders section.

   d. Click OK or press [ENTER]

   e. Click cell E19.

   f. Repeat steps b-d, above.

10. Double underline the net income figure.

   a. Click cell E20.

   b. Choose Border from the FORMAT menu.

   c. Click the box labeled Bottom in the Border section and the box containing the double line in the Line Style section.

   d. Click OK or press [ENTER].

11. Click in any empty cell to deselect and see the results of the formatting changes.

Many people prefer reports without lines. To display and print the file without grid lines,

12. Choose Gridlines from the VIEW menu.

This is a toggled command that controls the screen display. Your screen should resemble the one shown in Figure 8-6.

FIGURE 8-6

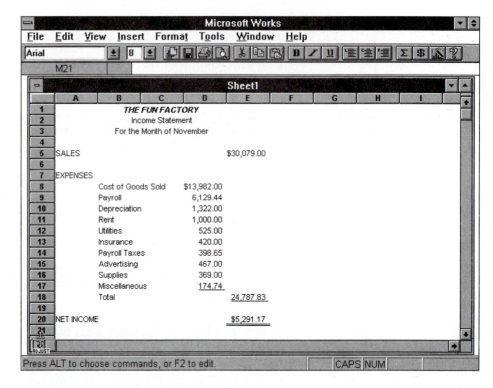

To print the file without grid lines,

13. Choose Page Setup from the FILE menu and click the Other Options tab when the dialog box appears.

14. If necessary click Print Gridlines to deselect that option.

15. Click the OK button or press [ENTER].

DETERMINING SPREADSHEET MARGINS

It is sometimes difficult to determine what the printout of a spreadsheet will look like before printing. Fortunately, as you know from working with it in earlier chapters, *WORKS 3.0* has a preview screen which you can use to decide whether to increase or decrease the margins or whether to print vertically or horizontally.

IT'S YOUR TURN

1. Choose Print Preview from the FILE menu or click the PRINT PREVIEW button on the toolbar.

The Print Preview screen shown in Figure 8-7 appears, showing what this spreadsheet would look like if printed with the present settings.

Although you cannot read the file, you can see that the spreadsheet will be printed high on the page and to the left side. If you wanted to magnify any part of the file (the heading, for example),

2. Move the pointer (magnifying glass) over the title lines and click twice.

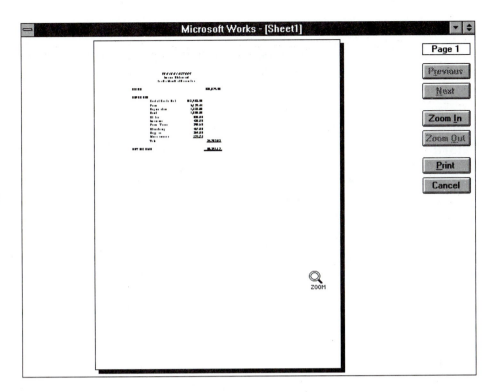

FIGURE 8-7

Since this spreadsheet is quite small, the entire spreadsheet displays. You can scroll vertically and horizontally through the Print Preview screen by using the scroll bars and arrows. To move back to the reduced preview screen,

3. Click the magnifying glass on the screen once, or click the ZOOM OUT button at the side of the screen twice.

Clicking the PRINT button at this point will display the Print dialog box; the PREVIOUS button will display the previous page, if there is one; and the NEXT button will display the next page, if there is one. To return to the spreadsheet,

4. Click the CANCEL button.

   You will increase the left side margin to 2.5 inches and the top margin to two inches to place this income statement more attractively on the page before actually printing.

To change the margins,

5. Choose Page Setup from the FILE menu.

   The Page Setup dialog box appears,

6. If necessary, click the Margins tab to bring that section to the top.

7. If necessary, double click the Top Margin box to select it.

8. Type: 2

9. Press [TAB] twice to advance the highlight to the Left Margin box.

10. Type: 2.5

11. Click OK or press [ENTER] to return to the spreadsheet.

To see the effect of the changes,

12. **Click the** PRINT PREVIEW **button on the toolbar.**

When you are finished with the print preview screen,

13. **Click** CANCEL **to return to the spreadsheet.**

FINISHING UP PROJECT 1

Because this file is not very long, you were not previously instructed to save it. However, you should save frequently (every ten to fifteen minutes) when you are creating any long, important file. Before you save, however, you will create a header to help you identify this document.

IT'S YOUR TURN

1. **Choose Headers & Footers from the VIEW menu.**

    Headers are typed using the same codes as footers, which you have already used. You want this header to contain your name at the left margin, the date in the center, and the filename at the right margin. Since the insertion point is already in the Header text box of the Headers & Footers dialog box,

2. **Type:** &LYour Name&C&D&R&F

    The dialog box should look like the one shown in Figure 8-8.

FIGURE 8-8

Headers and Footers	
Header: &LA Student&C&D&R&F	OK
Footer:	Cancel
☐ No header on 1st page ☐ Use header and	Help
☐ No footer on 1st page footer paragraphs	

3. **Click** OK **or press [ENTER].**

You will be returned to the spreadsheet. To see the header as it will be when printed,

4. **Click the** PRINT PREVIEW **button on the toolbar.**

When the Print Preview screen appears,

5. **Zoom in on the header line at the top of the sheet.**

Because you have not yet named this document, the name "Sheet1" appears in the header. However, as long as you save the file with another name before you print, the actual document name will appear on the final document. To return to the spreadsheet,

6. **Click the** CANCEL **button.**

    Now you are ready to save this file.

7. **Insert your data disk into the internal disk drive.**

8. **Choose Save As from the FILE menu and save this file as** *STATEMNT* **in your name directory on your data disk.**

    Since you have already used Print Preview many times with this file, you know it only uses one page to print.

9. Choose Print from the FILE menu and click OK when the Print dialog box appears.

The Printing dialog box will appear briefly and you will be returned to the spreadsheet.
Since you are finished with this file you will put it away, or close it.

10. Double click the CONTROL MENU button in the upper left corner of the *STATEMNT* window or choose Close from the FILE menu.

SETTING THE SCENE

PROJECT 2 The Reorder Form

One of your managers has suggested the use of a reorder form to determine the number of products to be purchased from each of your major suppliers. She has created a draft of her idea for the stuffed animals she orders from Pandas and Such. You have examined the draft and you agree that it could be helpful in operating The Fun Factory.

GETTING STARTED

The spreadsheet draft appears in Figure 8-9 and is stored on your data disk as *REORDER*. You will provide the formulas and functions to complete the file, add cell protection so the formulas can't be changed, create a header, and change the margins to make a more pleasing printout.

FIGURE 8-9

```
┌────────────────────────────────────────────────────────────────────────┐
│  ─                        Microsoft Works                          ▼ ▲  │
│  File   Edit   View   Insert   Format   Tools   Window   Help           │
│ ┌──────┐                                                                 │
│ │Arial │ ▼  8  ▼  □□□□□ ✂□□ B I U ≡≡≡ Σ $ ▨ ?                           │
│ └──────┘                                                                 │
│        │ B2 │                                                           │
│ ┌──────────────────────────────────────────────────────────────────┐  │
│ │ ▫                      REORDER.WKS                         ▼ ▲     │  │
│ │      A        B         C        D        E        F     G   H  I  │  │
│ │  1 REORDER FORM                                                    │  │
│ │  2 Date:    [        ]          Vendor:  Pandas and Such          │  │
│ │  3                                                                 │  │
│ │  4 Item No. Description  Needed  On Hand Short    Order           │  │
│ │  5    135  Alligator       5        3   FORMULA  FORMULA          │  │
│ │  6    102  Brown Bear     12        3   FORMULA  FORMULA          │  │
│ │  7    142  Dolphin        11        6   FORMULA  FORMULA          │  │
│ │  8    109  Duck            6        2   FORMULA  FORMULA          │  │
│ │  9    141  Frog            5        3   FORMULA  FORMULA          │  │
│ │ 10    113  Giraffe         6        4   FORMULA  FORMULA          │  │
│ │ 11    153  Panda Bear      9        3   FORMULA  FORMULA          │  │
│ │ 12    122  Seal            7        5   FORMULA  FORMULA          │  │
│ │ 13    107  Tiger           9        4   FORMULA  FORMULA          │  │
│ │ 14         TOTALS     FORMULA  FORMULA  FORMULA  FORMULA          │  │
│ │ 15                                                                 │  │
│ │ 16                                                                 │  │
│ │ 17                                                                 │  │
│ │ 18                                                                 │  │
│ │ 19                                                                 │  │
│ │ 20                                                                 │  │
│ │ 21                                                            ▼    │  │
│ │ ◄ ►                                                          ►    │  │
│ └──────────────────────────────────────────────────────────────────┘  │
│ Press ALT to choose commands, or F2 to edit.            NUM            │
└────────────────────────────────────────────────────────────────────────┘
```

IT'S YOUR TURN

1. Open the spreadsheet file *REORDER* from your data disk.

Your screen will display the file shown in Figure 8-9.
The first thing you will do is insert the current date into the file. Since you want the date to change every time the spreadsheet is updated, you will use the Now function. If the date is incorrect, make sure the internal clock used by your computer is set to the correct date and time. For information on setting the internal clock, see the

Microsoft Windows User's Guide. The Now function's syntax is NOW(). Even though it requires no arguments, the empty parentheses are still required. Incidentally, the Now function can be used to display the current time if the cell is formatted for time.

2. Click cell B2.

3. Choose Number from the FORMAT menu.

When the dialog box appears,

4. Click Date in the Format block.

Since the short date form is already selected in the Date block in the center of the dialog box,

5. Click the OK button or press [ENTER].

You will be returned to the spreadsheet with cell B2 still selected.

6. Type: =NOW( )

7. Click the ENTRY button or press [ENTER].

The current date will appear in the cell, and the formula will be displayed in the Formula bar.

MOVING CELL CONTENT

Look at the spreadsheet title "Reorder Form." You will perform an approximate centering of the title by placing it in cell C1, where it will dominate the columns even if it is not perfectly centered.

IT'S YOUR TURN

1. Click cell A1.

   It presently contains the title, as displayed in the Formula bar.

2. Choose Cut from the EDIT menu.

   The title disappears! Don't worry—it isn't lost. *WORKS* stored it on the clipboard in anticipation that you will paste it somewhere else.

3. Click cell C1

4. Choose Paste from the EDIT menu.

5. Click in any empty cell to deselect so you can view the effect of the move.

HINT ▶ You can also use the keyboard to move cells by using the keyboard shortcuts you learned in Chapter 5: simply highlight the cell to be moved, press [CTRL] + [X], (the shortcut for cut), highlight the destination cell, and press [CTRL] + [V], (the shortcut for paste).

REVIEWING FORMULAS AND FUNCTIONS

The form needs formulas in columns C through F. The formulas for cells C14 through F14 must sum the cells above them. The formulas for cells E5 through E13 must subtract the amounts in column D from the amounts in column C. The formula for cells F5 through F13 is a more complex conditional formula, which will be explained later in the chapter. You will use the point-and-click method to create them.

IT'S YOUR TURN

1. Click cell E5.

2. Create a simple formula that will subtract the items on hand (cell D5) from the items needed (cell C5). Try to do this on your own, using the point-and-click method. If you need help,

   a. Type: = (equal sign)

   b. Click cell C5.

   c. Type: - (hyphen)

   d. Click cell D5.

   e. Click the ENTRY button or press [ENTER].

3. Copy the formula in cell E5 down through E13. Try to do this on your own. If you need help,

   a. Drag from cell E5 to E13 to select those cells.

   b. Choose Fill Down from the EDIT menu.

4. Click cell C14.

   You now need to create a formula to calculate the total needed for stuffed animals. You can type a formula or function if you wish, but using the AUTOSUM button is by far the easiest method.

5. Click the AUTOSUM button on the toolbar.

Since the formula proposed in the Formula bar is correct,

6. Click the ENTRY button or press [ENTER].

7. Copy the formula in cell C14 to the three cells to the right. If you need help,

   a. Drag from cell C14 through F14.

   b. Choose Fill Right from the EDIT menu.

8. Click any empty cell to deselect.

You have one more column that needs a formula. This one is a much more complex logical function—the **_IF statement_**.

USING THE IF STATEMENT AND A LOGICAL OPERATOR

Your vender, Pandas and Such, requires a minimum order of three per animal ordered. To calculate the amount to be ordered, you will need to insert a formula in the order column which will print a number only if it is equal to or greater than three. _WORKS 3.0_ offers a logical function that can help with this problem.

IT'S YOUR TURN

1. Click cell F5.

2. Choose Function from the INSERT menu.

3. Click on Logical in the Category block on the left of the dialog box.

   A list of _WORKS'_ logical functions appears in the list box on the right.

4. Click on the function IF(Cond,ValueIfTrue,ValueIfFalse).

The text between the parentheses contains abbreviations standing for the arguments (the values needed for the calculation) for the IF function. The condition (cond) must be an expression that can be evaluated as either true or false. The other two arguments can be numbers, cell addresses, another function, or any combination that results in a number. This particular function looks at the condition (cond) and will print the first value (ValueIfTrue) if the condition is true or the second value (ValueIfFalse) if the condition is false.

To insert the IF function,

5. Click OK or press [ENTER].

The spreadsheet reappears with the function in the Formula bar. The abbreviation for the first argument is highlighted, waiting to be replaced.

You will use a logical operator in the conditional expression. Knowing that you need to know if cell E5 is at least three, can you guess what the conditional expression should be?

6. Type: E5>=3 (Translated, this means that if the amount in cell E5 is more than or equal to three)

As you typed the first letter, it replaced the highlighted dummy argument, Cond, in the Formula bar.

To replace the second dummy argument, ValueIfTrue,

7. Drag to highlight the dummy argument ValueIfTrue.

Be very careful not to select the commas separating the dummy arguments. If you do, be sure to replace them when you type. Commas must be used to separate the arguments.

To record that the content of E5 is to be displayed if the comparison in step 6 is true (if E5 is greater than or equal to three),

8. Type: E5

To replace the third dummy argument,

9. Drag to select ValueIfFalse, taking care not to select the comma or the right parenthesis.

To record that the value zero is to be displayed if the comparison in step 6 is false (if E5 is less than three),

10. Type: 0 (zero)

To record the function in the cell,

11. Click the ENTRY button or press [ENTER].

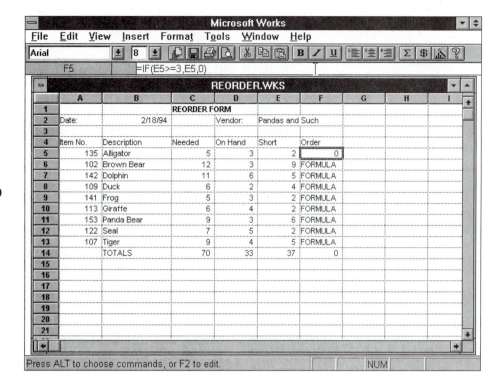

FIGURE 8-10

Since you are only two alligators short, the spreadsheet indicates in column F that none should be ordered. Your spreadsheet should now resemble the one shown in Figure 8-10.

12. Copy this formula down for the rest of the animals. If you need help,

   a. Drag from cell F5 through F13.

   b. Choose Fill Down from the EDIT menu.

The order amount is now calculated for all animals.

FORMATTING BLOCKS OF TEXT

Now you are ready to put the finishing touches on this spreadsheet.

Numbers are usually right aligned for ease of reading. But since all of the numbers in column A contain the same number of digits, they can be centered to better balance the column's heading. Centering column A will also prevent it from running into column B, which contains labels and is left-aligned.

IT'S YOUR TURN

1. Click column header A.

   The entire column, including the heading, becomes selected and can now be centered.

2. Click the CENTER alignment button on the toolbar.

   Column A is now centered.

The headings for columns of numbers are frequently aligned at the right to agree with the alignment of the numbers below. To make the headings for columns C through F conform to this standard,

3. Drag from cell C4 through F4.

4. Click the RIGHT alignment button on the toolbar.

Reports can also be made easier to read if the column headings are set off by underlining.

5. Drag from cell A4 through F4.

6. Click the UNDERLINE button on the toolbar.

7. Click any empty cell to deselect.

Placing a line between the last stuffed animal and the totals presents a small problem. If you underline the last line (data for Tigers) and later want to insert a new stuffed animal at the end of the list, you will have to remove the underline from the data for Tigers and underline the data for the new stuffed animal. You will avoid this problem by attaching the line to the totals in row 14.

8. Drag from cell C14 through F14.

9. Choose Border from the FORMAT menu.

10. Click the Top option from the Border block in the Format Cells dialog box.

Since the correct line style (thin) is already selected,

11. Click OK or press [ENTER].

12. Click any empty cell to deselect and see the effects of your formatting efforts.

The date in cell B2 is rather far removed from its label in cell A2. To correct that,

13. Click cell B2.

14. Click the LEFT alignment button in the toolbar.

To move the label in cell D2 closer to the vendor name in cell E2,

15. Click cell D2.

16. Click the RIGHT alignment button in the toolbar.

17. Click any empty cell to deselect.

Your finished screen should resemble the one shown in Figure 8-11.

PROTECTING CELLS

Whenever you create a spreadsheet that will be used by others, you should protect cells that should not be modified to prevent other users from accidentally changing them. Protecting designated cells in *WORKS 3.0* spreadsheets is a two-step process. Initially, *WORKS* locks all cells in a spreadsheet, but until you activate the Protection command, the locks have no effect. If you want to be able to change a specific entry, you must unlock its cell. Then when you activate protection, *WORKS* does not protect the cells you have unlocked. If anyone tries to enter data into a protected cell, the program will sound a warning beep and display a warning message.

You would not want anyone tampering with your formulas in the spreadsheet, so you will protect them.

	A	B	C	D	E	F
1			REORDER FORM			
2	Date:	2/18/94		Vendor:	Pandas and Such	
3						
4	Item No.	Description	Needed	On Hand	Short	Order
5	135	Alligator	5	3	2	0
6	102	Brown Bear	12	3	9	9
7	142	Dolphin	11	6	5	5
8	109	Duck	6	2	4	4
9	141	Frog	5	3	2	0
10	113	Giraffe	6	4	2	0
11	153	Panda Bear	9	3	6	6
12	122	Seal	7	5	2	0
13	107	Tiger	9	4	5	5
14		TOTALS	70	33	37	29

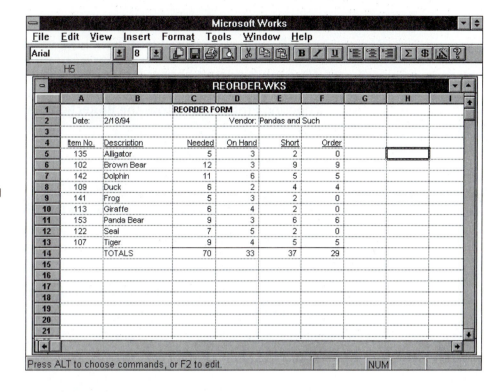

FIGURE 8-11

IT'S YOUR TURN

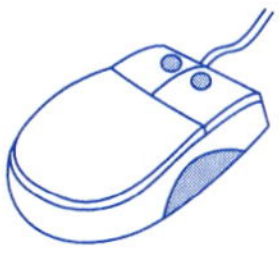

To unlock the cells which will be changed frequently,

1. Drag from cells C5 through D13.
2. Choose Protection from the FORMAT menu.

   The Protection dialog box shown in Figure 8-12 appears.

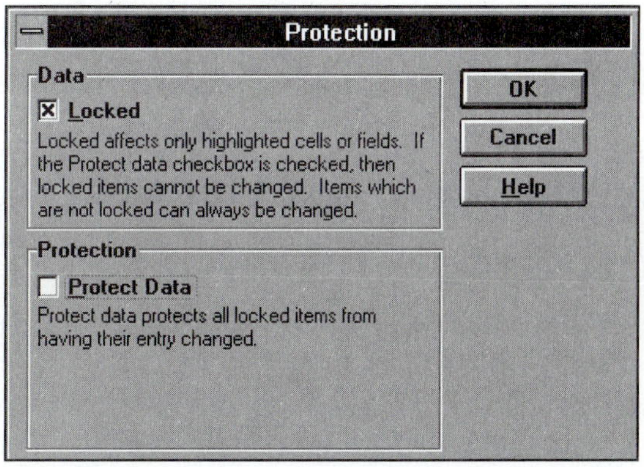

FIGURE 8-12

3. Click the Locked option to remove the "X" mark and unlock the highlighted cells.
4. Click OK or press [ENTER].

   You can now apply protection to the cells that remain locked.
5. Click any empty cell to deselect.
6. Choose Protection from the FORMAT menu.

   This time you will work with the Protection block of this dialog box.
7. Click the Protect Data option in the Protection block.

8. Click OK or press [ENTER].

Don't be concerned that there is no visible change on the screen.

Although it doesn't appear that anything has happened, data cannot be entered into the protected cells until the protection is removed by again choosing Protect Data from the Protection dialog box. To test this out,

9. Click cell C14.

10. Type: 57

11. Click the ENTRY button or press [ENTER].

A message box appears indicating that this cell is protected.

To put away the message box,

12. Click OK or press [ENTER].

As you can see, it would be difficult for anyone to accidentally change protected cells.

FINISHING UP PROJECT 2

You are almost finished. Before you type your header and print, you should check your margins. You can see by looking at the screen that this document has extra space on the right. This time you may bypass the Print Preview screen and simply guess that two-inch margins at the top and on the left and right will better balance the page.

IT'S YOUR TURN

1. Change your margins to two-inch side and top margins. If you need help,

   a. Choose Page Setup from the FILE menu.

Since the Top Margin box is already highlighted,

   b. Type: 2

   c. Press [TAB] twice to advance to the Left margin box.

   d. Type: 2

   e. Press [TAB] to advance to the Right margin box.

   f. Type: 2

   g. Click OK or press [ENTER] to return to the spreadsheet.

   WORKS will not allow you to add a header to a protected spread-sheet, so you will temporarily turn off the protection.

2. Choose Protection from the FORMAT menu.

3. Click the Protect Data option in the Protection block to turn off Protection and click OK or press [ENTER].

4. Create a header with your name on the left, the date in the center, and the document name at the right edge. If you need help,

   a. Choose Headers and Footers from the VIEW menu.

In the Header text box,

b. Type: &Lyour name&C&D&R&F

The Footer text box already has a default page number footer in it, so

c. Click OK or press [ENTER].

5. Choose Protection from the FORMAT menu and click the Protect Data option in the Protection block of the Protection dialog box.

To reinstate the protection,

6. Click OK or press [ENTER].

7. Insert your data disk into the internal disk drive if it is not already there.

8. Choose Save As from the FILE menu to save this file as *REORDER2* in your name directory on your data disk.

9. Click the PRINT PREVIEW button on the toolbar to view the spreadsheet.

10. Click the PRINT button, if you are directed to print the document.

11. Quit *WORKS,* as directed in previous chapters.

SUMMARY

Congratulations! You can now create new spreadsheets, insert functions, improve the appearance of spreadsheets through the use of formats and margins, create an IF statement, protect cells, and create headers. You should now be able to use the spreadsheet tool for creating your own projects. In the next chapter, you will learn some shortcuts and some advanced features, such as how to create charts from the spreadsheet.

REVIEW QUESTIONS

1. Which menu and options would you use to move the content of a cell? Is there another way to move cell content?

2. Which menu and option do you use to copy a formula down several rows?

3. How do you change the alignment of numbers?

4. Which menu and option would you use to prevent someone from accidentally changing your spreadsheet formulas?

5. TRUE OR FALSE—All functions or formulas must begin with a colon (:).

EXERCISES

EXERCISE 8-1   Changing labels and dates, inserting rows, entering data, creating formulas, copying formulas

1. Open the spreadsheet file *REORDER* from your data disk.

2. Make the following changes to the spreadsheet:

a. Change the title of the spreadsheet to "Weekly Orders."

b. Insert the current date.

    c.   Roughly center the title.

    d.   Insert a blank row above the Totals line.

    e.   Think of a new stuffed animal the company might have added to its offerings. Type it into the new blank row, including its item number and an amount you would need. Since you have none at the present time, type zero in the "On Hand" column.

    f.   Enter formulas for the "Short" and "Order" columns using an IF statement for column F with a minimum of three.

    g.   Copy the formulas down in columns E and F.

    h.   Enter the formulas to compute the totals.

3.   Create a header containing your name at the left, the date at center, and the name of the document at the right. (*Note:* Preview to see if the top margin and side margins fit. If not, make the necessary changes before saving.)

4.   Save the spreadsheet as *EX8-1* in your name directory on your data disk.

5.   Print the spreadsheet, if requested to do so by your instructor.

EXERCISE 8-2   Inserting columns and creating formulas

1.   Open the file called *REORDER* from your data disk.

2.   Another store has sent its extra inventory to you. Make the following changes to the spreadsheet:

    a.   Insert a new column between "On Hand" and "Short."

    b.   Title the new column "Transfer" and adjust the width of the column.

    c.   Make up some numbers for the new column E.

    d.   Insert the current date in cell B2.

    e.   Type your name in cell A3.

    f.   Insert two blank rows under your name.

    g.   Enter the correct formulas in columns F and G (add the "Transfer" to "On Hand"). Use four as the qualifying amount for the IF statement.

    h.   Enter the formulas in the Totals row.

    i.   Change font size to 10, top margin to two inches, and side margins to 1.5 inches.

    j.   Center cells A6–A15. Also, adjust the widths of some of the columns that are either too wide or too narrow.

3.   Create a header containing your name on the left, the date in the center, and the name of the document at the right.

4.   Protect all cells containing formulas.

5.   Save the spreadsheet as *EX8-2* in your name directory on your data disk.

6.   Preview and then print the spreadsheet, if requested to do so by your instructor.

EXERCISE 8-3

1. Create a loan spreadsheet similar to the one shown in Figure 8-13 using the Arial font and 10 for the font size. If you need help with the formulas, see the example.

FIGURE 8-13A

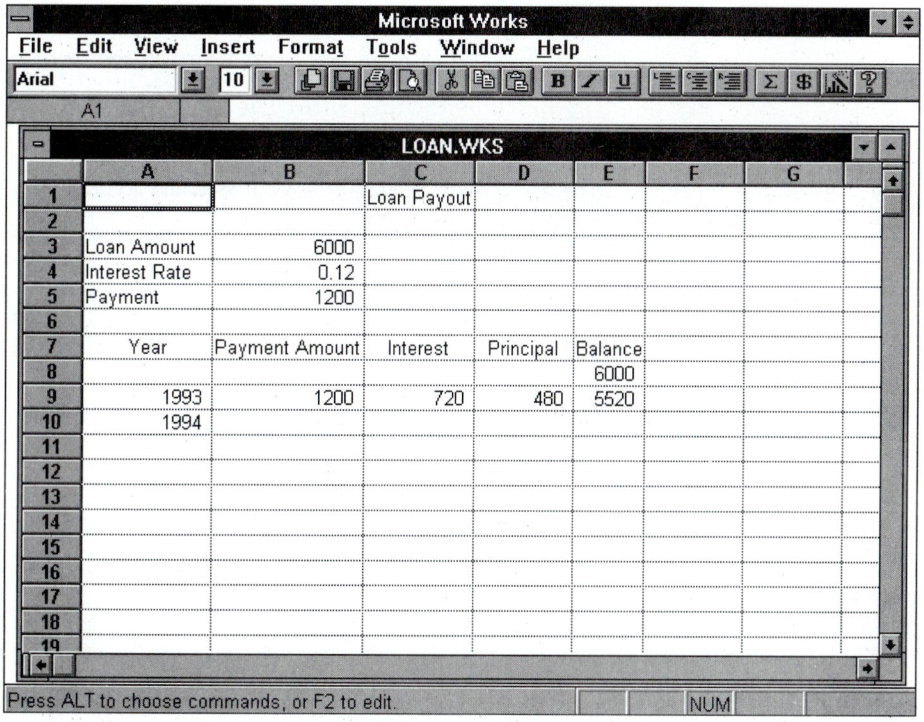

Loan Payment Spreadsheet with Values Displayed

FIGURE 8-13B

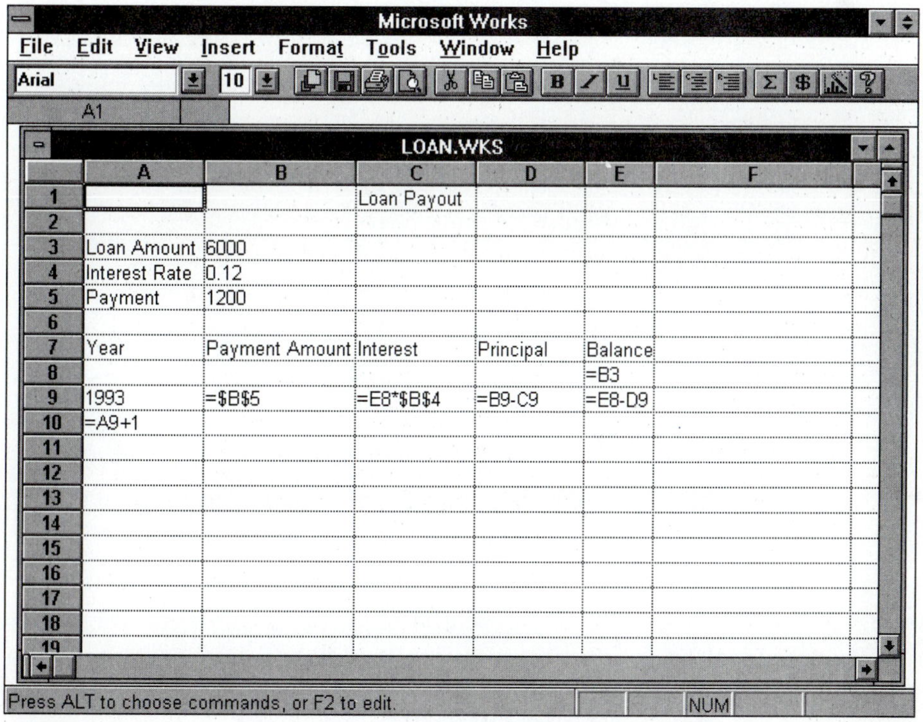

Loan Payout Spreadsheet with Formulas Displayed

2. Copy the formulas down through row 16, then format the amount columns with commas and two decimal places.

3. Type a footer with your name on the left and the filename on the right.

4. Right align cells B7–E7.

5. Center cells A7–A16.

6. Place your name in cell D3 and the current date in cell D4.

7. Save as *EX8-3* in your name directory on your data disk.

8. Preview and print the spreadsheet, if requested to do so by your instructor.

9. When will you owe less than $100? _____

10. If you paid $1450 per year, when would you owe less than $100? _____

11. Try other numbers for loan amounts, interest, and payment.

CHAPTER 9

Spreadsheet 4

OBJECTIVES

When you finish this chapter you will be able to

■ *use keyboard shortcuts*

■ *create spreadsheet templates*

■ *sort a file*

■ *enforce manual calculation*

■ *divide windows into panes and freeze titles*

■ *set page breaks*

■ *create and modify charts*

■ *print and save charts*

SETTING THE SCENE

This chapter completes the spreadsheet portion of this book and introduces you to more of the features that make this tool so popular.

As with the final word processing lesson, the instructions given in this chapter are sometimes less detailed and leave more to your imagination. We will start with a listing of keyboard shortcuts, some of which may have been introduced in prior chapters.

GETTING STARTED

You should open the spreadsheet file *REORDER* so you can experiment with the features presented in this chapter. When you finish with the Shortcuts section, leave the *REORDER* file open unless you have made changes to it; you will use it again later in this chapter.

SHORTCUTS

If you have not begun to use these shortcuts, make it a point to try them out while you work on this chapter. Many of the shortcuts are listed to the right of the command on the drop-down menus. If you follow the procedure of finding a shortcut on a menu, putting away the menu without selecting the option, then invoking the option using the keyboard shortcut, you will quickly learn commands you frequently use. Many shortcuts (such as copy, paste, and cut, for example) are common to all *WORKS* modules. A complete list of keyboard shortcuts is given in the on-line Help document, which can be accessed as follows:

1. Choose Search for Help On from the HELP menu.
2. Type "Keyboard" when the Search dialog box appears.
3. Click the SHOW TOPICS button.
4. Click the GO TO button.

163

An explanation paragraph followed by a list of keyboard shortcuts will appear. You can examine them as much as you wish. The following tables present some of the spreadsheet and charting shortcuts you may find helpful.

Keys for Changing Information and Making Menu Choices

To Do This	Press
Edit cell	[F2]
Copy the values of above cell	[CTRL] + [']
Go To	[F5]
Remove all font styles	[CTRL] + [SPACEBAR]
Apply Comma format	[CTRL] + [COMMA]
Apply Currency format	[CTRL] + [4]
Apply Percent format	[CTRL] + [5]
Get Help	[F1]
Choose the Tutorial	[SHIFT] + [F1]
Open the Font box on the toolbar	[CTRL] + [F]
Open the Font Size box on the toolbar	[CTRL] + [K]
Switch between spreadsheet and chart	[F3]

Keys for Highlighting Spreadsheet Information

You highlight a cell by moving to that cell; a border around the cell shows it is highlighted. When you highlight a range of cells, the background behind the selection changes color. You can then change the selection.

To Highlight	Press
The row containing the currently selected cell	[CTRL] + [F8]
The column containing the currently selected cell	[SHIFT] + [F8]
An entire spreadsheet	[CTRL] + [SHIFT] + [F8]
Left one cell	[SHIFT] + [LEFT ARROW]
Right one cell	[SHIFT] + [RIGHT ARROW]
Down one cell	[SHIFT] + [DOWN ARROW]
Up one cell	[SHIFT] + [UP ARROW]

Extending Selections

There are times when you will have one cell selected and you want to extend the selection to include other cells. The [F8] key can help you in these situations. First you press [F8] to signal that you wish to extend the selection, and then, after releasing [F8] you press the arrow keys in the desired direction. After extending the selection as much as you wish, press the [ESC] key to signal the end of extended selection.

To Do This	Press
Extend a selection	[F8] [ARROW KEYS]
Quit extending	[ESC]

Keys for Inserting Information

To Insert	Press
Autosum total	[CTRL] + [M]
The current date	[CTRL] + [SEMICOLON]
The current time	[CTRL] + [SHIFT] + [SEMICOLON]

Keys for Moving Around in a Spreadsheet

To Move	Press
To a particular range, cell, or row	[F5]
To the beginning of row	[HOME]
To the end of row	[END]
To the beginning of spreadsheet	[CTRL] + [HOME]
To the end of spreadsheet	[CTRL] + [END]

Keys for Aligning Text or Cells

To Achieve This Result	Press
Center text	[CTRL] + [E]
Left align text	[CTRL] + [L]
Right align text	[CTRL] + [R]

CREATING A SPREADSHEET TEMPLATE

Whenever a spreadsheet's format is to be used over and over again, it is productive to create and save a template so that the user may simply open that template document and fill in only the changing data before printing. The procedure for creating a spreadsheet template is similar to that for creating word processing templates. As in word processing, however, spreadsheet templates are saved to the *WORKS* system files, and if you are working on a network or in a school laboratory, you may not be able to utilize this feature. Refer to the *WORKS 3.0* manual or use on-line Help to find out more about templates.

SORTING A FILE

Another time-saver is to use the spreadsheet's matrix format to quickly create tables and sort them. If you wish to incorporate a table into a word processing document, you can easily do so. You can then use the word processor's additional formatting features (increasing the size of selected text, mixing fonts, etc.) to improve the table's appearance. For example, to write to Pandas and Such about a past order, you might want to sort the items by number and then incorporate that portion of the file into a letter or memo. The *REORDER* file should be open on your desktop.

IT'S YOUR TURN

1. Drag to select all rows containing the names of stuffed animals (row headers 5 through 13).

2. Choose Sort Rows from the TOOLS menu.

   The Sort Rows dialog box appears, as shown in Figure 9-1.

FIGURE 9-1

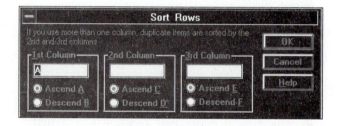

Notice that you can sort based upon one to three columns in ascending order (A to Z or numeric from 0) or descending order (Z to A or numeric down to zero). Since the dialog box is already set for sorting on column A in ascending order, and that is what you want to do,

3. Click OK or press [ENTER] to accept the default sort on the first column only, in ascending order.

   The list is now reorganized in numerical order from 102–153. You could now drag to select the area you want for your letter, copy it, and paste it into a word processing document. You will have the opportunity to use this integration feature in Chapter 15. Of course, once the material has been pasted into a word processing document, it ceases to function as a spreadsheet. "Cells" that contained formulas are now only numbers and cannot recalculate for you if you change any of the values upon which the formula was based.

Since you will not be using *REORDER* again, you should put it away.

4. Double click the CONTROL MENU button or choose Close from the FILE menu. Do not save any changes made to the file.

ENFORCING MANUAL CALCULATION

WORKS' default setting is to perform spreadsheet calculations automatically as you enter and change data. If your computer seems to be working sluggishly and you have a lot of data to enter, you may want to switch to manual calculation by choosing Manual Calculation from the TOOLS menu (a checkmark will appear next to that option when you select it). When you are finished inputting data and want *WORKS* to perform the calculations, choose Calculate Now from the TOOLS menu (or press [F9]). The Manual Calculation option is a toggle; so if you want to return to automatic calculation, choose Manual Calculation from the TOOLS menu again to turn it off.

DIVIDING WINDOWS INTO PANES

When a spreadsheet is very large, you will not be able to see all parts of it at any one time. However, *WORKS* allows you to divide the window vertically and horizontally into two or four panes. Thus, you can view two or four parts of the spreadsheet simultaneously. The next set of steps shows you how this works.

IT'S YOUR TURN

1. Open the file named *MONSAL* from your data disk.

To make the file larger so you can work with panes,

2. Click the SELECT ALL button in the upper left corner of the spreadsheet or choose Select All from the EDIT menu.

3. Choose 16 from the Size drop-down box of the toolbar.

    The spreadsheet now exceeds the margins of the screen (see Figure 9-2).

4. Click any empty cell to deselect. Widen the column(s) if #### appears.

FIGURE 9-2

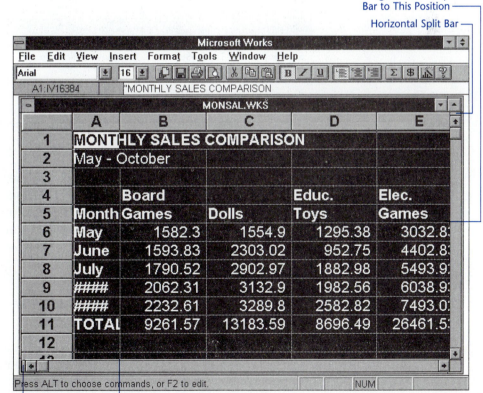

5. Point to the *horizontal split bar* (the pointer will change into a two-way arrow labeled "adjust" when it is in the correct position) and drag the split bar until it is between rows 5 and 6 (see Figure 9-2).

6. Drag on the *vertical split bar* until it is between columns A and B (see Figure 9-2).

Your screen should resemble the screen shown in Figure 9-3.

FIGURE 9-3

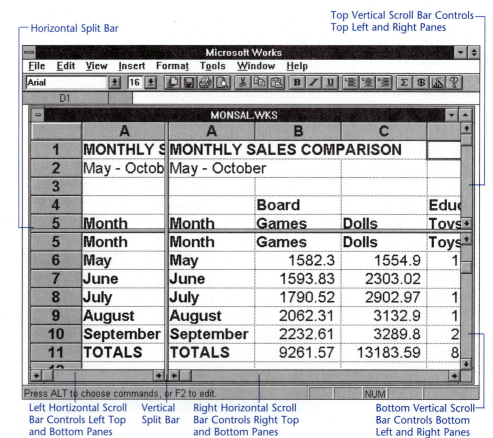

As you can see, there are two sets of horizontal and vertical scroll bars.

7. Use the scroll bar arrows to see how they affect the various panes.

Notice that two panes will move each time you use the scroll arrows, while the other two panes remain stationary. The two scroll bars at the bottom of the screen control the horizontal movement of the two windows above them. The two scroll bars at the right control the vertical movement of the windows on their left.

When you have finished experimenting,

8. Either double click on each split bar or drag each split bar back to its original position to put it away.

Your screen should again look similar to the screen shown in Figure 9-2, depending on how far you scrolled before putting the split bars away.

FREEZE TITLES

WORKS 3.0 enables you to *freeze* the column and row titles found above and to the left of the current cursor position. This is very useful when you have a large spreadsheet with headers at the top and/or left portions of the screen, which would otherwise disappear as you scrolled. The Freeze Titles command is available from the FORMAT menu. Freezing titles keeps those headers in place while enabling you to scroll through the remainder of the document. With the headers frozen, the spreadsheet is much easier to work with. If you want to test this feature, click on cell B6 and choose Freeze Titles from the FORMAT menu. Then you can experiment with the scroll bars. Don't forget to choose Freeze Titles again to turn it off before you continue to the next section.

SETTING PAGE BREAKS

When your spreadsheet contains more information than can be printed on one page, *WORKS* will divide it into pages by setting **page breaks**. If you would like to determine your own page breaks, you can adjust the widths of columns and/or margins, or you can insert manual page breaks by using the Page Break command from the INSERT menu.

To set a manual page break, highlight the row or column that should be the first row or column of the next page. Choose Page Break from the INSERT menu; a dotted line will appear, marking the break. If you select only one cell when you select Page Break, *WORKS* will display a dialog box asking if you want a row (horizontal) page break or a column (vertical) page break.

To delete a manual page break, highlight a cell immediately to the right of a vertical page break, or the one immediately below a horizontal page break, and choose Delete Page Break from the INSERT menu.

CREATING CHARTS

Charts help you analyze and interpret the numbers in your spreadsheet and can help reveal trends and patterns. Charts are visual representations of spreadsheet information. When you create a chart, you display numbers from your spreadsheet as lines, bars, markers, or pie slices in graphic form.

WORKS 3.0 can create twelve basic chart types:

- An **area chart** shows the relative importance of values over a period of time.

- A **bar chart** represents a series of values in a chart as a series of vertical bars to show the relationship between the values in the series. Bar charts can be used to compare two or more different series; and in that case, each series would be represented by a bar of a different color or pattern.

- A **line chart** represents a series of values in a chart as markers or points connected by a line to show trends. Line charts use lines to connect points that represent numbers on a spreadsheet. When you compare more than one set of numbers, each set is represented by a different line. Line charts are used to illustrate trends, e.g., increasing and decreasing profits by month during the year or by years over a period of time.

- A **pie chart** represents a series of values as slices in a pie to show the relationship of each value to the whole, as well as to each other; for example, a pie chart would allow you to see the portion contributed by each department toward the total revenue of The Fun Factory.

- A **stacked line chart** represents each series of values in a chart as markers, connected by a line. Individual lines are stacked on top of each other to represent a total. Stack charts can be used to display components of a total, e.g., each salesperson's contribution to monthly sales.

- An ***X-Y (scatter) chart*** represents a series of values in a chart as markers plotted in relation to corresponding category values.
- A ***radar chart*** shows changes or frequencies of data relative to a center point and to each other. A radar chart is useful for making relative comparisons between items.
- A ***combination chart*** can represent the different values in a chart as a combination of points, markers, bars, and lines. Combination charts can combine a bar chart with a line chart, displaying one set of numbers in bar form and another in line form.
- A ***3-D area chart*** is a three-dimensional representation of an area chart.
- A ***3-D bar chart*** is a three-dimensional representation of a bar chart.
- A ***3-D line chart*** is a three-dimensional representation of a line chart.
- A ***3-D pie chart*** is a three-dimensional representation of a pie chart.

You will use the *ANNSALES* spreadsheet file to create a chart graphically illustrating each department's contribution to total sales. Initially, *WORKS* always creates a bar chart when you choose the Create New Chart command, but you can always change the type of chart *WORKS* creates if your data would be better represented with another kind of chart.

IT'S YOUR TURN

1. Close *MONSAL* without saving the changes and open the *ANNSALES* spreadsheet file from your data disk.

   Your screen should look like the screen shown in Figure 9-4.

FIGURE 9-4

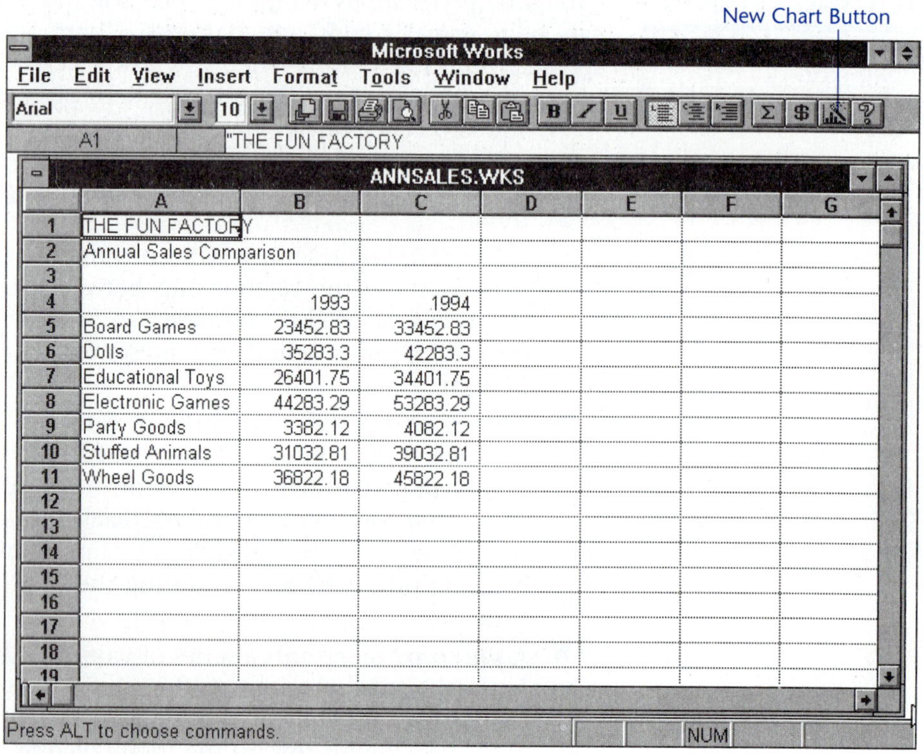

New Chart Button
Microsoft Works
File Edit View Insert Format Tools Window Help
Arial 10
A1 "THE FUN FACTORY
ANNSALES.WKS
A B C D E F G
1 THE FUN FACTORY
2 Annual Sales Comparison
4 1993 1994
5 Board Games 23452.83 33452.83
6 Dolls 35283.3 42283.3
7 Educational Toys 26401.75 34401.75
8 Electronic Games 44283.29 53283.29
9 Party Goods 3382.12 4082.12
10 Stuffed Animals 31032.81 39032.81
11 Wheel Goods 36822.18 45822.18
Press ALT to choose commands.
NUM

2. Review the *ANNSALES* screen.

   This data readily lends itself to a bar chart design, and since this is the type of chart *WORKS* creates by default, the steps are simple. Before *WORKS* can create the chart, you must first highlight the following information you would like to chart:

■ The values (dollar amounts in this spreadsheet) that define the points to be charted (these are in columns B and C)

🏴 The text (the types of toys in this spreadsheet and the years of sales) that becomes the chart's labels (this information is in column A and row 4)

Follow the next steps to define and create the chart.

3. Select the range from cells A4 through C11.

4. Click the NEW CHART button on the toolbar (the second button from the right, as shown in Figure 9-4) or choose Create New Chart from the TOOLS menu.

The New Chart dialog box shown in Figure 9-5 appears on your screen.

FIGURE 9-5

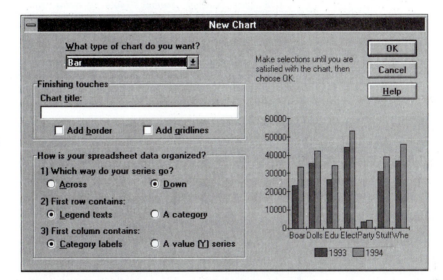

WORKS automatically creates your chart using the bar chart type. You can see a small sample of the chart in Figure 9-5. After you complete the dialog box, you will see the finished chart.

Even though Bar is already selected in the drop-down list box labelled "What type of chart do you want?," it is interesting to look at all the other types of charts that are available. Some of them are appropriate for the data selection you have made and some of them are not. As you browse through the samples in the next few steps, it will be readily apparent which chart types are appropriate and which are not.

5. Click the down arrow on the "What type of chart . . ." drop-down list box and select Area.

   Notice the small sample changes to show what an area chart would look like.

6. Continue selecting other chart types and note the way the data is displayed. You will have to click the DOWN ARROW button on the list box scroll bar to see all the types.

When you have finished viewing all the chart types,

7. Select Bar chart or 3-D Bar chart for this data.

8. Press [TAB] to advance to the Chart Title text box or click in the Chart Title text box in the Finishing Touches block.

9. Type: 1993 & 1994 SALES COMPARISON

10. Click the Add Border option.

11. Click the Add Gridlines option.

Since the selections made in the Organization block are correct,

12. Click the OK button or press [ENTER].

The spreadsheet menus are replaced with the Charting menus, and the chart is displayed in a new full-size window, as shown in Figure 9-6.

FIGURE 9-6

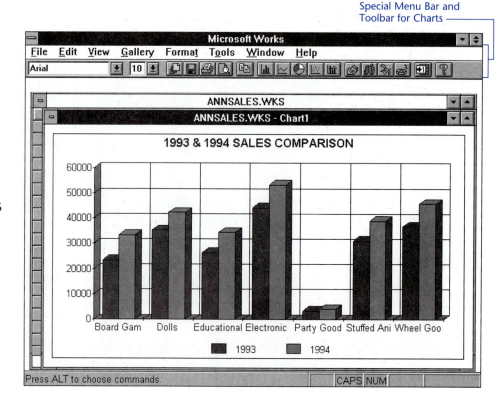

You can now choose any charting command, change the chart type, or modify any element in the chart.

MODIFYING THE CHART

WORKS provides many opportunities for changing the chart, a few of which you will practice in this session. You may have noticed that the category labels across the bottom of the bars are truncated.

IT'S YOUR TURN

To change the font size of the labels so they will print completely,

1. Choose Arial from the Font Name drop-down list box on the toolbar, if it is not already chosen.

2. Choose 6 from the Font Size drop-down box on the toolbar.

The horizontal and vertical titles are both reduced in size, and you can now read the entire name for each category.

To add a subtitle to the chart that identifies the store,

3.   Choose Titles from the EDIT menu.

The Titles dialog box shown in Figure 9-7 appears on your screen.

FIGURE 9-7

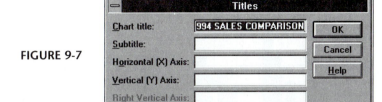

Titles	
Chart title:	994 SALES COMPARISON
	OK
Subtitle:	
	Cancel
Horizontal (X) Axis:	
	Help
Vertical (Y) Axis:	
Right Vertical Axis:	

Since you do not wish to change the Chart title,

4.   Press [TAB] to move the highlight to the Subtitle text box.

5.   Type: The Fun Factory

To label the horizontal and vertical axes,

6.   Press [TAB] to move the highlight to the Horizontal X-Axis text box.

7.   Type: Departments

8.   Press [TAB] to move the highlight to the Vertical Y-Axis text box.

9.   Type: Dollars

10.   Click OK or press [ENTER].

One of the advantages of having a chart tool within a spreadsheet program is that if you change the spreadsheet, the graph will also change. Suppose you discover the 1994 sales of educational toys is overstated by $10,000. Can you imagine how much trouble it would be to recompute all the figures and to redraw the chart by hand? You can easily complete this task with *WORKS*.

Before you enter the change, you will tile the windows so you can see the spreadsheet and the graph at the same time.

11.   Choose Tile from the WINDOW menu.

Your screen should now look like the one shown in Figure 9-8.

Look at the graph display for educational toys (the third set of bars from the left). As you can see, before the change, 1994 sales (the sixth bar) are higher than 1993 sales (the fifth bar). When you enter the change in the next step, the 1994 bar will immediately drop below the 1993 one.

12.   Click the *ANNSALES.WKS* title bar to make it the active window.

The spreadsheet window will now be the active window. If cell C7 is not presently visible,

13.   Use the scroll bars to bring cell C7 into view.

14.   Click cell C7 and change the entry to read "24401.75."

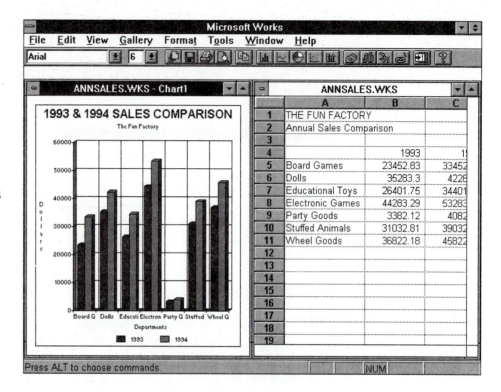

FIGURE 9-8

Keep your eyes on the Educational Toys bars (the third set from the left) as you complete the next step.

15. Click the ENTRY button or press [ENTER].

Did you see the change? If you wish, try changing some other numbers to assure yourself that the program is working properly. When you finish,

16. Click the chart window to activate it.

17. Choose Name Chart from the TOOLS menu.

The Name Chart dialog box shown in Figure 9-9 appears. Since there is only one chart now associated with this spreadsheet, it has been given the generic name "Chart1," which is already selected for you.

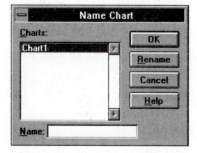

FIGURE 9-9

18. Press [TAB] to move the insertion point to the Name text box.

Since the name cannot exceed 15 characters,

19. Type: 1993vs1994Sales

20. Click the RENAME box.

21. Click OK or press [ENTER].

**DEFINING A
NEW CHART**

Now you will create a pie chart showing how much each department contributed to 1994 revenues. *WORKS 3.0* allows you to save eight charts with each spreadsheet.

IT'S YOUR TURN

To put away the bar chart window,

1.   Double click the CONTROL MENU button on the bar chart window.

2.   Click the MAXIMIZE button on the spreadsheet window to have it cover the full screen.

3.   Use the scroll bars to bring cell A1 into view.

4.   Refer back to Figure 9-4 and type in the original numbers for any cells you may have changed while working with the bar chart.

5.   Select cells C5 through C11.

6.   Click the NEW CHART button on the toolbar.

When the New Chart dialog box appears,

7.   Select Pie from the What Type of Chart Do You Want drop-down list box.

The sample pie chart will appear on the right-hand side of the dialog box. Don't worry that the sections aren't labelled. You will fix that in the next few steps.

8.   Press [TAB] to advance to the Chart Title text box.

9.   Type: Sales by Departments - 1994

The title appears on the sample.

10.   Click the Add Border option.

The basic pie chart is complete. To save it and enter the charting menus where you will add the titles to the pie sections,

11.   Click the OK button or press [ENTER].

The pie chart is displayed on the full screen.

To add labels to the pie sections,

12.   Choose Data Labels from the EDIT menu.

CAUTION | For keyboard users: When the [ALT] key is pressed to activate the menu bar, the button on the extreme left of the menu bar becomes shaded, instead of the usual highlighted menu title.

The Data Labels dialog box shown in Figure 9-10 appears.

13.   Click the Cell Contents option in the 1st Label block.

14.   Click the Cell Range text box to move the insertion point to that box.

15.   Type: A5:A11

This will cause the labels in column A of the spreadsheet to be applied to the values that were charted from column C. You must explicitly define the data labels in this manner, because the two columns are

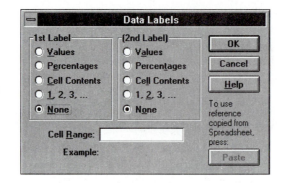

FIGURE 9-10

not contiguous. If you had been creating a pie chart for the values in column B, you could have simply selected both columns A and B, and *WORKS* would have known which were labels.

To have the percentage of each pie section calculated and displayed,

16. Click the Percentages option in the 2nd Label block.

17. Click the OK button or press [ENTER].

You are returned to the chart window where each section is labelled by name, as well as by its percentage of the total.

Suppose you are concerned about the small contribution the Party Goods department is making to total sales, and you wish to emphasize that slice.

18. Choose Patterns and Colors from the FORMAT menu.

The Patterns and Colors dialog box shown in Figure 9-11 appears.

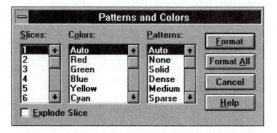

FIGURE 9-11

First you will select the Party Goods slice by number, and then you will check the Explode Slice option. To determine which number applies to which slice, you have to know that *WORKS* numbers the slices clockwise, starting from the slice at the one o'clock position of the pie. Board Games is slice number one, and Party Goods is slice number five.

19. Click 5 in the Slices scrolling list box.

20. Click the Explode Slice option at the bottom of the dialog box.

To apply the Explode option so you can see what it looks like,

21. Click the FORMAT button.

To confirm the option and put away the dialog box,

22. Click the CLOSE button.

Your screen should look like the screen shown in Figure 9-12.

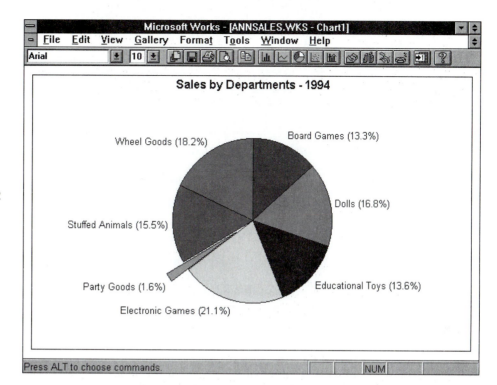

FIGURE 9-12

NAMING, SAVING, AND PRINTING A CHART

As you can see from the title bar of the chart window, the pie chart is still assigned the generic name given to it by *WORKS* when it was created. Do you remember how to give it a more descriptive name? The following steps will remind you of the process.

IT'S YOUR TURN

1. Choose Name Chart from the TOOLS menu.

When the Name Chart dialog box appears, the Charts list box will contain two names, with Chart1 highlighted. Since this is the chart you wish to rename,

2. Press [TAB] to advance the insertion point to the Name text box.
3. Type: 1994 Sales Pie Chart
4. Click the RENAME button.
5. Click the OK button or press [ENTER].

Charts are saved when the spreadsheet from which they are derived is saved. Charts do not exist as separate entities. To save the spreadsheet and its charts under a different name from the original file,

6. Choose Save As from the FILE menu and save this file as *ANNSALE2* in your name directory on your data disk.

   As was true with the bar chart, you can now print the chart as its own document or copy it into a word processing document or a database document. Charts can also be linked to either a word processing or a database document in such a way that when the spreadsheet data changes, the chart printed with the word processing or database document will also change. This feature is more fully explained in the user's manual.

CAUTION	If you print either the pie chart or the bar chart, the segments may not be clearly visible unless you are using a color printer. For a black and white printer, change the pattern of each slice or series using the Patterns and Colors option in the FORMAT menu.

You will now print the bar chart.

   7.   **Choose Chart from the VIEW menu.**

   8.   **Double click on the 1993vs1994Sales chart title.**

When the bar chart appears,

   9.   **Choose Patterns and Colors from the FORMAT menu.**

To differentiate the first series (which is already highlighted) from the second series,

   10.   **Choose Sparse from the Patterns box and click the FORMAT button.**

   11.   **Click the CLOSE button.**

   12.   **Choose Print from the FILE menu.**

When the Print dialog box appears,

   13.   **Click the OK button or press [ENTER].**

FINISHING UP

The charting feature of *WORKS 3.0* for windows is quite extensive and complex. The sections on charting in this chapter have just given you a small taste of the ways in which charts can be manipulated. To learn more about the subject, we suggest that you study both the on-line Help screens and the user's manual for *WORKS 3.0*.

IT'S YOUR TURN

To close both the spreadsheet window and the chart window and quit *WORKS*,

   1.   **Choose Exit Works from the FILE menu. If a query box appears, asking if you want to save changes to the file, click the YES button.**

Both the spreadsheet window and the chart window will be put away.

SUMMARY

Congratulations! You have tried keyboard shortcuts, learned how to create spreadsheet templates for quickly developing your commonly used worksheets, enforced manual calculations, sorted data, divided windows into panes so column and row headings never disappear from view, set page breaks wherever you wish, and created, modified, and printed charts to more effectively present spreadsheet data. We hope you feel comfortable using the *WORKS 3.0* spreadsheet and that you will take the time to learn more about it.

REVIEW QUESTIONS

1. Which menu do you use to sort the spreadsheet by rows?

2. What is the keyboard command to completely remove a selected row or column?

3. What menu do you use to set a manual page break?

4. How do you save charts?

5. How do you create a new chart?

EXERCISE

Create a chart using a spreadsheet of your choice. You can use a spreadsheet provided on the data disk or create one of your own.

CHAPTER

10

Database 1

OBJECTIVES

In this chapter, you will learn how to

■ *recognize fields and records*

■ *view a file as a list and as a form*

■ *query a database*

■ *add a record to a database*

■ *sort a database*

■ *add fields to a record*

■ *change the size of a field in Form view*

■ *search a database*

■ *print part of a database*

DATABASE BACKGROUND

The term *database* is broadly applied to any large collection of related information (data). Two familiar manual databases are the telephone directory (a collection of names with addresses and phone numbers) and a recipe file (a collection of recipe titles with the ingredients and instructions for preparation).

Databases are made up of *records*. A record describes one entity (or single item) in the collection. In a telephone directory, a record is the data about one subscriber. For the recipe file, a record is the data for one recipe.

Each record is composed of *fields*. For example, a record in the telephone directory could have a first name field, last name field, address field, and phone number field. A record in a recipe file could have a category field, ingredients field, and instructions field. Each record in the same database contains the same group of fields.

Obviously, the manner in which records are organized has a major effect on how easily you can find a specific record. For example, the telephone directory database is organized alphabetically by last name. Therefore, if you know the name of a person or company, you can search the telephone directory and easily find the telephone number.

Suppose, however, that you do not know a name—you only know a telephone number, and what you really want is to find out the name of the person or company to which that number belongs. Or suppose you have scribbled an address on a scratch pad and have forgotten the name of the company to which it belongs. You cannot find the company in a traditional telephone book. However, when a database is stored on a computer and managed by a database program, you are not limited to just one search field. The *WORKS 3.0* database tool allows you to search the database using any field as the key (or search) field.

INTRODUCING THE *WORKS* DATABASE

A *WORKS 3.0* database can have up to 32,000 records, with 256 fields per record.

You can view the *WORKS* database in four different ways. **Form view** shows information for individual records on separate forms. In Form view, you work with one record at a time on a customized form you create, such as an invoice or statement. **List view** shows all the fields and all the information in a column-and-row table format. In List view, you work with many records in a list at once, similar to a spreadsheet. **Report view**, which resembles List view in that it displays information in columns and rows, is used for printing information from the database. **Query view** allows you to search the database, looking for all records that match a particular criterion or set of criteria.

It is easy to switch from one view to another, thus allowing you to work with the database as individual records on the screen or as a list that displays all records (or just selected records). You can cause the same data (or portions thereof) to be presented in different formats. You can create reports from the database and print all or part of the data it contains. Some of these concepts are summarized in the following section, which uses as an example a database consisting of information about college students.

VIEWS

List view contains all fields and records in the database.

Last Name	First Name	Soc. Sec. #	Major	GPA
Takumi	Robert	345-21-9876	Astronomy	4.0
Vanderveldt	Hans	341-45-2341	Political Science	3.4
Flores	James	458-21-3847	English	3.8
Abbot	Zina	552-42-4821	Engineering	3.75
Allen	David	458-99-8932	English	2.8

Information on All Students

Form view displays fields and data for one record at a time in a database.

Last Name	Allen
First Name	David
Soc. Sec. #	458-99-8932
Major	English
GPA	2.8

Information on One Student

Query view is used to define complex search criteria which, when applied to the database, cause a subset of records to be displayed. This view contains only the field names in a database. The user can fill in one or more blank fields to establish the search criteria.

Last Name	.
First Name	.
Soc. Sec.#	.
Major	.
GPA	.

Field Names in Query View

Report view displays a special code in list format that can be used to create a report that contains selected fields in any order. Report view also allows the user to specify that certain statistics be calculated and displayed as part of the report.

Last Name	First Name	GPA
Takumi	Robert	4.0
Flores	James	3.8
Abbot	Zina	3.75
Vanderveldt	Hans	3.4
Allen	David	2.8

GPA Standings in Report View

BASIC DATABASE ACTIVITIES

Outlined below is information to guide you through database activities in *WORKS*.

1. Creating a database
   a. Type field names
   b. Enter data for each record
2. Adding fields to an existing database
   a. New fields can be added either in List view or Form view
3. Querying for information
   a. Use Query view or Query dialog box to set up field criteria and then apply the query, or
   b. Choose Find to select particular contents in fields
4. Creating output
   a. Choose Report view to print information on more than one record, with selected fields organized by rows and columns, including summary statistics
   b. Choose Form view to print all information, including field names and field contents on one record at a time
   c. Choose List view to print all information in each record in row-and-column format

SETTING THE SCENE

In order to manage The Fun Factory more efficiently, you need a simple database of information about the employees. You will use your database to keep track of addresses and phone numbers, as well as to create work schedules and identify employees due for raises.

GETTING STARTED

In this chapter's activities, you will use *WORKS* to retrieve a simple database file from your data disk, view the information stored in the file, search the database, add a record, and then save the revised file as a new database. After you have completed the chapter, you should be able to create a simple database of your own. First you will open the database file and select a view type.

IT'S YOUR TURN

1. Launch *WORKS 3.0* and open the database file *PROFILE* from your data disk.

   PROFILE contains data about the employees of The Fun Factory.

   Figure 10-1 presents two of the four previously discussed views of the database. (Query view will be discussed later in this chapter, and Report view will be presented in a later chapter.)
   Your screen should resemble the List view figure shown in Figure 10-1a.

2. If your screen looks like the Form view, press [F9] or choose List from the VIEW menu or click the LIST VIEW button on the toolbar (shown in Figure 10-1).

FIGURE 10-1A

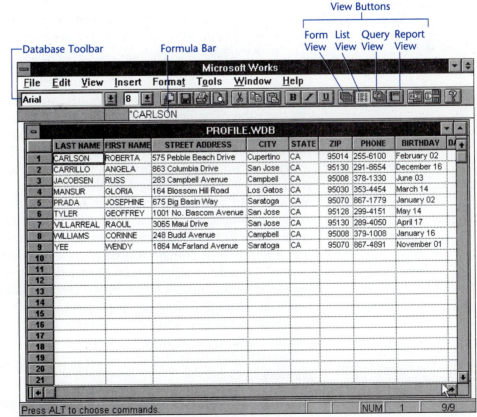

List View of Database

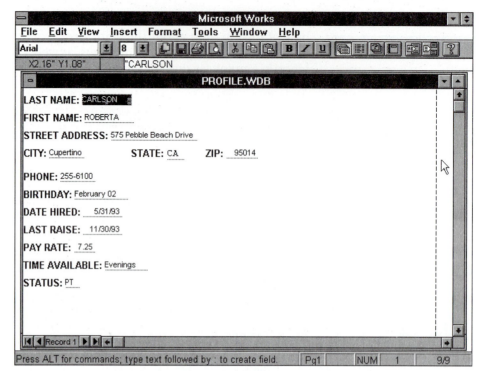

FIGURE 10-1B

Form View of First Record

THE LIST VIEW

The *PROFILE* database is now showing on your screen in List view.

IT'S YOUR TURN

1. Study the List view on your screen and in Figure 10-1.

   Note that the menu bar is similar to the word processor and spreadsheet menu bar. The Formula bar is similar to the spreadsheet Formula bar; you use it to enter data and to edit the contents of the active field.

   In a List window, each record (in our example, information relating to each employee) occupies one row in the list, and the records are listed one under the other. The field names (in our example, the labels for each item of information for each employee) are strung across the top of the columns (for example, you see LAST NAME, FIRST NAME, and so on).

   The List window lets you work with a database (file) much as you did with spreadsheets in the last section. Viewing your database as a list enables you to see many records at one time. It is, therefore, very handy when making comparisons or trying to get an overall picture of what records are in the database. One of the disadvantages of the List view is that if the records contain a large number of fields, it is not possible to display all the fields on the screen at one time, and you must scroll horizontally to view the hidden fields. When certain changes are made in List view (such as changing font or font size), they do not affect Form view. However, when you add or delete fields in List view, *WORKS* also adds and deletes them in Form view.

   You will now use the scroll bars to see the rest of the database in the List window.

2. Click to the right of the scroll box in the horizontal scroll bar at the bottom of the screen.

To move back to the first field (Last Name),

3. Click to the left of the horizontal scroll box.

Note that the number one is displayed in the Status bar, and that Roberta Carlson's last name is enclosed in a dark border and is also displayed in the Formula bar. These clues tell you that the Last Name field of the first record is currently selected. To move from one record to another in List view,

4. Press [DOWN ARROW].

Note that the number two is now displayed as the record number in the Status bar and that Carrillo is highlighted in the Last Name field and is displayed in the Formula bar.

To move up one record in List view,

5. Press [UP ARROW].

You are returned to the first record.

Instead of using the arrows, you can click to select any field of any record in the database. To move randomly to a distant record in List view,

6. Click the name "Josephine" in the fifth line and watch the record number, the Formula bar, and the highlight all change.

This is another advantage of the List view—the ability to jump easily from one record to another.

Now you will switch to explore the Form view. If you switch with the fifth record as the selected one, this will be the record displayed first in Form view. Since we want you to see the first record when you switch,

7. Click "Carlson" in the first record.

THE FORM VIEW

The List view is rather awkward when the database has a large number of fields (*PROFILE* has twelve fields or columns) that take more than one screen to display and you want to analyze all the field entries relating to one record.

To see all the information about one person, it is easier to use the Form view, which presents one record per screen. The default form includes the entire record for one person with the fields in the same order as they are shown in the List view. You can design the form with the fields completely rearranged from the order they occupy in List view. You can even add titles, labels, and graphics to the form. Form view allows you to move through the database one record at a time. Many people prefer Form view for entering information into the database.

IT'S YOUR TURN

To switch to the Form view for *PROFILE*,

1. Click the FORM button on the toolbar or press [F9] or Choose Form from the VIEW menu.

You see a layout of fields and entries similar to those shown in Figure 10-2.

FIGURE 10-2

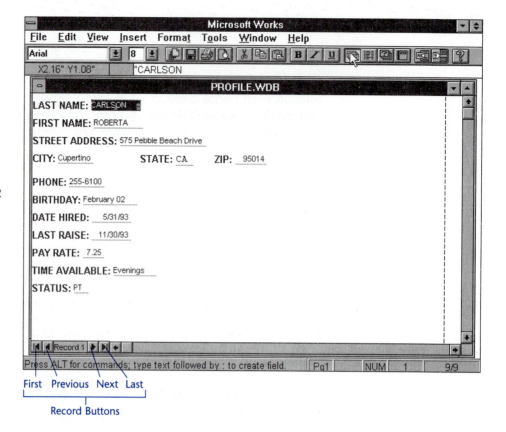

Notice that the Form view shows one record at a time. The information in this form is the same as the information in the list. The two formats are simply arranged differently. As you can see, the two views do not require that you use the same font name, style, or size. In general, the List view is more like looking at a page of a telephone book. The Form view is more like looking at one recipe card from a box of recipes.

To view the next record,

2. Click the NEXT RECORD button (the triangle on the immediate right of "Record 1" in the horizontal scroll bar shown in Figure 10-2).

To view the previous record,

3. Click the PREVIOUS RECORD button on the horizontal scroll bar (see Figure 10-2).

To view the last record in the database,

4. Click the LAST RECORD button on the horizontal scroll bar (see Figure 10-2).

    The last record in all *WORKS* databases is an empty record, for your convenience in adding records. We will discuss this subject later in this chapter.

To return to the first record,

5. Click the FIRST RECORD button on the horizontal scroll bar.

    Your screen should now be displaying Roberta Carlson's record again.

To choose the next field in this record,

6. Press [TAB].

   The highlight will move to the next field shown on the form. If you keep pressing [TAB], the highlight will eventually reach the last field in this record then will continue to the first field in the next record.

To move back to the previous field in this record,

7. Press [SHIFT] + [TAB].

   The highlight will return to the previous field. If you keep pressing [SHIFT] + [TAB], the highlight will eventually reach the first field in this record and then will continue to the last field in the previous record.

To select any field's contents in this record,

8. Click on the contents portion of the desired field.

To select any field name in this record,

9. Click on the name portion of the desired field.

You should use the Go To command from the EDIT menu to switch to a non-adjacent record in Form view.

10. Choose Go To from the EDIT menu or press the shortcut key [F5].

    The Go To dialog box shown in Figure 10-3 will appear.

FIGURE 10-3

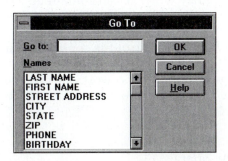

This dialog box can be used to jump directly to any record in the database or to any field in the current record. If you click one of the field names shown in the scrolling list box and then click the OK button, the selected field name will be highlighted in the current record. To use the Go To dialog box to advance to a distant record, you must use the record number. With the insertion point blinking in the Go To text box,

11. Type: 5

12. Click the OK button or press [ENTER].

    Record number five (Josephine Prada) will be displayed.

To return to the first record,

13. Choose Go To from the EDIT menu.

14. Type: 1

15. Click the OK button or press [ENTER].

Record number one (Roberta Carlson) will be back on the screen.

To return to the list,

16. Click the LIST VIEW button in the toolbar or choose List from the VIEW menu.

**SELECTING
A SUBSET
OF RECORDS**

Suppose you wanted to see a list of all part-time employees whose last names begin with a C and who live in the 95014 zip code area. You could create a *query* containing these rules and apply it to the database. When you set up and use queries, *WORKS 3.0* finds specific records that meet those rules. Queries are created within and belong to a specific database, and you can delete queries when they are no longer needed. When you create a query, you should give it a meaningful name to help you remember the conditions it contains. By using queries, you can look at database information in different ways, without changing the original information.

To set up a simple query, you build query sentences in the Create New Query dialog box. More complex queries must be defined using Query view, which is explained in the *WORKS 3.0* user's manual. In the Query dialog box you indicate which fields you want *WORKS* to search and specify what conditions to use as the search is made. *WORKS* automatically saves each query that you build so that you can use it again or modify it to find different information. A query is always applied to the entire database.

To build a query sentence, you specify a field name, choose a comparison phrase from a list *WORKS* displays, and then type the record comparison information. Each query sentence can contain up to three conditions linked together with the word "and" or "or." If the conditions are linked with "and," all conditions must be satisfied for a record to be included. If the conditions are linked with "or," only one of the conditions must be satisfied for a record to be included.

Suppose Angela Carrillo, who works in the afternoons, calls in sick. You can find all the employees who are available to work the afternoon shift by creating and using a query.

IT'S YOUR TURN

To create a new query,

1. Choose Create New Query from the TOOLS menu or click the QUERY button on the toolbar.

The New Query dialog box shown in Figure 10-4 appears on your screen.

The text box labeled "Please Give This Query A Name" is used to name the query so you can quickly identify it. Since you may want to use this query again, you will give it a meaningful name. The name you choose should have less than fifteen characters. If you choose a longer name, *WORKS* will only display the first fifteen characters. To highlight the generic "Query1" in order to replace it,

2. Double-click Query1 in the Please Give This Query A Name text box (or press [SHIFT] + [TAB] to move the highlight back to the Name box).

FIGURE 10-4

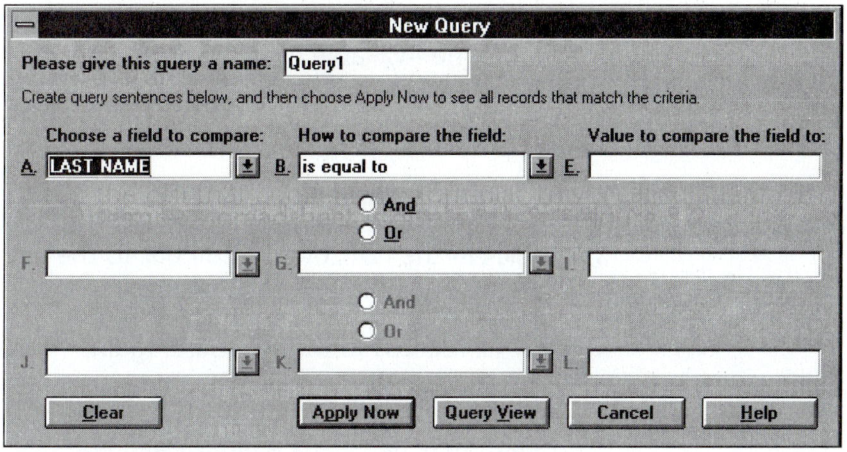

```
┌─────────────────────────────────────────────────────────────────┐
│ ▬                          New Query                              │
├─────────────────────────────────────────────────────────────────┤
│  Please give this query a name:  │Query1                     │    │
│                                                                   │
│  Create query sentences below, and then choose Apply Now to see all records that match the criteria. │
│                                                                   │
│   Choose a field to compare:    How to compare the field:    Value to compare the field to: │
│  A. │LAST NAME        │ ▲▼│  B. │is equal to          │ ▲▼│ E. │                    │ │
│                                                                   │
│                          ○ And                                    │
│                          ○ Or                                     │
│  F. │                 │ ▲▼│  G. │                     │ ▲▼│ I. │                    │ │
│                                                                   │
│                          ○ And                                    │
│                          ○ Or                                     │
│  J. │                 │ ▲▼│  K. │                     │ ▲▼│ L. │                    │ │
│                                                                   │
│  ┌─────────┐          ┌───────────┐ ┌──────────┐ ┌────────┐ ┌────────┐ │
│  │  Clear  │          │ Apply Now │ │Query View│ │ Cancel │ │  Help  │ │
│  └─────────┘          └───────────┘ └──────────┘ └────────┘ └────────┘ │
└─────────────────────────────────────────────────────────────────┘
```

3. Type: Afternoons OK

    That title will appear in the Query Name box.

The Choose A Field To Compare box is a drop-down scrolling box that lists all the fields in the database.

4. Click the down arrow on the Choose A Field To Compare text box to drop down the list, then scroll down the list, until the Time Available field name is visible in the list box.

5. Click the Time Available field name to highlight it.

    The list box will close and Time Available will be displayed as the field of choice.

6. Open the How To Compare The Field scrolling box and select Contains.

To advance the insertion point to the box labeled "Value To Compare The Field To,"

7. Click in the box or press [TAB].

8. Type: afternoon

When *WORKS* applies the query, the comparison is not sensitive to upper- or lowercase. Therefore, even though your comparison value is typed in lowercase letters and the item is capitalized in the database, the search will be successful. Note also that the comparison item is typed as singular "afternoon" and that it appears in the database as plural. The search will still be successful, because the comparison criterion is "Contains." If you choose "Is Equal To" for the comparison, the search will not be successful unless you type the exact contents of the field.

9. Click the APPLY NOW button or press [ENTER].

    WORKS 3.0 will now find all the records that contain "afternoon" in the Time Available field. You will quickly see a list of the employees who can work in the afternoons.

Because the Time Available field is one of the last fields and, therefore, does not show on the screen, you can check the accuracy of this search by scrolling to the right.

10. Click in the horizontal scroll bar to the right side of the scroll box so the Time Available field becomes visible.

Now you can see that all the listed employees are available in the afternoons.

To return to the name fields,

11. Click in the horizontal scroll bar to the left of the scroll box to return to the beginning of each record.

To view all records in the database again,

12. Choose Show All Records from the VIEW menu.

Now that you have a query defined and named, you can invoke it any time from the VIEW menu.

13. Choose Apply Query from the VIEW menu.

The Apply Query dialog box shown in Figure 10-5 will appear.

FIGURE 10-5

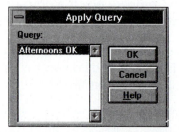

Since only one query has been defined for this database, its name is highlighted, waiting for you to accept it. If more than one query had been defined, the Query scrolling list in the dialog box would contain all query names, and you could select the one of interest by clicking on it.

14. Click OK or press [ENTER].

The selected records are displayed again.

15. Choose Show All Records from the VIEW menu again.

The full database is displayed once more.

ADDING A RECORD TO THE DATABASE

A new part-time employee has been hired recently, and you need to add her record to the database. You can add a new record in either the List or Form view. Since you have only one record to add, you could insert it manually into the correct alphabetical position. However, if you had many records to add, it would be simpler to type them at the end of the list and have *WORKS* sort the entire list alphabetically. For the sake of learning the technique, you will add the record to the end of the list then let *WORKS* sort the records so you can see how easy it would be if you had a lot of new names to insert in the database.

IT'S YOUR TURN

Your screen currently shows the List view. Because it is easier to add a record in Form view,

1. Click the FORM VIEW button on the toolbar or choose Form from the VIEW menu.

You will switch to the last record.

2. Click the LAST RECORD button on the horizontal scroll bar.

> You see a blank form with the Last Name field selected. This puts you in position to add a new employee record. *WORKS* always maintains an extra blank record at the end of every database to facilitate this add-on technique.

3. Type: HIRVONEN

> As you can see, HIRVONEN appears in the Formula bar. Also note that the familiar CANCEL and ENTRY buttons are displayed in the Formula bar. If you make a typing mistake at this point, you can use [BACK-SPACE] to erase errors and retype. Now that you know how to make corrections,

4. Press [TAB].

> This accomplishes two things. First, you confirm the entry and insert the name into the field. Second, you get ready to type an entry into the next field.

5. Type: PIA

To insert this first name and to move to the Street Address field,

6. Press [TAB].

If you notice a mistake in a field after you have pressed [TAB] and continued on to the next field, you can return to the previous field to correct your mistake by pressing [SHIFT] + [TAB] until the field you want to correct is selected.

7. Use the following data to complete the form.

STREET ADDRESS:	823 Barcelona Drive
CITY:	San Jose
STATE:	CA
ZIP:	95130
PHONE:	298–8489
BIRTHDAY:	August 23
DATE HIRED:	3/5/94
LAST RAISE:	
PAY RATE:	5.25
TIME AVAILABLE:	Evenings
STATUS:	PT

8. Click the ENTRY button or press [ENTER] or [TAB] to record the last field.

Clicking the ENTRY button or pressing [ENTER] will record the last field and keep the highlight on that field. Pressing [TAB] will record the last field and move the highlight to the first field of the next record, which is another empty record.

SORTING A DATABASE

WORKS can sort a database file in alphabetical, numerical, or chronological order, either backward or forward. It can sort on any field in either List or Form view, although it is easier to observe the results of the sort from the List view. When you sort, the new order is displayed in both database views.

WORKS can also sort on as many as three different fields at the same time so you are able to group your records just the way you want them. You control such a multi-level sort by specifying more than one sort field in the Sort Records dialog box. (If you want more information on sorting, consult your *WORKS* manual.) For this exercise, we will do a simple alphabetical sort from the List window.

IT'S YOUR TURN

1. Click the LIST VIEW button on the toolbar or choose List from the VIEW menu.

2. Press [HOME], if necessary, to view the Last Name field.

3. Choose Sort Records from the TOOLS menu.

   The Sort Records dialog box shown in Figure 10-6 will appear, with LAST NAME suggested as the first sort field. Note also that the Ascend option is already selected for all sort fields.

FIGURE 10-6

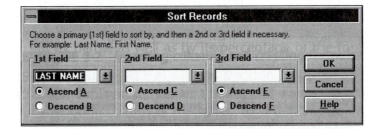

Since this is the field on which you wish to sort, and since you want an ascending sort (A to Z),

4. Click the OK button or press [ENTER].

   The dialog box will go away, and the records will be sorted with the new record for Pia Hirvonen in its proper place.

ADDING FIELDS TO RECORDS

One of your employees, Raoul Villarreal, resigned from work on March 18 because he wanted to return to school as a full-time student. You decide to add two fields to the database (Termination and Comments) to keep track of resignations and the reasons for them. After adding the fields, you will fill them in for Raoul's record.

IT'S YOUR TURN

1. Click the FORM VIEW button on the toolbar.

   The Form view window will appear.

2. Point in the blank white space at the right of the Status field and click the mouse.

   The insertion point will blink in the position where you clicked.

3. Type: TERMINATION:

Field names can contain up to fifteen characters. Note the colon at the end of the field name. When inserting a field in Form view and typing the field name directly on the form, as you did in step 3, the name must end with a colon to signal the end of the field name. There is another way to insert a field name, which doesn't require you to type the colon. That method will be used to insert the next field.

4. Click the ENTRY button or press [ENTER].

The Field Size dialog box shown in Figure 10-7 will appear.

FIGURE 10-7

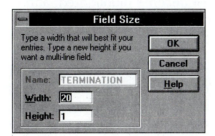

The suggested width for this field is 20 characters, and its suggested height is one line. You can accept the suggested size, because it is easy to change the size of the field when you find it is necessary.

To accept the settings in the Field Size dialog box,

5. Click OK or press [ENTER].

The new field appears at the position you clicked on the form. You can move it to a different location later if you wish.

You will use a slightly different method to add the next new field.

6. Click immediately below the STATUS field name to set the insertion point.

7. Click the INSERT FIELD button on the toolbar (the third button from the right end of the toolbar).

The Insert Field dialog box shown in Figure 10-8 appears.

FIGURE 10-8

Note the similarity of the Insert Field dialog box to the Field size dialog box. The main difference is that you must type the field name into the Insert Field dialog box, and when you do, you do not need to type the colon to end the field name.

8. Type: COMMENTS

9. Click on the OK button or press [ENTER].

Look at the placement of the two fields you just added. If you are not satisfied with the placement of a field,

10. Move the pointer to the field name, hold down the mouse button, and drag the field to a better position. Release the mouse button.

The space for comments should be made as long as possible. To allow more space for that field on all records in the file,

11. Click to select the field contents area, if it is not already selected.

The field will become highlighted, and three small gray square dots will appear on it; one in the middle bottom, one at the middle of the right edge, and one at the bottom corner of the right edge. These dots are called *handles* and are used for resizing the field. The first (Vertical Resize) handle is used to make the field taller or narrower. Dragging on the second (Horizontal Resize) handle is used to make the field longer or shorter, and the third (Diagonal Resize) is used to change both dimensions at the same time.

12. Position the pointer on the Horizontal Resize handle in the middle of the right edge of the rectangle. When it is in the proper position, it will turn into a horizontal two-way arrow labelled "resize." Hold down the mouse button and drag all the way to the right side, then release the mouse button (see Figure 10-9).

FIGURE 10-9

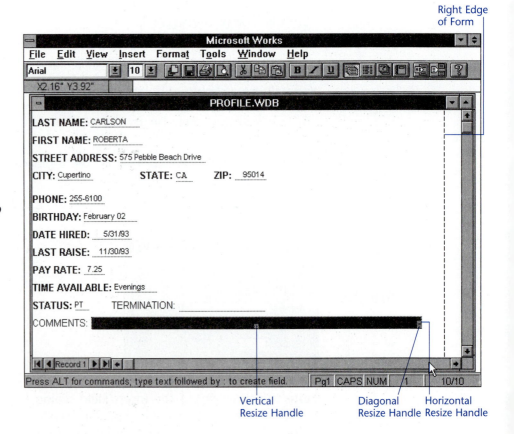

Your Comments field is now long enough to accommodate a sentence.

The Termination field should be long enough to accommodate the date. If not,

13. Repeat steps 11 and 12 to adjust the size of the Termination field.

You may have noticed that the font size of 10 (shown in the Font Size box in the toolbar) when one of the new field contents lines is selected is different from the old field contents font size of 8. To make the font size the same,

14. Hold down the [CTRL] key while you click the field contents line for both new fields.
     This selects both fields for formatting.

15. Pull down the Font Size box on the toolbar and set the selected field contents font and size to Arial 8.

16. Click anywhere in the white space to deselect the field contents lines.

It is also noticeable that the original field names are in bold, but the new ones are not. To set the new field names to bold style,

17. Hold down the [CTRL] key while you click both new field names (TERMINATION and COMMENTS).

18. Click the BOLD button on the toolbar.

The form is now finished, and the new fields have been added both to the Form and List view. To verify that the new fields are included in the List view,

19. Click the LIST VIEW button on the toolbar or choose List from the VIEW menu.

20. If necessary, use the horizontal scroll bar to move to the right to see the two new fields.

Because fields are independently sized in List view and Form view, the fields you see in List view are quite small. To enlarge them,

21. Move the pointer to the right border of each field heading until the pointer turns into a two-way arrow with the legend "adjust," and drag the right border to the right to make each field larger.

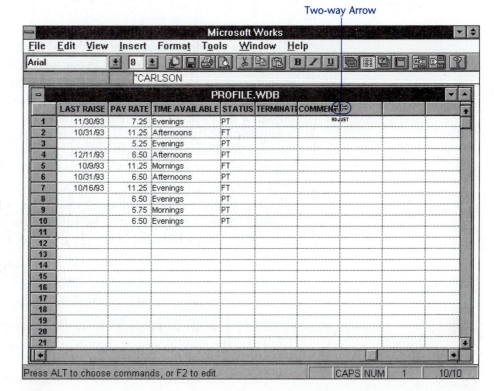

FIGURE 10-10

To return to the Form view to assure yourself that the size of the fields did not change in Form view,

22. Click the FORM VIEW button on the toolbar.

SEARCHING THE DATABASE

You are now ready to enter data about Raoul's resignation. First you need to find his record. You will use a *WORKS* search feature similar to the Find feature in the word processor.

IT'S YOUR TURN

1. Choose Find from the EDIT menu.

   The Find dialog box appears, with the blinking cursor in the Find What text box.

2. Type: VILLARREAL

   Your screen should look like the one shown in Figure 10-11, except that the name does not have to be typed in all capitals; the search is not case-sensitive. Also, if you were not sure how to spell Raoul's last name, you could just enter the first few letters in the Find What box. For example, entering "Vill" would result in a successful search.

FIGURE 10-11

Note that the Next Record option should be selected, as illustrated in Figure 10-11. If it is not, move the pointer to the Next Record option and click once.

3. Click OK or press [ENTER].

   The form window reappears, with VILLARREAL highlighted. The Find command is equally effective in List view. You can also use the Find command to locate a subset of the database by selecting the All Records option. When the All Records option is selected in Form view, *WORKS* displays the first record matching the Find What box and waits for you to press the [F7] key to display the next record. When the All Records option is chosen in List view, *WORKS* displays a list of all records that match the Find What box. In both views, after examining all the records that were found, you must choose Show All Records from the VIEW menu to return to the full database.

   You are now in Form view, with the Villarreal record displayed on your screen and the Last Name field contents highlighted.

4. If the entire name is not displayed,

   a. Move the pointer to the Horizontal Resize handle in the center of the right edge of the highlighted field contents area until the pointer turns into the two-way Resize arrow.

   b. Drag the field contents box to the right approximately one-half inch and release the mouse button.

The full name should now be displayed. If it is not, repeat steps 4a and 4b until the field contents line is long enough.

5. Click on the Termination field contents line to select it.

6. Type today's date.

7. Click the ENTRY button or press [ENTER] or [TAB].

If the field contents are displayed as "#########," the line is too short to display the full date. In that event,

8. Use the dragging procedure you learned earlier to lengthen the Termination field contents line.

The date is now entered on his record.

9. If necessary, click (or press [TAB]) to select the Comments field contents line.

10. Type: Returned to school full time

11. Click the ENTRY button or press [ENTER].

The data will be entered in the field, and Raoul's form will stay on the screen. This completes the entry; Raoul's record is now updated.

| CAUTION | If you accidentally press [TAB] after entering data into the Comments field, the data will be entered, but the next form will be displayed. If that happens and you want to return to Raoul's form, simply click the PREVIOUS RECORD button on the horizontal scroll bar. |

To return to the first record in preparation for the activities in the next section,

12. Click the FIRST RECORD button in the lower left corner of the form.

PRINTING FROM THE DATABASE

You can print a database from Form view, List view, or Report view. Printing from Form view prints every record currently active. Printing from List view produces all active records organized in row-and-column format. If the database contains more fields than can fit on one sheet, a multi-page document will be printed. Printing from Report view is presented in detail in Chapter 12. For now, you will limit the printing output from Form view by creating a query that will be useful in the future but that will only select the Villarreal form for the present.

IT'S YOUR TURN

1. Choose Create New Query from the TOOLS menu.

When the New Query dialog box appears,

2. Double click to highlight the generic name in the Please Give This Query A Name text box.

3. Type: Resign

4. Click the Down Arrow to drop down the scrolling list in the Choose a Field To Compare box.

5. Scroll down the list and click TERMINATION when that field name appears.

    The scrolling list will close, and the TERMINATION field name will appear in the box.

6. Click the down arrow to drop down the scrolling list box for How To Compare The Field.

7. Click the Is Not Equal To option.

    The scrolling list box will close, and the chosen option will appear in the text box.

8. Click in the text box labeled Value to Compare The Field To.

9. Press the [SPACE BAR] several times to insert blanks into the text box.

10. Click the APPLY NOW button or press [ENTER].

    The dialog box will be put away, and the Villarreal record will appear. It is the only record in the database that matches the query criterion you just established.

11. Choose Print from the FILE menu.

    The Print dialog box similar to the one shown in Figure 10-12 will appear.

FIGURE 10-12

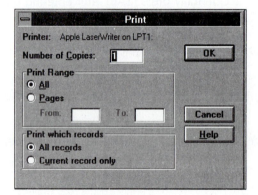

As you can see, the print dialog box gives you the option to print selected pages of a document. You could use that option to print a single form by typing the record number in both the From box and the To box. Two of the exercises at the end of this chapter direct you to use this method of limiting the records to be printed. Also, the Print dialog box includes an option to print the current record only; since your selection only includes one record, you can leave the dialog box as it is.

12. Click OK or press [ENTER].

    Raoul's record will be printed, and you will be returned to the Form view.

13. Choose Show All Records from the VIEW menu.

FINISHING UP PROJECT 1

You will now save all of your work under a different filename and quit *WORKS*.

IT'S YOUR TURN

To return to the beginning of the database,

1. Click the FIRST RECORD button in the lower left corner.

2. Choose Save As from the FILE menu, and save the database as *PRO-FILE2* in your name directory on your data disk.

3. Quit *WORKS,* as directed in previous chapters.

SUMMARY

In this chapter you have learned some basic database terms (records, fields, form, list, and query). You have also performed basic database tasks (such as searching, sorting, adding fields to records, and adding a record to a file). Now you are ready to create your own database in the next chapter.

REVIEW QUESTIONS

1. Which menu allows you to switch between List view and Form view?

2. Which view is suggested when sorting? Which view is suggested when adding data to new records?

3. Which menu and which option is used to display a certain selection of records?

4. Which menu and option allows you to insert a field?

5. Which views allow you to print?

6. What are the four views of a file available in *WORKS?*

EXERCISES

EXERCISE 10-1   Exploring an existing database

(Use the Find and Sort features, create a query)

1. Open the file *PROFILE* from your data disk.

2. Use the Find feature to locate "Gloria."

3. In the List view, sort the database by zip code, from zero to nine.

4. Create a query named "San Jose" that displays all records that contain "San Jose" in the "City" field. How many are there?

5. Do not save or print this exercise.

EXERCISE 10-2   Modifying a database

(Add a record and footer, sort, and print a record)

1. Open the file *PROFILE* from your data disk.

2. Add the following person to the database:

    LAST NAME: SMITH

    FIRST NAME: JANE

    STREET ADDRESS: 222 Station Road

    CITY: Sunnyvale

STATE:	CA
ZIP:	95111
PHONE:	777–7777
BIRTHDAY:	July 7
DATE HIRED:	4/4/93
LAST RAISE:	10/4/94
PAY RATE:	5.75
TIME AVAILABLE:	Evenings
STATUS:	PT

3. Sort the database by LAST NAME, A to Z.

4. Obtain the Form view of Jane Smith's record.

5. Use the skills you already know to create a footer with your name on the left, the filename in the center, and the date on the right.

6. Save the file in your name directory on your data disk as *EX10-2*.

7. To print the screen that contains the new record for Jane Smith using the Form view, choose Print from the FILE menu and click the Current Record Only option. An alternate way to print only this record is to click the Pages option in the Print Range block and type "6" (Jane's record number) in both the From box and in the To box. Only record six will print.

EXERCISE 10-3   Modifying an existing database

(Create a new field and data for it, experiment with searches and sorts, type a footer, print a blank form in Form view.)

1. Open the file *PROFILE* from your data disk.

2. Choose Form view.

3. Insert two new fields of your choice and add them to the database (for example, Vacation, Termination, or Memo).

4. If necessary, change the font, size, and style to match the other fields in the database.

5. Make up and enter some data for the new fields for each employee.

6. Try some searches and sorts on your new fields.

7. Type a footer with your name on the left, the filename in the center, and the date on the right.

8. Save the file as *EX10-3*.

9. In Form view, use the LAST RECORD button on the horizontal scroll bar to advance to the last record. It will be blank. Print the blank form to show the new fields.

Database 2

OBJECTIVES

In this chapter, you will learn how to

- create a simple database
- design a form
- format fields
- change the size and location of fields on a form
- change the size of a column (field) in the List View
- do multi-level sorts
- create mailing labels from the database

SETTING THE SCENE

Remember the Birthday Club letter you composed with the word processor? (If you want to review the sample letter, see Figure 4-1 in Chapter 4.) In this chapter, you will create a simple database of Birthday Club members to go with the letter. Once you have the database (see Figure 11-1), you can use *WORKS 3.0* to create mailing labels and personalized letters from your standard letter.

FIGURE 11-1

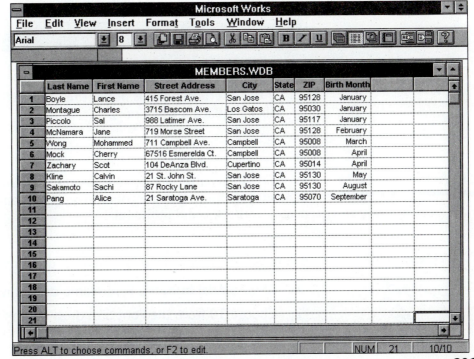

GETTING STARTED

You are going to be typing more in this chapter. There is no file already prepared for you. If you are not a good typist, just take it slow and easy so you will not get frustrated.

IT'S YOUR TURN

1. Launch *WORKS.*

   You will see the Startup dialog box on your screen.

2. Click the DATABASE button in the block labelled "Create a New."

   A blank window titled "Data1" appears, ready for you to design the form. Your screen should look like Figure 11-2. The insertion point should be blinking in the upper left corner.

FIGURE 11-2

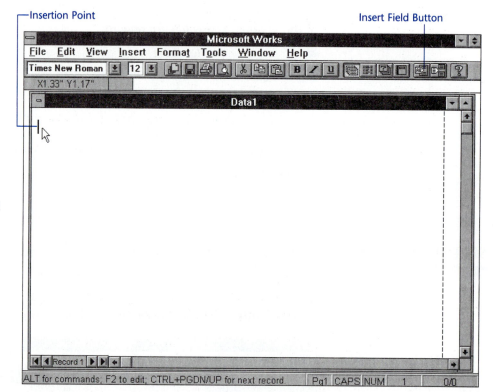

3. If the insertion point is not in the upper left corner as in Figure 11-2, click to place it there now.

CREATING A FORM

The INSERT FIELD button shown in Figure 11-2 is used to create the various fields in a database form. You are going to create a simple database with fields for names, addresses, and birthdays.

IT'S YOUR TURN

Before you create any field, you will set the font name, size, and style.

1. Choose Arial from the Font Name drop-down list on the toolbar.

2. Choose 10 from the Font Size drop-down list on the toolbar.

3. Click the BOLD button on the toolbar.

You are now ready to type the field names. It is easier to type the field names directly onto the form. Don't forget to include the colon as part of the field name.

To create a field for last names,

4. Type: Last Name:

5. Press [ENTER].

    The Field Size dialog box will be displayed. To make it easier for you to type in the field names, you will simply accept the suggested field width of 20 characters for each field and then go back later and adjust the size of any fields that need to be changed.

To accept the suggested field width,

6. Press [ENTER].

    The insertion point moves to the next line of the form.

7. Type: First Name:

8. Press [ENTER] twice.

9. Continue typing and pressing [ENTER] as in steps 7 and 8 to enter the following five field names:

    Street Address:

    City:

    State:

    ZIP:

    Birth Month:

    These are all the fields in your database. However, you have some more work to do in designing the look of your form before you are ready to enter data into the database.

FORMATTING THE FIELDS

Since the database fields will be carrying different kinds of information, now is the time to set their formats properly. Also, since the field names are in bold, it is a good idea to format the field contents for plain text to make it easier to distinguish between the two.

In all of the following instructions in this book, when you see the phrase "click on the XXX field," you should click on the field contents line. If you are to click on the field name, the phrase "click on the XXX field name" will be used.

IT'S YOUR TURN

1. Hold down the [CTRL] key and keep it down while you click on each field, one at a time.

    The blank lines following the field names will be highlighted.

2. Click the BOLD button on the toolbar to deselect it for all fields.

    All fields should still be highlighted.

3. Click 8 in the Font Size drop-down box to choose that font size for all fields.

4. Click anywhere in the white space to deselect the fields.

To format the numeric fields,

5. Click the ZIP field.

6. Choose Number from the FORMAT menu.

When the Number dialog box appears,

7. Select Fixed from the Format block, type "0" in the Number of Decimals text box, then click OK or press [ENTER] to return to the database form.

8. Click the Birth Month field.

9. Choose Number from the FORMAT menu.

When the Number dialog box appears,

10. Select Date from the Format block, select the the month name only (the last option in the Date block), then click OK or press [ENTER] to return to the database form.

The fields are now formatted properly. You will next concentrate on making your form look like the application form that was filled out by each Birthday Club member.

CHANGING FIELD SIZE AND LOCATION

You now have an opportunity to build upon the skills you learned in the previous chapter by changing the length and position of some of the fields so they will look similar to those shown in Figure 11-3.

FIGURE 11-3

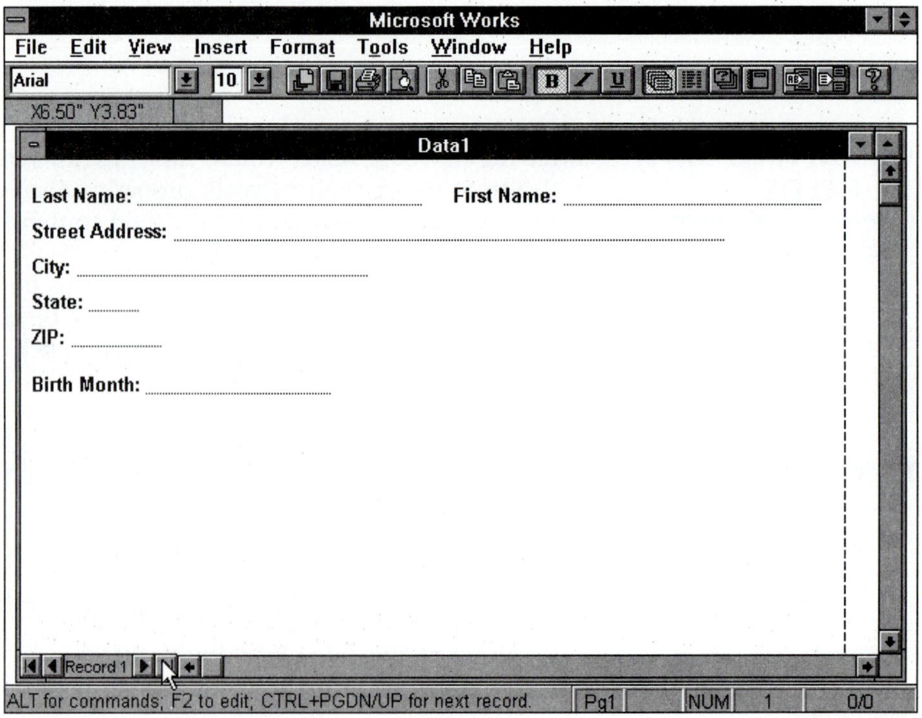

Look carefully at the length of the fields on your screen and compare them with those shown in Figure 11-3. Some of them may seem long enough, but others may seem too long or too short.

Use the following steps to make your form look as much like Figure 11-3 as possible. You will probably have to change the size of all data fields and move most fields.

IT'S YOUR TURN

To lengthen or shorten fields, complete the following steps.

1. Click the field contents line of the field you wish to resize. As in Chapter 10, you will use the handles to resize the field contents lines (see Figure 11-4).

FIGURE 11-4

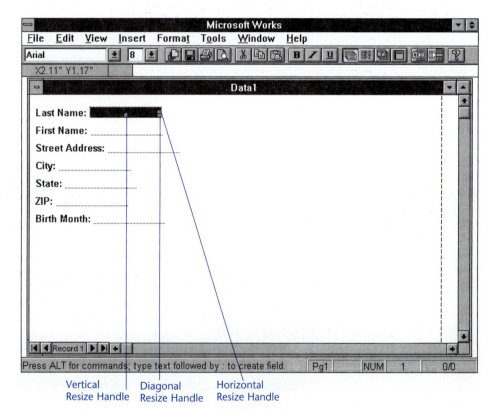

2. Position the pointer on the Horizontal Resize handle in the middle of the right edge of the highlighted field.

3. Hold down the mouse button and drag the outline to the right or left until the field reaches the length you want.

4. Release the mouse button.

To move a field to a new location,

5. Click the field name of the field you want to move.

6. Hold down the mouse button and drag the field outline to the position you want. Release the mouse button.

ENTERING NEW DATA

Now enter the following club members into your new database. Follow the directions given in steps 1–17 to enter the first member's data. You are then on your own to enter the data for the other nine members shown in the Membership List following the instructions.

You can enter data in either the Form View or List View, but Form View is normally preferred because the entire record is usually visible from that view.

IT'S YOUR TURN

1. If you are not in Form view, click the FORM VIEW button on the toolbar or choose Form from the VIEW menu.
2. Click in the first field (Last Name).
3. Type: McNamara

To enter the last name and move to the First Name field,

4. Press [TAB].
5. Type: Jane

To enter the first name and move to the Street Address field,

6. Press [TAB].
7. Type: 719 Morse St.

To enter the street address and move to the City field,

8. Press [TAB].
9. Type: San Jose

To enter the city name and move to the State field,

10. Press [TAB].
11. Type: CA

To enter the state abbreviation and move to the ZIP field,

12. Press [TAB].
13. Type: 95128

To enter the ZIP code and move to the Birth Month field,

14. Press [TAB].
15. Type: February

To enter the birth month and move to the next record,

16. Press [TAB].

    Note that pressing [TAB] this last time moved you to the next record. ("Record 2" is displayed in the lower left corner, between the PREVIOUS RECORD and NEXT RECORD triangle buttons. This indicates that you are in the second record of this file.)

17. Repeat steps 2–16 to enter the data for the rest of the club members shown in the following Membership List.

    When you finish, you will have entered ten records; the screen will show a blank form with "Record 11" displayed in the lower left corner.

Birthday Club Membership List

Last Name: McNamara
First Name: Jane
Street Address: 719 Morse St.
City: San Jose
State: CA   **ZIP:** 95128
Birth Month: February

Last Name: Kline
First Name: Calvin
Street Address: 21 St. John St.
City: San Jose
State: CA   **ZIP:** 95130
Birth Month: May

Last Name: Boyle
First Name: Lance
Street Address: 415 Forest Ave.
City: San Jose
State: CA   **ZIP:** 95128
Birth Month: January

Last Name: Pang
First Name: Alice
Street Address: 21 Saratoga Ave.
City: Saratoga
State: CA   **ZIP:** 95070
Birth Month: September

Last Name: Montague
First Name: Charles
Street Address: 3715 Bascom Ave.
City: Los Gatos
State: CA   **ZIP:** 95030
Birth Month: January

Last Name: Sakamoto
First Name: Sachi
Street Address: 87 Rocky Lane
City: San Jose
State: CA   **ZIP:** 95130
Birth Month: August

Last Name: Wong
First Name: Mohammed
Street Address: 711 Campbell Ave.
City: Campbell
State: CA   **ZIP:** 95008
Birth Month: March

Last Name: Mock
First Name: Cherry
Street Address: 6516 Esmeralda Ct.
City: Campbell
State: CA   **ZIP:** 95008
Birth Month: April

Last Name: Piccolo
First Name: Sal
Street Address: 988 Latimer Ave.
City: San Jose
State: CA   **ZIP:** 95117
Birth Month: January

Last Name: Zachary
First Name: Scot
Street Address: 104 DeAnza Blvd.
City: Cupertino
State: CA   **ZIP:** 95014
Birth Month: April

CHANGING COLUMN SIZE IN LIST VIEW

Now that you have entered the names, you will switch back to List View, where all records are visible. None of the cosmetic changes carry over from one view to the other, so you will find that some of the fields (columns) are not wide enough to display all the information they contain, and some of them may seem unnecessarily wide for the data they contain. Since you are going to be using List view to make some structural changes (i.e., sorting the database) that do carry over from view to view, you will spend some time making the List view as easy to read as possible.

IT'S YOUR TURN

1. Click the LIST VIEW button on the toolbar or choose List from the VIEW menu.

   As you can see, the font name is the same as you chose when you first started to design the form, but the font size is larger than needed.

To change the font size to a smaller one that will allow all fields to be displayed on the screen,

2. Click the SELECT ALL button at the intersection of the column headers and row headers in the upper left corner of the List view.

   The entire window will become highlighted.

3. Select 8 from the Font Size drop-down scrolling box.

   The Font Name box should now read "Arial" and the Font Size box should contain "8".

To change the size of the columns for the best fit, all fields should still be selected.

4. Choose Field Width from the FORMAT menu.

When the Field Width dialog box appears,

5. Click the Best Fit option and then click OK or press [ENTER].

6. Click any empty field to deselect.

   Your screen should now look somewhat like the one shown in Figure 11-5.

FIGURE 11-5

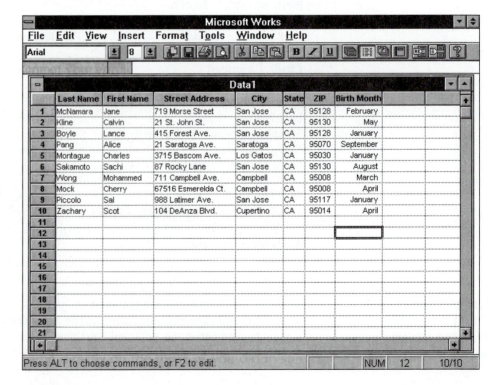

MULTI-LEVEL SORTING

One of the many benefits of a database program is that you can use it to sort a file in different ways. For example, you can sort by ZIP code for mailing purposes or by birth month for your birthday letters. Now that you have entered data for the Birthday Club members, you can alphabetize the list for clarity and to find any duplicated entries. (You don't want anyone to get more than one letter.)

If you have a database with duplicated last names, you can do a multi-level sort. You can use the Sort Records dialog box to sort on as many as three levels. You will now do a multi-level sort, first by last name and then by birth month.

IT'S YOUR TURN

You should be in List view so you can see the effect of the sort.

1. Choose Sort Records from the TOOLS menu.

   The Sort Records dialog box appears, as shown in Figure 11-6.

FIGURE 11-6

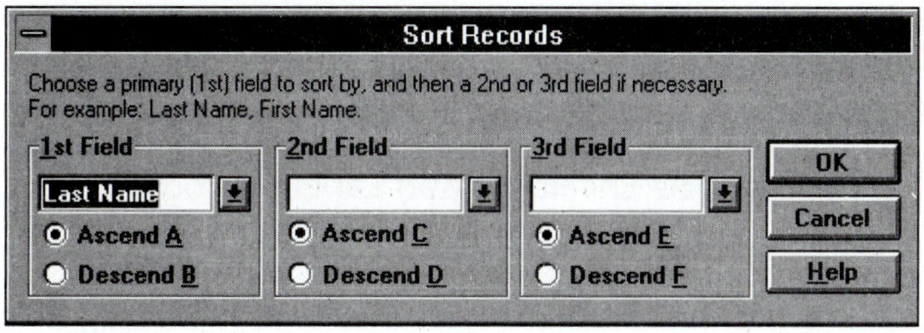

2. Select Birth Month from the drop-down scrolling list in the 1st Field block.

3. Check to be sure that the 1st Field block has the Ascend option selected. If it does not, select it now.

4. Select Last Name from the drop-down scrolling list in the 2nd Field block.

5. Check to be sure that the 2nd Field block has the Ascend option selected. If it does not, select it now.

   The 3rd Field block should be empty.

6. Click OK or press [ENTER].

   The records are now listed in alphabetical order by birth month. Note that because the Birth Month field was originally formatted as a date, the sort correctly placed January first. If you had entered Birth Month as text, April would have been placed first. There are three members with January birthdays, and they are listed in alphabetical order within the January block. Look down the Birth Month column, and you will see that there are two members with April birthdays; the two are correctly alphabetized within the April block. Also notice that the birth months are aligned on the right, because you formatted them as numbers, not text.

   You have created a new database that you will use again in a later chapter. Therefore, you should save it under an appropriate name.

7. Choose Save As from the FILE menu and use the file name *MEMBERS* to save this database in your name directory on your data disk.

   Your screen now shows the new title and should resemble the screen shown in Figure 11-1.

CREATING MAILING LABELS

An important feature of *WORKS 3.0* is the ease with which you can combine a word processing document and a database to create and print mailing labels and envelopes. In a later chapter you will learn how to create and print personalized form letters using a database. For now you will prepare the mailing labels for the club members. Before you can create mailing labels, you must have open the database document that contains the addresses for the labels. You can then use a word processing document to hold the mailing label specifications.

IT'S YOUR TURN

To create mailing labels from the already open Members database,

1. **Choose Create New File from the FILE menu.**

When the Startup dialog box appears,

2. **Click the WORD PROCESSOR button in the Create A New block.**

   An empty word processing window will appear with the generic title "Word1."

3. **Choose Envelopes and Labels from the TOOLS menu.**

   The Envelopes and Labels dialog box will appear, as shown in Figure 11-7.

FIGURE 11-7

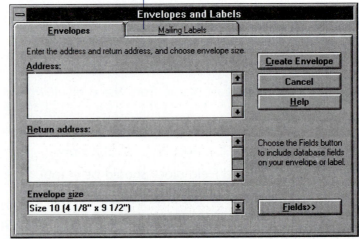

This dialog box can be used for creating either a single envelope or mailing label from an address that you type in, or a set of envelopes or mailing labels based on fields contained in a database. Each database can support either mailing labels or envelopes, but not both. You will be creating mailing labels from the *MEMBERS* database. To enter the proper section in the dialog box,

4. **Click the Mailing Labels tab.**

   The dialog box now resembles the one shown in Figure 11-8.

To include database fields in your mailing labels,

5. **Click the FIELDS>> button in the lower right corner of the dialog box.**

FIGURE 11-8

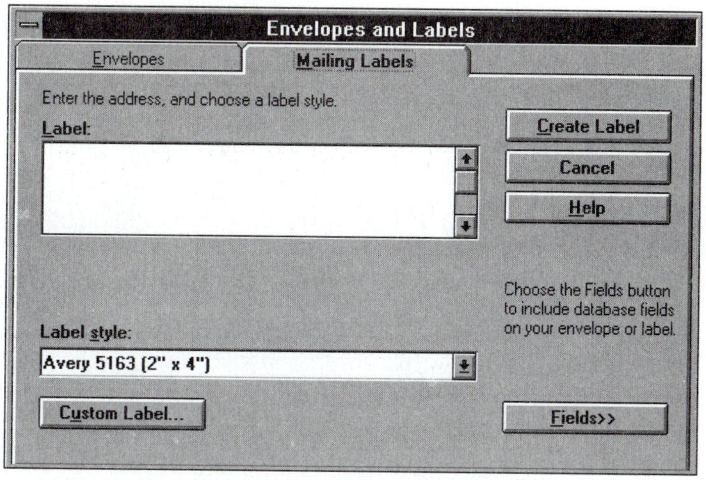

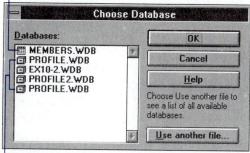

The dialog box will become larger and show a database portion at the bottom.

6. Click the DATABASE button in the lower left corner.

    A separate Choose Database dialog box will appear with a listing of all databases on your data disk. The open databases will be marked with an open document icon, and the other databases will be marked with a file cabinet icon (see Figure 11-9).

Open Database File

FIGURE 11-9

Closed Database Files

7. Click the *MEMBERS.WDB* filename in the Databases list box.

8. Click OK or press [ENTER].

The Mailing Labels dialog box will reappear, but now the insertion point is blinking in the Label text box. To insert placeholders for the mailing labels,

9. Click FIRST NAME in the Fields scrolling list box.

10. Click the INSERT button.

    The <<FIRST NAME>> placeholder will appear in the Label text box as shown in Figure 11-10.

You must set up the placeholders exactly as you wish the addresses to appear when printed. To separate the first and last names,

11. Press [SPACEBAR].

To enter the last name,

FIGURE 11-10

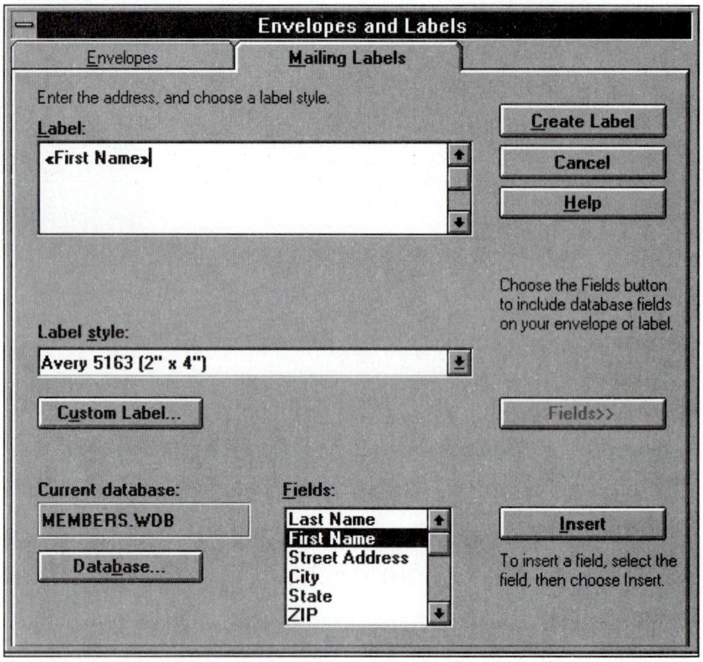

12. Click LAST NAME in the Fields text box and then click the INSERT button.

To move the insertion point to the next line,

13. Press [ENTER].

To enter the address,

14. Click STREET ADDRESS in the Fields text box and then click the INSERT button and press [ENTER] to move to the next line.

To enter the placeholders on the third line,

15. Click CITY, click the INSERT button, type a comma, press [SPACEBAR], click STATE, click the INSERT button, press [SPACEBAR] twice, click ZIP, and click the INSERT button.

Your screen should now resemble Figure 11-11.
    You will now select a label style from the Label Style box—a drop-down box that contains the names of over three dozen commercially available labels together with their associated sizes. You may create your own custom label size if you wish.

16. Click the down arrow on the Label Style box, and scroll through the list to get a sense of the tremendous variations available to you.

When you have finished exploring the list,

17. Click Avery 5163 (2" x 4") to select it.

    The Label Style list will close, leaving your choice highlighted in the box.

18. Click the CREATE LABEL button in the upper right corner of the dialog box.

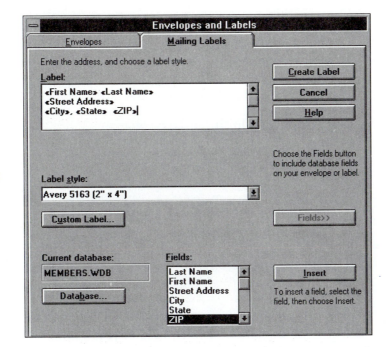

FIGURE 11-11

The dialog box goes away, and you are transferred to the word processing document where you will see the placeholders that you have chosen as shown in Figure 11-12.

You are not ready to print the labels now, but you can still see what they would look like if they were printed.

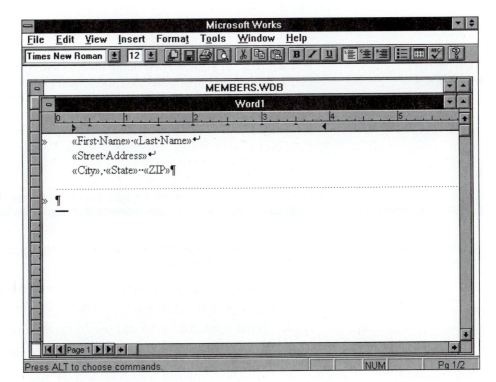

FIGURE 11-12

19. Click the PRINT PREVIEW button on the toolbar.

The Choose Database dialog box will appear once again, with the *MEMBERS.WDB* filename highlighted in the Databases list box.

20. Click the OK button or press [ENTER] to confirm the selection of the members database.

    The Print Preview screen will be displayed, showing all ten addresses as they would appear on a mailing label sheet. You can use the ZOOM IN button to examine the labels more closely if you wish.

When you finish,

21. Click the CANCEL button to return to the word processing document.

FINISHING UP

You will be using the word processing and database documents to print the mailing labels in another chapter, so you must save them now.

IT'S YOUR TURN

1. Choose Save As from the FILE menu, and save the word processing document as *MEMLBLS* in your name directory on your data disk.

2. Close the *MEMLBLS.WPS* file.

    The *MEMBERS.WDB* file is now showing on your screen.

3. Choose Save from the FILE menu to save any late changes you made in the file.

4. Quit *WORKS*, as directed in previous chapters.

SUMMARY

You are well on your way to being able to use the Database tool productively. You have learned and practiced some basic database operations, such as creating, sorting, and formatting a new database. You can also create mailing labels. The database application is complex and powerful, and in the next chapter, you will learn how to create special reports from your database.

REVIEW QUESTIONS

1. Which view allows you to view as many records of a database as the screen can hold?

2. Name a situation in which the cursor changes into a two-way arrow when you are doing something to the *WORKS 3.0* database.

3. What application do you use to create a labels document?

4. Which key do you press to move from field to field in the Form view?

5. Which menu and which option do you use to sort records?

EXERCISES

EXERCISE 11-1 Modifying the *REFER* file

(Add records, sort, print labels)

1. Open the *REFER.WDB* file from the Exercise directory of your data disk.

2. Add information about yourself to the database in the List View.

3. Sort the file by last name within city. The cities should be in alphabetical order and if more than one person lives in one city, the names should be in alphabetical order.

4. Create labels for all names in this file.

    a. Choose Avery 5163 as the size.

    b. Select the following fields for printing: First Name, Last Name, and Birth Month.

    c. Leave one space between the first and last names.

    d. Place Birth Month on a separate line.

5. Save the word processing file as *EX11-1* in your name directory on your data disk.

6. Print the labels on a plain sheet of paper, if directed to do so by your instructor.

7. Do not save changes to *REFER* file.

EXERCISE 11-2 Creating a database

(Create and fill in forms, sort records, and print custom labels)

1. Open a new database file.

2. Create a form with the following field names in Arial 10 Bold:

	Width
Item #	8
Description	20
Needed	5
On Hand	5
Order	5

3. Enter the data from the Reorder Form spreadsheet in Figure 8-11 of Chapter 8 for Item #, Description, Needed, On Hand, and Order (nine items).

4. Choose List View.

5. Sort the database by the Order field from nine to zero.

6. Create labels using Avery 5161 label size. Select Fields: Item #, Description, and Order. Arrange fields all on one line with two spaces between them. (*Note:* Click OK if message appears about margins not wide enough.)

7.   Save the database document as *EX11-2* and the labels document as *LBL11-2* in your name directory on your data disk.

8.   From the labels document, choose Print Preview.

9.   Print the labels on plain paper, if directed to do so by your instructor.

EXERCISE 11-3   Creating a database from scratch

1.   Open a new database file.

2.   Create an address list of five people with Last Name, First Name, Address, City, State, and ZIP fields. Use an appropriate filename. Use font name, size, and style of your choice.

3.   Sort the file by ZIP.

4.   Create labels to fit your data.

5.   Save the word processing file as *LBL11-3* in your name directory on your data disk. Save the database file as *EX11-3* in the same directory.

7.   Choose Print Preview from the FILE menu. If you don't like the labels, use another label size.

8.   Print the labels on plain paper.

Database 3

OBJECTIVES

In this chapter, you will learn to

■ *create calculated fields*

■ *insert new fields*

■ *use the IF function*

■ *change a field name*

■ *create a new report*

■ *create totals and subtotals in a report*

■ *sort records for a report*

■ *name and save a report*

■ *select records for a report*

■ *format and print a report*

SETTING THE SCENE

PROJECT 1 Board Game Inventory

Maintaining the proper inventory is extremely important to the operation of The Fun Factory. Each department manager is responsible for taking a physical inventory of the toys in his or her department. You have designed a database form that can be adapted to any department or section of a department.

In order to introduce your managers to the use of the form, you have prepared a hypothetical inventory of board games. The board game database includes fields titled Stock Number, Game Title, Vendor, Maximum, Unit Cost, On Hand, Balance, and Order. The first two field names are self-explanatory; the Vendor field indicates the source for the game; the Maximum field gives the largest number of each game that should be in stock; Unit Cost is the cost to The Fun Factory for each game; On Hand tells how many of each game are currently in stock; Balance is the difference between Maximum and On Hand; and Order tells how many games to order to maintain a working inventory. You will be printing two reports from this database. One report will show the current inventory level, and the other report will show the number of items that need to be ordered to maintain a proper level of inventory. The finished reports are illustrated in Figures 12-1a and 12-1b.

GETTING STARTED

You will be using the file named *INVENT.WDB*. You may notice a functional similarity between this file and the spreadsheet file *REORDER.WKS*. The similarity is intentional. Although both the spreadsheet tool and the database tool provide the ability to make the calculations necessary to maintain an in-

217

FIGURE 12-1A

Board Games Inventory

Stock#	Game Title	Vendor	Unit Cost	Maximum	On Hand	Amt Sold	Order	Total Cost
101	Monopoly	World Entertainment, Ir	18.50	15	6	9	9	166.50
102	Trivial Pursuit	World Entertainment, Ir	23.75	15	5	10	10	237.50
103	Mousetrap	Games Supply Co.	20.00	7	5	2	0	0.00
104	Chess	World Entertainment, Ir	20.00	8	4	4	4	80.00
105	Scattergories	California Board Games	18.50	15	5	10	10	185.00
106	Scrabble	World Entertainment, Ir	20.00	14	4	10	10	200.00
107	Trump	World Entertainment, Ir	23.75	10	5	5	5	118.75
108	Checkers	California Board Games	20.00	15	6	9	9	180.00
109	Candyland	Games Supply Co.	18.50	10	4	6	6	111.00
110	Life	Games Supply Co.	23.75	6	2	4	4	95.00

SUM:
1,373.75

FIGURE 12-1B

The Fun Factory Order List

Stock#	Game Title	Unit Cost	Order	Total Cost	Vendor
105	Scattergories	18.50	10	185.00	California Board Games
108	Checkers	20.00	9	180.00	California Board Games
				365.00	
109	Candyland	18.50	6	111.00	Games Supply Co.
110	Life	23.75	4	95.00	Games Supply Co.
				206.00	
101	Monopoly	18.50	9	166.50	World Entertainment, Inc.
102	Trivial Pursuit	23.75	10	237.50	World Entertainment, Inc.
104	Chess	20.00	4	80.00	World Entertainment, Inc.
106	Scrabble	20.00	10	200.00	World Entertainment, Inc.
107	Trump	23.75	5	118.75	World Entertainment, Inc.
				802.75	

TOTAL ORDER 1,373.75

ventory file, the database tool is superior for this application because of its reporting capabilities.

IT'S YOUR TURN

1. Launch *WORKS 3.0*.

When the Startup dialog box appears,

2. Open *INVENT.WDB* from your data disk.

The *INVENT* file in Figure 12-2 will be displayed when the file opens.

FIGURE 12-2

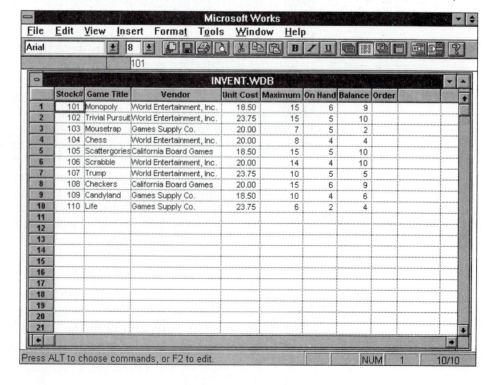

As mentioned earlier, when viewed in List format, this database file strongly resembles a spreadsheet. As you will see, however, the database form has some distinct advantages over the spreadsheet for inventory purposes.

UNDERSTANDING A CALCULATED FIELD

Notice that the Order field is blank for all records. (If you cannot see the Order field, use the horizontal scroll arrows to bring it into view.) Now, direct your attention to the Balance field. This is a *calculated field.* It contains a formula that is based on other fields in the database. Whenever one of those other fields changes, the value displayed in the calculated field also changes (exactly as they do in spreadsheets).

You are going to change the Order field to a calculated field and add another new calculated field before you print your reports.

IT'S YOUR TURN

1. Click on the number 9 under the Balance field name.

   The Balance Field for Stock #101 will be displayed, as shown in Figure 12-3.

Formula Displayed in Formula Bar   Value Displayed in Cell

FIGURE 12-3

	Stock#	Game Title	Vendor	Unit Cost	Maximum	On Hand	Balance	Order	
1	101	Monopoly	World Entertainment, Inc.	18.50	15	6	9		
2	102	Trivial Pursuit	World Entertainment, Inc.	23.75	15	5	10		
3	103	Mousetrap	Games Supply Co.	20.00	7	5	2		
4	104	Chess	World Entertainment, Inc.	20.00	8	4	4		
5	105	Scattergories	California Board Games	18.50	15	5	10		
6	106	Scrabble	World Entertainment, Inc.	20.00	14	4	10		
7	107	Trump	World Entertainment, Inc.	23.75	10	5	5		
8	108	Checkers	California Board Games	20.00	15	6	9		
9	109	Candyland	Games Supply Co.	18.50	10	4	6		
10	110	Life	Games Supply Co.	23.75	6	2	4		

Microsoft Works — File Edit View Insert Format Tools Window Help — Arial — =Maximum-On Hand — INVENT.WDB — Press ALT to choose commands, or F2 to edit. — NUM — 1 — 10/10

A calculated field displays the result of a calculation based upon the contents of other fields. Notice in Figure 12-3 that while the selected cell simply shows the number 9, the Formula bar contains the formula that occupies that cell and calculates the displayed value (=Maximum – On Hand). The = (equal) symbol is used to introduce formulas or functions. The formula indicates that the value stored in the On Hand field is to be subtracted from the value stored in the Maximum field and that the result is to be stored in the Balance field. Maximum and On Hand are called operands; the minus symbol is called the operator. (Operands and operators were introduced in Chapter 6).

In addition to making up your own formulas, you can also use *WORKS* functions (also introduced in Chapter 6) in a calculated database field. You can use a number, a formula, a field name, or another function as an argument in a database calculated field. You can use almost all of the functions you used in spreadsheets, but you cannot use a range value as an argument in a database function. We will return to the discussion of functions later in this chapter when we work with the Order field. For now, let's continue with adding a new calculated field.

INSERTING A NEW FIELD

You need a new field in the database—the Total Cost of each game to be ordered. Since the new field will contain a calculation, you will designate it as a numeric field.

IT'S YOUR TURN

Although it is possible to insert a field in List view, it is easier to use the Form view. In Form view, you can place the field where you want it. New fields inserted in List view seem to occupy random positions when viewed in Form view and have to be moved and reformatted before they can be used in Form view.

1. Click the FORM VIEW button on the toolbar.

2. Click at the left margin immediately below the Order field name to place the insertion point.

3. Choose Arial from the Font Name drop-down box and 10 from the Font Size drop-down box; then click the BOLD button on the toolbar to finish formatting the field name.

4. Click the INSERT FIELD button (third icon from the right) in the toolbar.

When the Insert Field dialog box appears, with the insertion point blinking in the Name text box,

5. Type: Total Cost

6. Click OK or press [ENTER].

    The new field appears at the bottom of the form, with the Field Contents line highlighted. The field contents line now has the same character attributes as the field name (Arial 10 Bold).

To remove the Bold style from the highlighted field so the field contents will match the rest of the form,

7. Click the BOLD button on the toolbar.

    The Total Cost field should still be highlighted, with handles showing on the field.

8. Drag the Horizontal Resize handle in the middle of the right edge of the highlighted field to the left to reduce the field to about half of its original size.

With the field still highlighted,

9.   Choose Number from the FORMAT menu.

When the Number dialog box appears,

10.   Click the Comma option in the Format block.

Since this field will contain dollar and cent values, leave the Number of Decimals text box at 2.

11.   Click OK or press [ENTER].

Now that the field has been entered and properly formatted, you can return to the List view where you can see all the records.

12.   Click the LIST VIEW button on the toolbar.

The new field appears in the List view of the database to the right of the Order field. You may have to scroll a little to the right or resize the window to see the entire column.

CREATING THE CALCULATED FIELD FORMULA

To calculate the total cost for each game, you will multiply the Unit Cost field times the Order field. (*Note:* Both of these fields have already been designated as numeric.) Although you could type the formula, you may prefer the following "selection" method.

IT'S YOUR TURN

You should be in List view.

1.   Click the Total Cost field for the first record, if it is not already selected.

To introduce the formula,

2.   Type: =

The equals sign appears in the formula bar, with the insertion point immediately following it. Also note that the CANCEL and ENTRY buttons appear in the Formula bar.

To record Unit Cost into the formula,

3.   Click the Unit Cost field for the first record.

The Unit Cost field name appears immediately following the equals sign in the Formula bar, as well as in the Total Cost field for the first record.

To insert the multiplication operator,

4.   Type: *

To multiply by the Order field,

5.   Click the Order field (presently empty) for the first record.

The formula is now complete. It should read "= unit cost*order"

6. Click the ENTRY button or press [ENTER].

Note that the Total Cost field is still selected. However, since individual database fields must be the same for all records, values for all records appear in the Total Cost field. Also note that the formula is showing in the Formula bar and that all records contain zeros in the Total Cost field. They contain zeros because one of the operand fields, Order, is still undefined. As soon as it is defined in the next section, amounts will display.

USING THE IF FUNCTION IN THE DATABASE

You will recall that you were introduced to the IF statement when you studied the Spreadsheet tool. An IF statement is also needed in this database to determine how many games of each type should be ordered. The database Menu bar does not contain an Insert Function command like the spreadsheet Menu bar, so to refresh your memory, we will tell you that the format for the IF function is

=IF(condition,ValueIfTrue,ValueIfFalse)

When you wish to use a function in a database and cannot remember its format, you can always use the HELP menu.

IT'S YOUR TURN

1. Click on the column header for the Order field.

   The entire column becomes highlighted to show that this field is selected in all records of the database. Note that the Formula bar is blank.

2. Choose Number from the FORMAT menu, and use the skills you have learned in this chapter to format this field as a Comma field with zero decimal places. Put away the Number dialog box by clicking OK or pressing [ENTER] when you have finished making the proper selections.

   You will be returned to List view.

3. Click the Order field in the first record.

   You will insert the following function to calculate the number of each game to order,

   =If(Balance>3,Balance,0)

   Translated, this formula means that if the amount in the Balance field (amount sold since the last order) is greater than three, then insert the Balance value in the Order field. If the Balance is not greater than three, insert a zero in the Order field.

4. Type: =IF(

5. Click the Balance field in the first record to insert the field name into the formula.

6. Type: >3,

7. Click the Balance field for the first record again.

8. Type: ,0)

The Formula bar should now contain the complete formula. It should read =If(Balance >3,Balance,0).

To confirm the formula and complete the entry,

9. Click the ENTRY button or press [ENTER].

    Now you can see values in both the Order and Total Cost columns. As you can see from your screen, the only game that has not sold more than three is Mousetrap. As a result, all of the games except Mousetrap should be included in the next order. Check the values to be sure the logic of the IF function is correct.

CHANGING A FIELD NAME

The field name Balance is somewhat ambiguous and should be changed. This field really represents the number of games sold during the current inventory period. To change the field name,

IT'S YOUR TURN

1. Click on the column header for the Balance field.

    That entire column becomes selected.

2. Choose Field Name from the EDIT menu.

    The Field Name dialog box appears with Balance highlighted in the Name box.

3. Type: Amt Sold

4. Click OK or press [ENTER].

5. Adjust the width of the Amt Sold column so you can see the entire field name.

6. Click on one of the numbers in the Order column, and look at the Formula bar to verify that the name change from Balance to Amt Sold is also reflected in the formula controlling the amount to order.

CREATING A REPORT

When you are in List view or Form view, you can only print the records of your database that are currently active. In List view you can also elect to print gridlines and record and field labels by selecting those options from the Page Setup dialog box. The Page Setup dialog box for Form view allows you to select to print more than one record on a page or to limit printing to field entries only. These printing capabilities are fine for certain situations, but they do not satisfy the need to rearrange or limit the fields printed. You also cannot print totals or other summary values from either List or Form view. However, report view gives you the tools to make such reports.

Report view allows you to design a report for printing that either includes every record in the file or only selected records and/or fields. When you print reports, you can group items in the database by category and create subtotals of each category. In this chapter, you will create two reports. The first report will include the entire database, showing games in each group with subtotals representing the total cost information per vendor. The second report will consist of selected fields and selected records of the database.

IT'S YOUR TURN

To begin defining the first report,

1. Click the REPORT VIEW button on the toolbar, or choose Create New Report from the TOOLS Menu.

   The New Report dialog box will appear with the insertion point blinking in the Report Title text box, as shown in Figure 12-4.

FIGURE 12-4

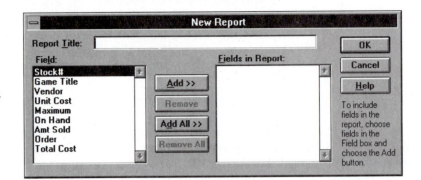

2. Type: Board Games Inventory

   This report name will be printed on the first page of the report.
   The Field list box contains the names of all the fields in the database. You can select the fields you wish to include in the report.

Since you want all fields included in this first report,

3. Click the ADD ALL button.

4. Click the OK button or press [ENTER].

   The Report Statistics dialog box shown in Figure 12-5 will appear.

FIGURE 12-5

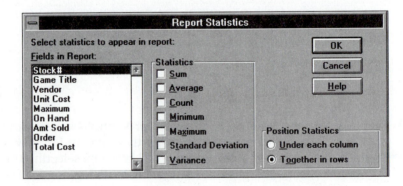

To have *WORKS* calculate the total cost if you ordered all of the games,

5. Click Total Cost in the Fields in Report list box.

6. Click Sum in the Statistics block.

7. Click Under Each Column in the Position Statistics block.

8. Click the OK button or press [ENTER].

   An information box appears, which offers you the opportunity to see your report by using the Print Preview screen.

9. Click the OK button in the information box.

The information box goes away, and you can now see the Report Definition view (REPORT displays in the lower right corner). (See Figure 12-6.)

FIGURE 12-6

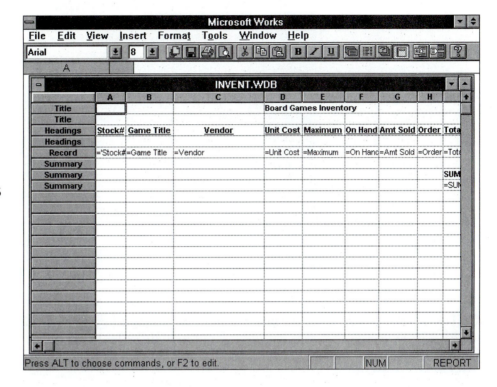

The items that are displayed in bold type on your screen will be printed on the report just as you see them on the screen. Those not displayed in bold are codes for selecting items from the database.

The two Title rows contain information that will be printed on the first page of the report. The first one contains the report title, and the second one is blank to separate the title from the rest of the report.

The Heading rows will appear at the top of every page of the report. There are two Heading rows. The first one contains field names that will be printed, and the second one is blank to separate the headings from the rest of the report.

The Record row contains codes that will cause the contents of the named fields to be printed. Even though there is only one record row, one line will be printed on the report for every record in the database.

The Summary rows will be printed at the end of the report.

10. If necessary, use the right horizontal scroll arrow to display column I so you can see the format of the summary rows shown in Figure 12-7.

Note that there are three Summary rows. The first one is blank to leave space between the body of the report and the calculated sum. The second Summary row only contains the word "Sum": in column I. The third Summary row contains the code that will cause the calculated total of all values in the Total Cost column to be printed.

FIGURE 12-7

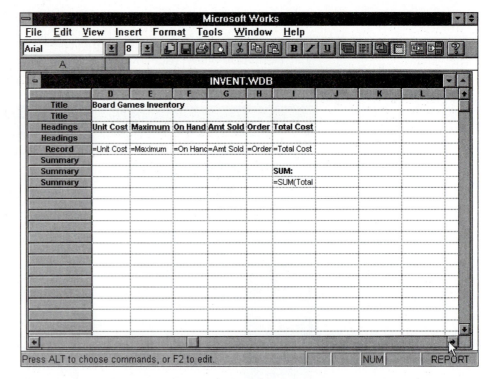

SORTING THE DATABASE FOR THE REPORT

In *WORKS,* sorting can be done in any view. Since the database may have been left in an inappropriate order by another report, you should include a sorting step every time a report is created.

IT'S YOUR TURN

With the database in Report Definition view,

1. Choose Sort Records from the TOOLS menu.

When the Sort Records dialog box appears,

2. Choose Stock # from the drop-down list in the 1st Field block.
3. Choose the Ascend option in the 1st Field block.
4. Click OK or press [ENTER].

To view the report as it will look when printed,

5. Click the PRINT PREVIEW button on the toolbar.

When the print preview screen appears,

6. Use the ZOOM buttons to examine it more closely.

You will not print the report at this time.

7. Click the CANCEL button to return to the Report Definition view.

NAMING AND SAVING THE REPORT

Before you save and print the report, you will add a footer with your name and the date. *WORKS 3.0* automatically stores the report definition with the database document from which it retrieved the information. Normally you would use the Save option, and the report definitions would be saved with it. However, since you will be using the original *INVENT* file for later exercises, you will use Save As and save this file under a different name.

IT'S YOUR TURN

1. Choose Headers and Footers from the VIEW menu.

2. Press [TAB] to advance to the Footer text box.

3. Type: &LYOUR NAME&R&D

4. Click OK or press [ENTER].

5. Choose Name Report from the TOOLS menu.

The Name Report dialog box appears, as shown in Figure 12-8.

FIGURE 12-8

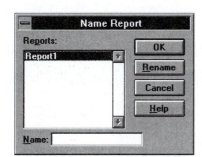

Since there is only one report, it has been given the generic name *Report1* and is highlighted in the Reports list box.

6. Press [TAB] to advance the insertion point to the Name text box.

Report names are limited to fifteen characters.

7. Type: BoardGameInvent

8. Click the RENAME button.

9. Click the OK button or press [ENTER].

Now you are ready to save the file and print the report.

10. Choose Save As from the FILE menu, and save the file as *INVENT2* in your name directory on your data disk.

11. If directed to do so, choose Print from the FILE menu and click the OK button when the Print dialog box appears, or click the PRINT button on the toolbar to bypass the Print dialog box.

This has been a long lesson. If you decide to end your session at this point, close your file and quit *WORKS* as usual. If you wish to continue working, go on to the next section.

MORE SCENE-SETTING

PROJECT 2 Vendor Report

As mentioned at the beginning of this chapter, you will be creating a second report using the same database. This second report, identifying the board games to be ordered and the vendors with which to place the order, will use only a portion of the *INVENT2* database. You will create a query to limit the items included in the report to only those games with a nonzero order amount. Also, you will not include all the fields in this report.

IT'S YOUR TURN

1. If *INVENT2* is not open, open it now.

2. If the file does not display in List view, click the LIST VIEW button on the toolbar.

SELECTING RECORDS FOR A REPORT

You may recall that one of the games in your inventory list did not need to be ordered. You can verify that the Mousetrap game is not to be ordered by looking at the Order field for the Mousetrap record in the list showing on your screen.

IT'S YOUR TURN

To eliminate Mousetrap from the report you will prepare,

1. Choose Create New Query from the TOOLS menu.

   The New Query dialog box will appear.

2. Double click Query1 in the Please Give This Query a Name text box.

3. Type: NonZeroOrders

4. Click Order in the drop-down list box in the Choose A Field To Compare section.

5. Click Is Not Equal To in the drop-down list box in the How To Compare The Field section.

6. Press [TAB] to advance the insertion point to the Value To Compare The Field To text box.

7. Type: 0 (zero)

   Your dialog box should look like the one shown in Figure 12-9.

FIGURE 12-9

New Query
Please give this query a name: NonZeroOrders
Create query sentences below, and then choose Apply Now to see all records that match the criteria.

Choose a field to compare:	How to compare the field:	Value to compare the field to:
A. Order	B. is not equal to	E. 0

○ And
○ Or

F.	G.	I.

○ And
○ Or

J.	K.	L.

| Clear | Apply Now | Query View | Cancel | Help |

8. Click the APPLY NOW button.

   You will be returned to the List view screen, where you can see that the Mousetrap record is not among the ones that are now displayed.

**CREATING THE
SECOND REPORT**

Now that you have the records selected, you can proceed with the report.

IT'S YOUR TURN

1. Choose Create New Report from the TOOLS menu.

    The New Report dialog box appears, with the insertion point blinking in the Report Title box.

2. **Type:** The Fun Factory Order List

In the first report, you wanted to print the entire database; however, this time you want this new report to contain only the Stock #, Game Title, Unit Cost, Order, Total Cost, and Vendor fields (in that order) for the games that need to be ordered.

   To select the fields for the report,

3. If necessary, click Stock # in the Field list box.

4. Click the ADD button.

5. Click Game Title in the Field list box, and click the ADD button.

6. Click the Unit Cost field name and the ADD button.

7. Click the Order field name and the ADD button.

8. Click the Total Cost field name and the ADD button.

9. Click the Vendor field name and the ADD button.

    The completed New Report dialog box should look like the one shown in Figure 12-10.

FIGURE 12-10

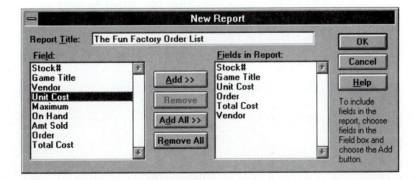

10. Click the OK button or press [ENTER].

When the Report Statistics dialog box appears,

11. Click Total Cost in the Fields in Report list box.

12. Click the Sum option in the Statistics block.

13. Click the Under Each Column option in the Position Statistics block.

14. Click OK or press [ENTER].

    The Information box appears, telling you that the report definition has been created.

15. Click the OK button or press [ENTER].

The report definition for the second report is displayed on your screen. To see what this report would look like if it were printed now,

16.   Click the PRINT PREVIEW button on the toolbar.

When the Print Preview screen appears,

17.   Zoom in to examine the report more closely.

There are still several changes that need to be made to the report to complete it. You need to center the title, sort the report by vendors, and create subtotals for each vendor.

18.   Click the CANCEL button to return to the Report Definition screen.

To sort the report and create subtotals,

19.   Choose Sort Records from the TOOLS menu.

When the Sort Records dialog box appears, the insertion point is blinking in the 1st Field block text box,

20.   Click Vendor in the 1st Field drop-down list.

Since the Ascend option is already selected in this block, you will not change it. There is, however, another option in this block that you must select. It is the Break option, which causes *WORKS* to create a subtotal whenever any part of the sort field changes.

21.   Click the Break option in the 1st Field block.

With the Break option selected, the final option in this block becomes available. Selecting the 1st Letter option will cause *WORKS* to create the subtotal only when the first letter of the sort field changes. You will not select the 1st Letter option, because the subtotal for this report should be calculated when any part of the sort field changes.

22.   Click OK or press [ENTER].

FORMATTING AND PRINTING THE REPORT

You will not change fonts, sizes, or styles for this report, but you can make those changes for each field if you wish. Fields in the Report Definition will take on any changes you specify. This report contains some unnecessary statistics, which you will remove. It would also look better if the title were more centered and some blank lines were inserted.

IT'S YOUR TURN

The title needs to be centered over the entire width instead of being over near the right edge. To achieve that appearance,

1.   Click the title in column F of the Title row.

2.   Choose Cut from the EDIT menu.

3.   Click the empty field in column C of the first Title row.

4. Choose Paste from the EDIT menu.

    The Report Definition should resemble the one shown in Figure 12-11.

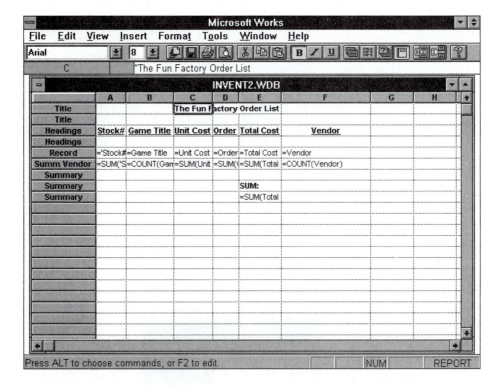

FIGURE 12-11

Note that a new line has been inserted just below the Record line. It is labeled Summ Vendor, and it contains codes that will cause *WORKS* to calculate sums for all dollar fields and to count the number of items for all other fields whenever the first letter of the Vendor field changes. Since you only want the sum for the Total Cost field to be calculated, you will delete the codes from all other fields in the Summ Vendor line.

5. Drag to select the fields in the Summ Vendor line in columns A through D.

6. Choose Clear from the EDIT menu.

7. Click column F in the Summ Vendor line, and choose Clear from the EDIT menu.

To see how your report looks now,

8. Click the PRINT PREVIEW button on the toolbar, and zoom in to examine the Print Preview screen more closely.

The following changes would make the report look better: A line separating the subtotals from the grouping above them, a blank line after each subtotal, and centering the entire report on the page. The rest of the steps in this section will achieve these changes. To return to the Report Definition screen,

9. Click the CANCEL button.

To create the line separating the subtotals from the groupings above them,

10. Click the field containing the sum code in the Summ Vendors line.

11. Choose Border from the FORMAT menu.

When the Border dialog box appears,

12. Click the Top option in the Border block.

13. Click the OK button or press [ENTER].

You will be returned to the Report Definition screen, where you may be able to see the line between the entries in column E on the Record line and the Summ Vendor line.

To insert a blank line following each subtotal,

14. Click the row header for the first Summary line.

15. Choose Row/Column from the INSERT menu.

The Insert Row dialog box shown in Figure 12-12 will appear.

FIGURE 12-12

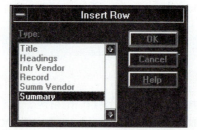

Since you want the blank line to be printed every time a subtotal is printed,

16. Click the Summ Vendor line name in the Type block, then click OK or press [ENTER].

You are returned to the report definition with a new blank Summ Vendor line inserted and highlighted.

17. Click in any empty field to deselect the line.

It is not necessary to print the word "Sum" above the final total for the Total Cost column, so you will eliminate it.

18. Click the row header for the Summary line that contains the word "Sum" in column E.

The entire line becomes highlighted.

19. Choose Cut from the EDIT menu.

To label the final total,

20. Click in column C of the Summary line that contains the sum formula.

21. Type: TOTAL ORDER

22. Press [ENTER].

To create a line dividing the final total from the rest of the report,

23. Click the field containing the sum formula in the second Summary line.

24. Choose Border from the FORMAT menu, click the option labeled Top in the Border block of the dialog box, then click OK or press [ENTER] to return to the report definition.

You are almost finished. The only thing left to do is to change the margins so the report will be better centered on the page.

25. Choose Page Setup from the FILE menu, and click the Margins tab if it is not currently visible.

26. Press [TAB] twice to advance to the Left Margin text box.

27. Type: 2

28. Press [TAB] to advance to the Right Margin text box.

29. Type: 2

30. Click OK or press [ENTER].

   Once again, you are returned to the report definition screen. If you wish, you can use Print Preview again to check the appearance of your report.

FINISHING UP PROJECT 2

You are now ready to add a footer, then name, save and print the report.

IT'S YOUR TURN

1. Create a footer with your name on the left and the date on the right.

2. Choose Name Report from the TOOLS menu.

When the Name Report dialog box appears,

3. If it is not already selected, click Report1 in the Reports list box to select it.

4. Press [TAB] to advance to the Name text box.

5. Type: Order List

6. Click the RENAME button, then click the OK button or press [ENTER].

7. If you are directed to print, click the PRINT button on the toolbar.

Printing should begin shortly. Your copy should be similar to the copy shown in Figure 12-1b.

8. Click the LIST VIEW button on the toolbar to leave the report definition.

You may be surprised to see that the database is still in order by vendors and that the query is still in effect.

To eliminate the query and change the sort order back to stock number order,

9. Choose Show All Records from the VIEW menu.

10. Choose Sort Records from the TOOLS menu, and sort the database in ascending order by the Stock # field.

11. Choose Save from the FILE menu.

12. Quit *WORKS,* as directed in previous chapters.

SUMMARY

In this chapter you have learned how easy it is to create and print customized reports from your *WORKS 3.0* database. In addition to the skills you learned earlier, you are now able to select records and fields for a database report, create calculated fields, use formulas, sort records, specify totals and subtotals, and add labels to the report.

REVIEW QUESTIONS

1. Which form is recommended when inserting new fields?

2. Which menu do you use to designate a field as numeric?

3. Which view does not allow sorting of records?

4. What is a calculated field?

5. How do you get a total printed for a field?

EXERCISES

EXERCISE 12-1   Sorting and creating a report using part of a database file, formatting, and printing using the *PROFILE* file

1. Open the *PROFILE* file from your data disk.

2. Create a report with Last Name, First Name, and Pay Rate. Title the report PAY RATE.

3. Sort the report definition by pay rate.

4. Select All and change font size to 14 point, then choose Page Setup to change the document's top margin to two inches and left and right margins to one inch.

5. Move the title to column B. (You may have to scroll to see the title.)

6. Increase the width of columns A and B to 20 and the Pay Rate to 10.

7. Add a footer with the current date on the left and your name on the right.

8. Preview and print the report.

9. Rename Report1 as "Pay Rate," and save the file as *EX12-1* in your name directory on your data disk.

EXERCISE 12-2   Sorting and creating a report using the entire database file, formatting the report, typing a footer, and printing from the *REFER file*

1. Open the *REFER* file from the *EXERCISE* directory of your data disk.

2. Create a report using the Last Name, First Name, and Birth Month fields. Title the report BIRTHDAY LIST.

3. Sort the report by the Last Name field.

4. Use the Page Setup option from the FILE menu to change the top margin to two inches.

5. Change font size for the entire report to 14.

6. Move the title to column B.

7. Increase the width of Last and First Name columns to 18 and the Birth Month to 15.

8. Left align the column headings. Also, left align the months in column C.

9. Type a footer with the current date on the left and your name on the right.

10. Rename the report "Birth Month," and save the file as *EX12-2* in your name directory on your data disk.

11. Preview and print the report.

EXERCISE 12-3   Creating a report using part of a database, selecting certain records, adding a footer and header, changing the top margin, and formatting the fields

1. Open the *INVENT* file from your data disk.

2. Create a query to select only records of World Entertainment, Inc. (Type an appropriate name for your query.)

3. Create a report with only the Stock #, Game Title, Vendor, and On Hand fields. Title the report WORLD ENTERTAINMENT LIST.

4. Use Page Setup to change the top margin to two inches, and the left margin to 1.5 inches.

5. Change font size of all fields to 12.

6. Increase the Game Title column to 15, Vendor column to 25, and Stock # and On Hand to 8.

7. Move the title to column C and center align it. Center align column headings and Stock # and On Hand columns.

8. Type a footer with the date on the left and your name on the right.

9. Rename the report as "WorldEnt," and save the file as *EX12-3* in your name directory on your data disk.

10. Preview and print.

Database 4

OBJECTIVES

In this chapter, you will learn to

- *use database keyboard shortcuts*
- *copy within and between documents*
- *copy a file format*
- *divide a window into panes*
- *Use Microsoft Note-It*

SETTING THE SCENE

As you worked with the *PROFILE*, *MEMBERS*, and *INVENT* databases in the previous chapters, you probably thought of several modifications you would have made if you had designed them. You can use this chapter to guide you in making those files more meaningful. Or, if you feel confident, you can design a completely different database!

This chapter gives you an opportunity to explore the *WORKS 3.0* database application on your own. You will notice that the instructions in this chapter are less precise and leave more to your imagination. See how much of what you have learned you can apply to one project.

GETTING STARTED

Since it is always easier to learn an application by working with it, you should open the database file *PROFILE*, so you can experiment with the features being presented.

DATABASE SHORTCUTS

As with *WORKS 3.0* word processing and spreadsheets, you can use keyboard shortcuts to invoke many commands. By now, you probably are using many shortcuts. The following table lists some of the database keyboard shortcuts; others can be found in the *WORKS* on-line Help document by following the steps given in Chapter 9.

Keys For Editing and Changing Text

To Achieve This Result	Press These Keys
Edit selected field	[F2]
Copy the content of above field (List view)	[CTRL] + ['] (apostrophe)

To Achieve This Result	Press These Keys
Go To	[F5]
Make text bold	[CTRL] + [B]
Make text italic	[CTRL] + [I]
Underline text	[CTRL] + [U]
Remove all font styles	[CTRL] + [SPACEBAR]
Repeat format	[SHIFT] + [F7]
Apply Comma format	[CTRL] + [,] (comma)
Apply Currency format	[CTRL] + [4]
Apply Percent format	[CTRL] + [5]
Apply Query	[F3]

Keys for Highlighting Database and Reporting Information

When you highlight, the background behind the selection changes color. You can then change the selection. Use the following keyboard shortcuts to highlight in a database or report.

To Highlight This	Press These Keys
A record (list view) or row (report view)	[CTRL] + [F8]
A field (list view) or column (report view)	[SHIFT] + [F8]
An entire database (list view or report view)	[CTRL] + [SHIFT] + [F8]

To Extend the Highlight in This Direction (List or Report Views)	Press These Keys
To the beginning of record or row	[SHIFT] + [HOME]
To the end of record or row	[SHIFT] + [END]
To the beginning of database or report	[CTRL] + [SHIFT] + [HOME]
To the end of database or report	[CTRL] + [SHIFT] + [END]
In any Direction	[F8] [ARROW KEYS]

**To Extend the Highlight in This Direction
(List or Report Views)**   **Press These Keys**

Quit extending after using F8   [ESC]

Cancel an extended selection   [ESC]

Keys for Moving Around in a Database or Report
Use the following keyboard shortcuts to move the insertion point within a database or report.

To Move	Press
Left through the database or report	[LEFT ARROW]
Right through the database or report	[RIGHT ARROW]
To previous field	[SHIFT] + [TAB]
To next field	[TAB]
To the beginning of database (first field or record)	[CTRL] + [HOME]
To the end of database (last field or record)	[CTRL] + [END]
Up one field, record, or line	[UP ARROW]
Down one field, record, or line	[DOWN ARROW]
Go to a particular field or record	[F5]
Switch between Form view and List view	[F9]

To Move in List View	Press
To the beginning of record	[HOME]
To the end of record	[END]
Left to the first field	[CTRL] + [LEFT ARROW]
Right to the last field	[CTRL] + [RIGHT ARROW]

To Move in Form View	Press
To the left edge of a form	[HOME]
To the right edge of a form	[END]

To Move in Form View	Press
To the previous record	[CTRL] + [PAGE UP]
To the next record	[CTRL] + [PAGE DOWN]

Keys for Aligning Text or Cells
Use the following keyboard shortcuts to change the alignment of highlighted fields in a document.

To	Press
Center text	[CTRL] + [E]
Left align text	[CTRL] + [L]
Right align text	[CTRL] + [R]
General alignment	[CTRL] + [G]

USING THE TOOLBAR

The toolbar is a useful way to switch between views, insert fields and records, and quickly change the appearance of a database. If the toolbar is not already showing, you can display it by choosing Toolbar from the VIEW menu.

Spend some time playing with the toolbar until you are certain that you know how each tool works.

COPYING INFORMATION

You can copy within and between documents. Copying saves retyping the same information when you need it in more than one place. You can copy a record, field, or single entry, or you can copy a block of records, fields, or entries. For example, you might have in a database two people who live at the same address. You can save time by copying the address and phone number fields from the first person's record into the second person's record.

Although you can copy in both List and Form views, copying is easier in a List window, because you can then copy multiple records or fields at one time. The next three sections lead you through the copying process.

COPYING A RECORD

To copy a record within the same database,

IT'S YOUR TURN

1. Make sure you are in a List window.
2. Click on the row header box to the left of the record you want to copy.

   The entire record will become highlighted.
3. Choose Copy from the EDIT menu.
4. Click on the row header box to the left of the empty row in which you want the copy to appear.

Remember that because you are copying an entire record, the receiving fields must match the sending fields (e.g., a text field cannot be pasted into a numeric field).

  5.   Choose Paste from the EDIT menu.

COPYING A SINGLE ENTRY

You can copy a single field into any other field of any record in any database, whether or not the sending field and the receiving field are compatible formats.

IT'S YOUR TURN

To copy a single field,

  1.   Select (highlight) the field you want to copy.
  2.   Choose Copy from the EDIT menu.
  3.   Select the receiving field.
  4.   Choose Paste from the EDIT menu.

At times you might want to copy a single field entry into the same field of one or more records below. To accomplish this quickly,

  5.   In List view, drag to highlight the field you want to copy plus the fields below that you want to receive the copy.
  6.   Choose Fill Down from the EDIT menu.

COPYING A BLOCK OF FIELDS

To copy a block of adjacent fields,

IT'S YOUR TURN

  1.   Make sure you are in the List view.
  2.   Select the block you want to copy by dragging until all desired fields are highlighted.
  3.   Choose Copy from the EDIT menu.
  4.   Click the field in the upper left corner of the block that is to receive the copy.
  5.   Choose Paste from the EDIT menu.

COPYING A FILE FORMAT

If the database you are creating is similar to another existing database, you can use the old one to create the new one. For example, suppose you need a vendor mailing list. You can copy the format of your old *MEMBERS* file and then modify it to suit your new Vendors file. (If you did not create the *MEMBERS* file earlier, you can use the file named *REFER* instead.)

IT'S YOUR TURN

  1.   Open *MEMBERS* from your personal directory (or *REFER* from the Exercise Directory) on your data disk, and put it in List view.
  2.   Choose Select All from the EDIT menu or press [CTRL] + [SHIFT] + [F8] to select the entire database.

3. Choose Clear Field Entry from the EDIT menu.

   You have erased the data in each record.

4. Move the pointer to the column header for the Last Name field and click once.

   The entire column will be highlighted.

5. Choose Field Name from the EDIT menu.

   A dialog box appears.

6. Type: VENDOR

7. Click OK or press [ENTER].

8. Click on the column header for the First Name field.

9. Choose Delete Record/Field from the INSERT menu.

   The field is deleted and the Street Address column becomes highlighted. You will retain that field.

10. Click on the column header for the Birth Month field to select that column.

11. Choose Delete Record/Field from the INSERT menu.

    The Birth Month field is deleted, and you are left with five columns representing the fields Vendor, Street Address, City, State, and Zip

12. Increase the size of the first three columns (Vendor, Street Address, and City) so that the State and ZIP columns move to the far right of the screen.

13. Choose Save As from the FILE menu. Save your newly designed file as Vendors in your name directory on your data disk.

    The new database is now ready to be used.

USING TEXT IN A FORMULA

Suppose you have a database file of addresses, all from the same state. Instead of typing the state abbreviation over and over, you can use a text formula to enter it automatically. To enter the state abbreviation "CA" in the state field of all records, simply select one state field and enter the formula ="CA". That abbreviation will then appear in all records. If you need to change one or more of the records, you can easily do so by using normal editing techniques.

DIVIDING A LIST WINDOW INTO PANES

Sometimes a database has so many fields and/or records that it becomes difficult to compare information in distant fields and records. To make it easier, you can divide a List window into side-by-side and/or top-and-bottom panes by dragging on the horizontal and vertical split bars as you did with spreadsheets.

USING NOTE-IT

From the Word Processor and Database (Form view), you can use Microsoft Note-It to annotate your documents with pop-up notes. Note-It creates reminders for yourself, notes to colleagues, or instructions to users about how to use a particular document.

You can move a Note-It note, copy it, or delete it. When you print a document that contains notes, *WORKS* prints the Note-It icon but does not include the text of the note. You can also change the Note-It picture that appears in your document. You will now use Note-It to add a short note to one of your database files.

IT'S YOUR TURN

1. If your *VENDORS* file is not already open, open it.

2. Switch to Form view.

3. Click to position the insertion point under the last field (ZIP).

4. Choose Note-It from the INSERT menu.

When the Note-It dialog box appears, the Caption box will be highlighted.

5. Type: Hint.

Your screen should now resemble Figure 13-1.

FIGURE 13-1

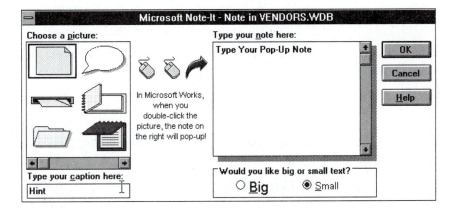

6. Select an icon from the Choose a Picture box.

7. Press [TAB] until the highlight moves to the Type Your Note box and type:

    Click on the USE A TEMPLATE button in the Startup dialog box for ready-made templates whenever you need a form quickly.

8. Click the Small option for the size of the text.

    Your dialog box should resemble Figure 13-2.

FIGURE 13-2

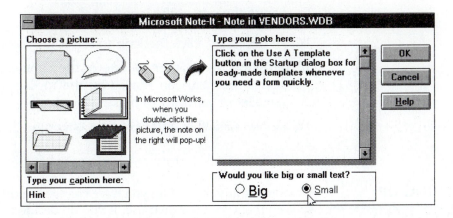

9. Click the OK button.

Your note icon now appears at the end of the file, surrounded by handles. To see the note:

10. Double click on the icon. Your screen will resemble Figure 13-3.

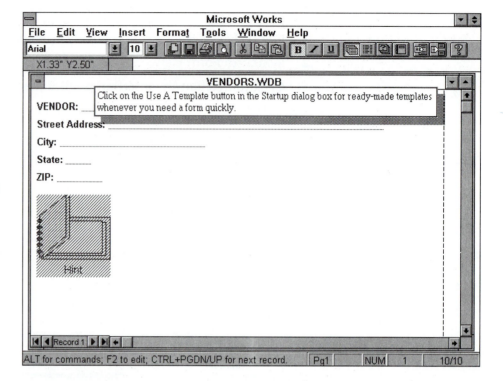

FIGURE 13-3

To hide the note:

11. Click anywhere outside the icon.

To edit your text,

12. If necessary, select your icon (handles appear).

13. Choose Microsoft Note-It Object from the EDIT menu, and select Edit from the pop-up box, which will appear on the right of the menu..

14. Make any changes you wish.

15. Click the OK button.

To change the size of the icon,

16. If necessary, click the icon to select it (handles appear).

17. Position the pointer on one of the handles. The word "resize" indicates that you can now drag the mouse inward to make the icon smaller or outward to make it larger.

18. Close *VENDORS* and save your changes.

FINISHING UP

Do not save any of the files you have changed in this chapter unless you want to keep them for your own use. If you do decide to save anything, be sure to use a different filename than the original one.

SUMMARY

As you can see, there are many possibilities for using a database. You can use it to compile and manipulate lists of any kind of information. You can use it to calculate new data and to provide a basis for more databases. You can use it as a research and report tool. For more information, select Help from the WINDOW menu or refer to the *WORKS 3.0* manual.

REVIEW QUESTIONS

1. What special key is used most often with letter keys to invoke menu options from the keyboard?

2. If you were in List view and you wanted to see a specific record in Form view, what would you do to switch directly to the desired record?

3. Following is the sequence of steps for copying a record within the same database. Fill in the missing steps.

   a. Select the record to be copied.

   b. _____.

   c. _____.

   d. Choose Paste from the EDIT menu.

4. What is the keyboard command that could substitute for step d in question 3?

5. Which WORKS tools support Note-It?

EXERCISE

Use WorksWizards or Templates to create a new database on any subject of your choice—perhaps a research bibliography or reference notes, a tape or CD collection, or a household inventory.

14

Advanced Tasks 1: Drawing

OBJECTIVES

When you finish this chapter you will be able to

- ■ *use MICROSOFT DRAW while creating a word processing document*
- ■ *identify draw tools*
- ■ *draw shapes and lines*
- ■ *move objects*
- ■ *resize objects*
- ■ *correct mistakes*
- ■ *fill objects with color or patterns*
- ■ *copy and paste objects*
- ■ *type and place objects*
- ■ *use the WordArt accessory*

INTRODUCTION

WORKS 3.0 includes some versatile tools used to enhance a document with drawings and special effects. On the simplest level, you can draw boxes around text or numbers, add arrows to label items in charts, or draw diagrams to add emphasis to documents created by any other *WORKS* module. You can also insert charts and spreadsheet tables, use the built-in ClipArt gallery, use the WordArt program to create special effects for text, and use the *MICROSOFT DRAW* program to create original artwork for inclusion in a document.

MICROSOFT DRAW is a drawing program that can be used from within many Windows-based applications. The application from which you invoke *MICROSOFT DRAW* is called the **destination application**. When you finish a drawing in *MICROSOFT DRAW* and return to the destination application, the drawing is automatically inserted. *MICROSOFT DRAW* can be used to create new drawings and edit them, edit clip art, or to import and edit drawings created in other applications. Your first project in this chapter is to use *MICROSOFT DRAW* from the *WORKS 3.0* word processing module to create a new drawing.

WordArt is an accessory that is included with *MICROSOFT WORKS 3.0*, but it is not a separate program like *MICROSOFT DRAW*. You can use WordArt to create distinctive headlines and titles. You can position text vertically down the page, curve text around a circle, stretch letters to make them wider, or condense letters to make them taller. Your second project in this chapter uses WordArt to create a letterhead for The Fun Factory.

SETTING THE SCENE

PROJECT 1 The Map

You will be creating a map that can be used in company literature, which shows the location of your store in relation to nearby major streets. When you are finished, the map should resemble the map shown in Figure 14-1.

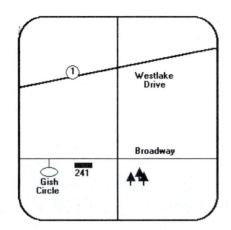

FIGURE 14-1

GETTING STARTED

It is extremely important that you read this chapter about draw before you begin working at the computer. Please pay special attention to the "Undoing a Mistake" section. Stop reading when you reach the section titled "Finishing Up the Map" (a reminder will appear at that point), and return to this section to begin following the detailed instructions for drawing the map.

If this is the first time you have used a draw program, do not despair if you do not succeed the first, second, or even third time. Your pictures may not be as good as you would like them to be, but you will improve with practice.

IT'S YOUR TURN

1. Launch *WORKS 3.0*.

   You can open *MICROSOFT DRAW* from a word processing window or a database Form view window. For this activity, you will use a word processing window.

The Startup dialog box should be on your screen, with the NEW & RECENT DOCUMENTS button selected. To open a blank word processing document,

2. Click the WORD PROCESSOR button in the Create A New block.

To place the insertion point in the center of the page where the drawing should appear,

3. Click the CENTER ALIGNMENT button on the toolbar.

To open *MICROSOFT DRAW*,

4. Choose Drawing from the INSERT menu.

   It will take a few moments for the *DRAW* window to open, as shown in Figure 14-2.

Note that *DRAW* has its own menu bar, which includes a HELP menu. Anytime you need help with the draw program, you can access it through this menu.

5. Click the MAXIMIZE button in the upper right corner of the *DRAW* window.

   The window will expand to fill the screen.

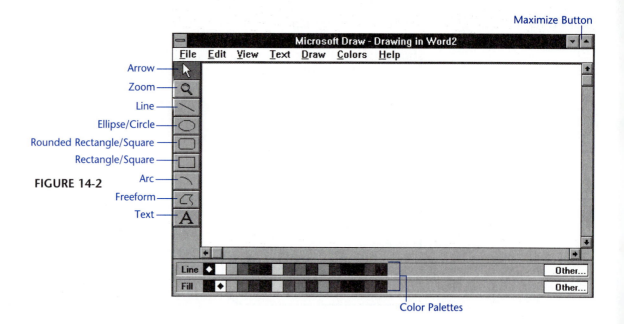

Maximize Button

Arrow
Zoom
Line
Ellipse/Circle
Rounded Rectangle/Square
Rectangle/Square
Arc
Freeform
Text

FIGURE 14-2

Color Palettes

GETTING ACQUAINTED WITH THE DRAW TOOLS

The tools in *MICROSOFT DRAW* are very similar to the tools available in other drawing programs. They enable you to draw various shapes in different line widths and to type text. They also provide options for changing the colors of shapes and text (if your computer monitor and/or printer have color capability), background patterns, and fonts (size and style). The tools are marked in Figure 14-2 and are described in the following table.

Tool	Function
Arrow	Is used for selecting and manipulating objects.
Zoom In/Zoom Out	Is used to change the magnification of a drawing. You can also use the VIEW menu to choose a specific level of magnification. There are seven levels of magnification—25%, 50%, 75%, Full Size, 200%, 400%, and 800%. When the Zoom In/Zoom Out tool is selected and you click on an object, the magnification increases one level. To decrease magnification, hold down [SHIFT] when you click.
Line Tool	Is used to draw straight lines. With the [CTRL] key held down, the line will be drawn from its center point. With the [SHIFT] key held down, the line will be constrained to the nearest 45-degree angle. With both the [CTRL] and [SHIFT] keys held down, the line will be drawn from the center and constrained to the nearest 45-degree angle.

Tool	Function
⬭ Ellipse/Circle Tool	Is used to draw ellipses and circles. With the [SHIFT] key down, a circle is produced. With the [CTRL] key down, the ellipse or circle is drawn from its center.
▢ Rounded Rectangle/Square Tool	Is used to draw rectangles and squares with rounded corners. The [SHIFT] key must be held down while dragging to produce squares with rounded corners. Holding down the [CTRL] key causes the rectangle or square to be drawn from the center.
▭ Rectangle/Square Tool	Is used to draw rectangles and squares with 90-degree corners. With the [SHIFT] key held down, the tool will draw a square, and with the [CTRL] key held down, the rectangle or square will be drawn from the center.
◥ Arc Tool	Is used to draw arcs that are 90-degree segments of ellipses. Arcs can be filled to create wedge shapes. Holding down the [SHIFT] key while using the Arc tool creates a 90-degree segment of a circle. Arcs can be edited by dragging to change the angle more or less than 90 degrees.
◿ Freeform Tool	Is used to draw closed or open polygons (with angles) or freehand objects (with curves), or combinations of angles and curves. Clicking the mouse causes a line to be generated; dragging creates curves.
A Text Tool	Is used to add a single line of text to a drawing.

DRAWING SHAPES AND LINES

Before drawing the map itself, you will draw a box to serve as a border for the map. You will be making some selections from the DRAW menu, which is shown in Figure 14-3.

FIGURE 14-3

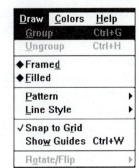

Note carefully the keyboard shortcuts that appear next to some of the commands. Keyboard shortcuts are especially helpful in a drawing program; you may want to try using them. The commands in the DRAW menu are explained in the following table.

Command	Function
Group [CTRL] + [G]	Is used to combine the selected objects in such a way that they can be treated as a single object. Grouped objects remain associated until you explicitly ungroup them.
Ungroup [CTRL] + [H]	Is used to change the selected grouped object back to its original state of several individual objects.
Framed	Certain objects can be drawn with or without a frame. If the Framed command is selected, a diamond will appear before it and any object that is drawn (except lines, bitmaps, and text) will include a frame. If Framed is not selected (no diamond) the object will not be framed. The frame color will be the same as the line color marked on the color palette.
Filled	Certain objects can be drawn filled with a color or a pattern. If the Filled command is selected, a diamond will appear before it, and any object that is drawn will be filled. If Filled is not selected (no diamond), the object will not be filled. The fill color is marked on the color palette.
Pattern	Choosing this command causes a pop-out menu to appear, from which you can select one of seven patterns to be used for filling.
Line Style	Choosing this command causes a pop-out menu to appear, from which you can select any one of five nonsolid line styles and six standard widths of solid lines. You can also customize the width of a solid line.
Snap To Grid	*DRAW* includes an invisible grid to align and place objects with precision. There are 12 grid lines per inch. If Snap To Grid is selected (there will be a check mark in front of it) even though you can't see the grid, any objects or groups that you create, move, or resize will snap to the nearest grid intersection. Snap To Grid is a toggled command; if it is on, clicking it will turn it off.
Show Guides [CTRL] + [W]	Guides are horizontal or vertical lines that can be used as a straightedge to align and place objects precisely. Guides can be dragged to any point on the screen. As you drag a guide, a readout tells you the distance in inches from the top left corner of the drawing area. When an object's edge or center gets close to a guide, that edge or center automatically snaps to the guide.

Command	Function
Rotate/Flip	Is used to rotate an object or a group of objects 90 degrees right or left.

IT'S YOUR TURN

1. Choose Show Guides from the DRAW menu.

    A vertical and a horizontal dotted line will appear on your screen, dividing the *DRAW* window into four quadrants, as shown in Figure 14-4.

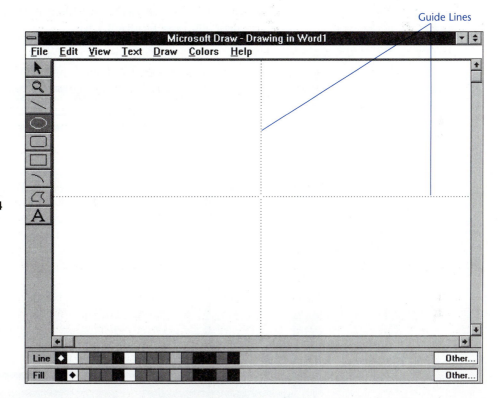

FIGURE 14-4

When you point to one of the lines and hold down the mouse button, a number appears, telling you the relative distance from the edge of the window (correct to three decimal places).

2. Point anywhere on the vertical guide line, hold down the mouse button, and note the number that appears with the small horizontal arrow pointing to the right.

    This is the middle of your screen in the horizontal direction. Ours says 3 inches, but yours may be different.

3. Point anywhere on the horizontal guide line, hold down the mouse button, and note the number that appears with the small downward pointing arrow.

    This is the middle of your screen in the vertical direction.

4. Click on the Rounded Rectangle/Square tool.

    The icon box becomes shaded, and your cursor will change to a crosshair when it enters the working area.

To give the lines of the box a little depth,

5. From the DRAW menu, choose 6 Point from the Line Style pop-out menu. If you have trouble getting to the pop-out menu, try the following steps:

   a. Click DRAW on the main menu bar to drop down that menu.

   b. Click the Line Style command to pop out that menu.

   c. Click the 6 point option.

6. To draw a square centered on the screen, position the crosshair at the center of the guidelines.

7. Hold down the [CTRL] + [SHIFT] keys with one hand while you drag down and to the right until you have a square that almost fills the screen vertically (see Figure 14-5).

FIGURE 14-5

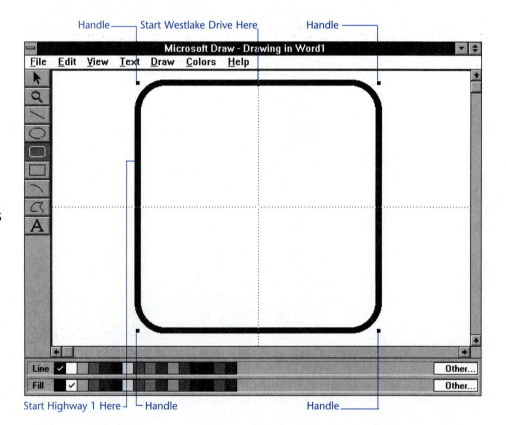

Handles appear on the object as soon as you release the mouse button. Handles indicate the object is selected and can be modified or deleted. Let's assume that you are not satisfied with the square you have drawn and you want to try again.

To delete this object,

8. Choose Cut from the EDIT menu or press the [BACKSPACE] key.

   The square disappears and you can try again.

9. Follow steps 6 and 7 above to create the square again.

   The first street you will place on your map is Westlake Drive, which should appear down the center of the box in a thinner line than you used for the border.

10. Click on the Line tool.

11. Choose Line Style from the DRAW menu and select 2 Point from the pop-out menu.

12. Position the crosshair in the middle of the top line of the border, aligned with the vertical guideline (see Figure 14-5).

Normally you simply drag to draw a line in any direction. You have to be very careful and precise to draw a perfect horizontal, vertical, or diagonal (45-degree) line; however, if you hold down [SHIFT], as you did when drawing the perfect square, *WORKS* will draw a perfectly straight line for you in the direction you drag.

13. Hold down [SHIFT] and drag down to the bottom border.

    Note that even if you wobble a bit, *WORKS* keeps the line perfectly vertical.

The line representing Highway 1 is the next one you will draw. Highway 1 is a large state highway, so it is slightly wider than Westlake Drive and is labeled with a circled number 1 on Figure 14-1. You will not use the [SHIFT] drag method of drawing Highway 1, because the slope is somewhat less than 45 degrees.

14. Click anywhere in the white space outside the square border to deselect the line you just drew.

15. Click on the Line tool again, then choose Line Style from the DRAW menu, and select 4 Point from the pop-out menu.

16. Move the crosshair about one-third of the way down the left side of the border (see Figure 14-5).

17. Drag up and to the right to draw Highway 1, as shown in Figure 14-1.

If you are not satisfied with your line, press [BACKSPACE] and repeat steps 16 and 17.

18. When you are satisfied, click the mouse button anywhere outside the border to deselect the line.

Broadway and Gish Circle are smaller streets than Westlake Drive and Highway 1, so you will reduce the line width again before adding them to your map.

19. Choose Line Style from the DRAW menu, and select 1 Point from the pop-out menu.

20. Click on the Line tool again.

Since Broadway is a straight, horizontal line,

21. Move the crosshair about one-third of the way from the bottom of the left side, hold down [SHIFT], and drag across to the right border (see Figure 14-1).

To draw the short street representing the stem of Gish Circle,

22. Move the cursor approximately one-third of the way along Broadway, between the left edge of the map and Westlake Drive (see Figure 14-1).

23. Hold down [SHIFT] and drag down approximately ¼ inch.

To draw Gish Circle,

24. Click on the Ellipse/Circle tool to select it.

25. Position the crosshair a little to the left of the short line drawn in step 23, and drag down and to the right, until the shape resembles Gish Circle, as shown in Figure 14-1.

    Handles appear around the ellipse, indicating that you can modify or move it.

26. If the placement of the ellipse or any other draw object is not right, try the following steps to move it where it should be:

    a. Drop down the DRAW menu, and turn off Snap To Grid if it is active (preceded by a check mark).

    b. Click the Arrow tool.

    c. Drag the object into proper position.

You may have to try several times before you are satisfied. Stop at any time to adjust your developing map.

To create a perfect circle for the Highway 1 sign,

27. Click on the Ellipse/Circle tool again (if it is not already selected), hold down [SHIFT], and draw the circle, as shown in Figure 14-1. Use the Arrow tool to move the circle into the proper position, if necessary.

To eliminate the guide lines,

28. Choose Show Guides again from the DRAW menu.

29. Click anywhere outside the border of the large rounded square to de-select all objects.

CORRECTING A MISTAKE

If you are unhappy with any part of the project so far and would like to redo one or all of the objects, follow these steps:

a. Click the Arrow tool.

b. Click the object to be redone to select it (handles will appear around it). For lines, you must click on the line. For an enclosed object such as a circle or square, you can click on its border or inside the object.

c. Press [BACKSPACE].

d. Click the appropriate tool and redo that part of the drawing.

If you would like to modify an object, follow these steps:

a. Choose the Arrow tool.

b. Click the object to be modified (handles will appear around it).

c. Drag on the handles to make the modifications. When modifying a two-dimensional object, dragging diagonally on a corner will affect both adjoining sides; while dragging vertically or horizontally on a handle will affect only one dimension.

If you would like to move an object, follow these steps:

a. Choose the Arrow tool.

b. Move the pointer over the object but not over a handle.

c. Drag to reposition the object. A "ghost" outline will follow the mouse as you drag to make it easy for you to know where the new position will be.

Remember you can also use Undo from the EDIT menu to reverse the last action taken.

If you have not yet begun your drawing, return to the "Getting Started" section at the beginning of this chapter now, and follow the instructions to create your map.

DRAWING FILLED OBJECTS

The last objects to draw are the building and tree symbols shown in Figure 14-1. They are to be filled with a color or pattern. *DRAW* gives you a color palette with two kinds of color—line color and fill color. Line color is used for lines, frames, pattern foreground, and text. Fill color is used for the interiors of shapes and pattern backgrounds. There can be up to 100 line colors and 100 fill colors in a palette. You can show or hide the color palette by choosing the toggled command Show Palette from the COLORS menu. If the palette is not hidden, it will be displayed at the bottom of the *DRAW* screen, as shown in Figure 14-2.

The following instructions use black for the filler, but if you are working with a color system, you can pick any color you wish.

IT'S YOUR TURN

To select a filler,

1. Move the pointer to the black square on the Fill line of the Color Palette (white is presently selected, as indicated by the diamond) and click.

    The Fill Pattern is now black (a diamond appears in the black block). To draw the rectangle marking the location of The Fun Factory,

2. Click on the Rectangle/Square tool to select it.

3. Place the crosshair a little to the right of Gish Circle, where you think the rectangle representing the Fun Factory should be (see Figure 14-1), and drag down and to the right to draw the small rectangle.

4. Click anywhere outside of the map to deselect.

To draw the trees representing a nearby park area, you will use the Freeform tool, which can draw polygons of all types. You will use it to draw triangles that represent trees. With every click of the mouse in the steps below, *DRAW* will set a point on your triangle until you finish the figure. You may not be successful with your first attempt at the tree, but keep trying until you are comfortable with the tool.

5. Click on the Freeform tool (see Figure 14-2).

The following instructions give you directions for drawing the trees in position, but you do not have to draw the triangle exactly at its final position. You can draw it anywhere on the *DRAW* window and drag it to its proper position after you are satisfied with its shape.

You will begin by drawing the tree on the left, starting at the top.

6. Position the crosshair approximately ½ inch to the right of Westlake Drive and ¼ inch below Broadway and click once.

7. Position the crosshair down and a little to the left and click.

   Did you notice that as you moved the mouse after clicking, a line connected to the first click point followed your mouse movements? The second click (in step 7) set the position for the end of the first line of the triangle—the left side of the tree top.

To draw the remainder of the tree top,

8. Hold down the [SHIFT] key while you move the mouse to position the crosshair about ¼ inch directly to the right and click once. Release the [SHIFT] key.

9. Position the crosshair up and to the left near the first click point, and click once to complete the figure.

   See Figure 14-1 to check your positioning.
   When you release the mouse, handles should appear around a black triangle. To get a clearer picture of your tree,

10. Click anywhere outside of the map.

    The handles disappear, and you are able to view your drawing clearly. If you are not satisfied with your tree, click to select it, press [BACK-SPACE], and try again. When you are satisfied with your drawing, you are ready to copy the tree and duplicate it twice.

COPYING, PASTING, AND REPOSITIONING OBJECTS

As with the other *WORKS* modules, you must select what you want to copy before you can copy and paste. When draw objects are selected, handles display around them.

IT'S YOUR TURN

1. Click on the tree (triangle) to select it (if the handles are not already visible).

2. Choose Copy from the EDIT menu.

3. Choose Paste from the EDIT menu.

   A copy of the tree with handles will appear somewhere near the first tree.

To move it into position,

4. Place the selection arrow inside the tree, and drag it into position to match Figure 14-1.

   A "ghost" outline will move with the mouse movement; the copy will appear when you release the mouse button.
   The Clipboard still contains a copy of the tree that you placed in step 2.

To make the third tree.

5. Repeat steps 3 and 4 to paste and position the last tree.

To draw the three tree trunks,

6.   Click the Line tool, and increase the thickness to 2 (DRAW menu, Line Style option).

7.   Hold down [SHIFT] as you drag to draw the trunks for each tree, as shown in Figure 14-1.

8.   Click anywhere outside the border to deselect.

TYPING AND PLACING TEXT

The final touches to the map involve typing the street names and store address. Positioning the pointer and typing the text may be all that's necessary. However, you will probably want to move the text after typing for more exact placement.

IT'S YOUR TURN

1.   Click on the Text tool.

To preset the text for bold print,

2.   Choose Bold from the TEXT menu.

3.   Click the text down arrow slightly above the line representing Broadway.

An insertion point will start blinking at the click point.

4.   Type: Broadway

Note that the insertion point keeps blinking.

To terminate Text mode,

5.   Click anywhere outside the border or press [ENTER].

The text you just typed now has handles around it to show that is is selected.

If you are not satisfied with the placement of the text, position the arrow inside the selected text block, and drag it to another location.

To deselect the text,

6.   Click anywhere outside the border.

One text object can only contain one line of text, but you want Gish Circle to occupy two lines. You will have to divide it into two text objects.
   To type Gish Circle on two lines,

7.   Click the Text tool.

8.   Click just below Gish Circle.

9.   Type: Gish

10.   Press [ENTER].

11.   Click the text tool again to select it.

12.   Click a little below and to the left of Gish.

13.   Type: Circle

14.   Press [ENTER].

The Circle text block is now selected.

15. Move the Circle text block so that it appears centered, with respect to the Gish text block.

To deselect the text block and view its placement,

16. Click anywhere outside the border.

17. Follow steps 7 through 16 to type the label for Westlake Drive on two lines, as shown in Figure 14-1.

Placing the number 1 inside the circle may be awkward, because the text block is large and your circle may appear to be too small. Complete steps 18 through 22 before deciding to make changes.

18. Click to select the Text tool.

19. Position the text crosshair inside the circle, and click to place the insertion point.

20. Type: 1

21. Press [ENTER].

To deselect the text object so you can observe the effect,

22. Click anywhere outside the border.

23. If the number is not in the center of the circle,

    a. Click the number with the Arrow tool to select it.

    Handles will appear around the text.

    b. Drag the outline of the number to a better position inside the circle.

24. If the number is too large for the circle,

    a. Click the number to select it.

    b. Choose Size from the TEXT menu, and select a smaller font size from the pop-out menu, OR

    c. Click the perimeter of the circle to select the circle.

    d. Drag one or more handles of the circle in a diagonal direction to enlarge the circle.

To insert the store address and complete the map,

25. Use the skills you have learned in this section to type and place the company address, 241. Your screen should look somewhat like the screen shown in Figure 14-1 when you finish.

To combine all the objects into a single drawing,

26. Choose Select All from the EDIT menu.

27. Choose Group from the DRAW menu.

FINISHING UP THE MAP

Now that you have finished the map, you must place it in your word processing document. You cannot save a file directly from *MICROSOFT DRAW*. The FILE menu, as shown in Figure 14-6, contains a set of commands different from the ones you are accustomed to seeing. They are explained in the following table.

FIGURE 14-6

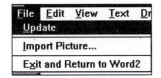

Command	Function
Update	To update a drawing means to save the current version of the drawing in the destination application (a word processing or database form document) without exiting *MICROSOFT DRAW*.
Import Picture	To import graphics files that were created in other graphics applications. Once you import a file, you can edit it with *DRAW* tools.
Exit and Return	To leave *DRAW* and return to the destination application. If the *DRAW* document is new, it becomes part of the destination document. If the *DRAW* document is an old one that was being edited, any changes you made will be saved to the destination document.

IT'S YOUR TURN

To return to the word processing document with the drawing,

1. Choose Exit and Return from the FILE menu.

    A dialog box appears asking if you want to update Word1.

2. Click the YES button.

    In a few seconds, you will be returned to your word processing document, with a copy of your drawing horizontally centered in the window.

3. If printing is required, click the PRINT button on the toolbar.

4. Choose Save As from the FILE menu, and save this document in your name directory on your data disk. Use the file name MAP.

5. To close MAP, choose Close from the FILE menu or double click on the CONTROL MENU button.

6. If you are finished for the day, quit *WORKS,* as directed in previous chapters; if you are not, continue with the next section.

SETTING THE SCENE

PROJECT 2   The Letterhead

The Fun Factory needs a distinctive new letterhead for general business use, as well as to dress up the newsletters that are sent to customers from time to time to keep them abreast of the latest sales, toys, etc. This month your newsletter will include the winning essays from the "How Toys Help Students Learn" contest, and you will use WordArt to create a new letterhead/logo to embellish that publication. Your finished product should resemble the letterhead shown in Figure 14-7.

FIGURE 14-7

THE FUN FACTORY
241 Broadway
Evergreen, CA 99999

GETTING STARTED

You can access WordArt from either a word processor window or a database Form view window. For this exercise, you will use a word processor window.

IT'S YOUR TURN

1. If you are returning to this lesson after exiting *WORKS,*

   a. Launch *WORKS 3.0.*

      The Startup dialog box will appear on your screen. If you just finished the last section and closed the *MAP* document, the startup dialog box will also be on your screen.

   b. Click the WORD PROCESSOR button in the Create a New block.

      A new word processor window should appear on your screen. Since you want the letterhead you are going to create to be in the center of the page,

2. Click the CENTER ALIGN button on the toolbar.

3. Use the Font Name box and the Font Size box on the toolbar to set the font to Arial 14.

4. Choose WordArt from the INSERT menu.

   It may take a few seconds for WordArt to open, but eventually your screen should resemble the one shown in Figure 14-8.

FIGURE 14-8

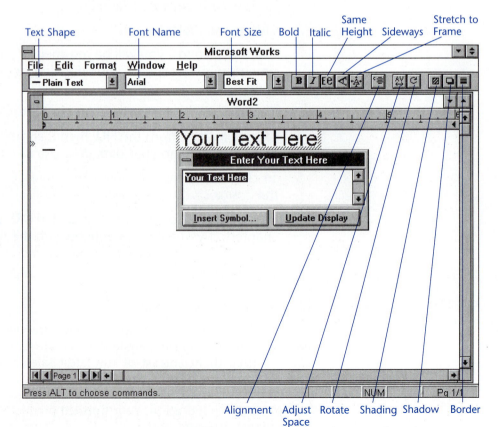

Notice carefully the changes that have occurred in the Menu bar and the toolbar.

UNDERSTANDING THE WORDART MENU BAR AND TOOLBAR

WORKS displays some new and different menus when WordArt is being used. The FILE menu and the WINDOW menu remain the same, but others change drastically, as does the toolbar. The HELP menu is totally devoted to help on WordArt, and you should feel free to use it. The other menus are shown in Figure 14-9.

FIGURE 14-9A

FIGURE 14-9B

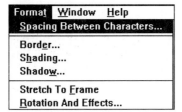

The EDIT menu only has one command, which is used to edit already existing WordArt objects. In the FORMAT menu, the command Spacing Between Characters allows you to control that characteristic if you wish. Spacing between characters is also referred to by the terms *kerning* and/or *tracking*, both of which are used in the dialog box that appears when you select this command. The Border, Shading and Shadow commands bring up dialog boxes that control those special effects. The Stretch To Frame command causes the WordArt text to expand to fill the entire frame, and the Rotation and Effects command can be used to freely rotate the WordArt text, as well as to manipulate it in other ways that are dependent upon the shape you have chosen.

The WordArt toolbar is shown again in Figure 14-10. The purpose of each item on the toolbar is explained in the table following the figure.

FIGURE 14-10

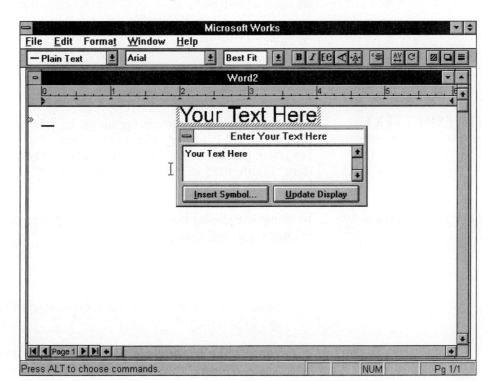

Button or Box	Purpose
`─ Plain Text ▼` Text Shape Box	Displays 36 different forms for shaping your text
`Arial ▼` Font Name Box	Used to change the font used for your text
`Best Fit ▼` Font Size Box	Used to select a specific size or select the Best Fit option (WordArt chooses the best font size)
B BOLD button	Makes text bold
I ITALICS button	Makes text italic (slanted to the right)
SAME HEIGHT button	Makes both uppercase letters and lowercase letters the same height
SIDEWAYS button	Turns all characters 90 degrees
STRETCH TO FRAME button	Stretches the text to fill the WordArt frame
ALIGNMENT button	Displays a drop-down menu, from which you can choose the method of alignment
ADJUST SPACE button	Adjusts the space between characters
ROTATE button	Rotates or inclines the text
SHADING button	Used to choose a shading pattern and colors for the pattern's foreground and background
SHADOW button	Adds one of several styles of shadow
BORDER button	Changes the thickness and color of the text's borders

ENTERING TEXT

Now that you know something about the possibilities of manipulating text with WordArt, it's time to enter some text and play with it. The Enter Your Text Here dialog box should be in the center of your screen, with "Your Text Here" highlighted in the dialog box.

IT'S YOUR TURN

To move the dialog box out of the way so you can more easily observe the changes you will make in the text,

1. Point to the title bar of the dialog box, and drag it to the lower right-hand corner of the screen.

   "Your Text Here" should be highlighted in the dialog box.

2. Type: THE FUN FACTORY

   Your typing will replace the contents of the dialog box. Now we are going to lead you through a short series of steps to produce the letterhead for The Fun Factory. Follow these steps exactly, or your results may not be as expected from step to step. After you finish with this section, you will have some idea of WordArt's capabilities, and you will be able to experiment all you wish.

3. Click the UPDATE DISPLAY button on the dialog box.

   The Fun Factory appears in the word processing window.

4. Click the down arrow on the TEXT SHAPE box in the toolbar.

   A block of shapes will drop as shown in Figure 14-11.

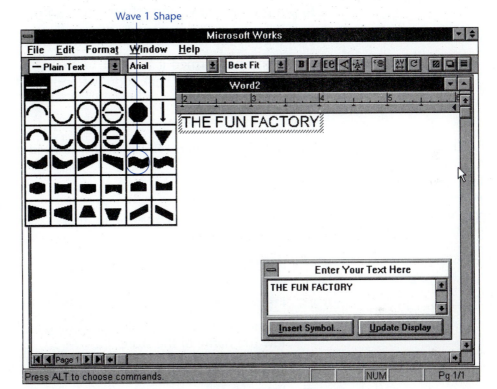

FIGURE 14-11

5. Click the Wave1 shape, as shown in Figure 14-11.

   The display in the word processing window changed, but it is so small that you can't see it very well.

6. Click the STRETCH TO FRAME button on the toolbar.

   Now you can see the display.

7. Click the BOLD button.

   That looks a little better, but it is still not jazzy enough. Instead of using Stretch to Fit, let's use a larger font size.

To remove Stretch to Fit,

8. Click the STRETCH TO FRAME button again.

9. Choose 12 from the Font Size drop-down list.

   The Size Change dialog box shown in Figure 14-12 appears.

10. Click the YES button to allow WordArt to resize the frame.

    Now the text looks much better. As a matter of fact, it can be the basis for a very attractive letterhead.

FIGURE 14-12

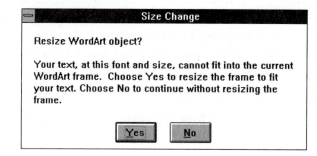

To put away WordArt and return to the word processing document,

11. Click in the white space in the word processing window.

Don't be alarmed if the text momentarily disappears from the window. It will come back soon, without the frame surrounding it.

ADDING THE ADDRESS TO THE LETTERHEAD

Your letterhead is almost finished; all you need to do is add the address.

IT'S YOUR TURN

1. Click anywhere in the white space on the right side of the Fun Factory's name.

2. If necessary, use the toolbar to set the font name to Arial and the font size to 12.

3. Press [ENTER] to go to the next line.

The insertion point should be blinking in the center, immediately below the name of the store.

4. Type: 241 Broadway

5. Press [ENTER].

6. Type: Evergreen, CA 99999

7. Press [ENTER].

Your letterhead is complete. To see how it looks,

8. Click the PRINT PREVIEW button and zoom up to full size.

When you have finished examining your creation,

9. Click the CANCEL button.

FINISHING UP THE LETTERHEAD

You will save your work so you can use it again and print a copy if you wish.

IT'S YOUR TURN

1. Choose Save As from the FILE menu, and save the document in your name directory on your data disk. Use the file name *LTRHD*.

In the future, you can open *LTRHD.WPS*, type a letter, and save it under a different name, thereby always leaving *LTRHD* ready to be used again.

Also, the store name can easily be copied into other documents, as you will do in later chapters.

2. If printing is required, click the PRINT button on the toolbar.

To close *LTRHD,*

3. Double click the CONTROL MENU button, or choose Close from the FILE menu.

If you wish to experiment with WordArt or *MICROSOFT DRAW*, go ahead and spend as much time as you like. When you are ready to stop,

4. Quit *WORKS 3.0,* as directed in previous chapters.

SUMMARY

Congratulations! You have used numerous tools from *MICROSOFT DRAW* to draw pictures, as well as to resize and move objects. You can fill objects with color and copy and paste them. Also, you know how to group objects to form one complex drawing.

You have also learned a little bit about the WordArt accessory. You know how to choose a shape and create an attractive letterhead.

REVIEW QUESTIONS

1. How can you tell that an object is selected and, therefore, can be moved or modified?

2. How can you be assured that you will draw a perfect square or straight line?

3. How can you move the Type Your Text Here dialog box?

4. If the Ellipse/Circle tool is selected from the *DRAW* toolbox, what form does the cursor take when it is moved into the work area?

5. How can you combine several objects you have drawn into one unit?

6. How can you select colors to fill objects you have drawn?

EXERCISES

EXERCISE 14-1   Creating a house using draw tools

1. Draw a simple house. (Open the House file from the Artwork folder on your data disk to see an example of a drawing created using *DRAW*. It may help you get started.)

2. Use the Text tool to write your name and the current date under the house.

3. Save the file as *EX14-1* in your name directory on your data disk.

4. Print the file, if requested by your instructor.

EXERCISE 14-2   Creating a letterhead using WordArt

1. Create a letterhead for yourself, using a shape other than Wave 1.

2. Add an address to the letterhead and embellish it.

3.   Save as *EX14-2* in your name directory on your data disk.

4.   Print if directed by your instructor.

EXERCISE 14-3   Creating a map

1.   Create a map to show the location of your school campus, your office, or your home. Or, create a logo for a company, a business, or your school.

2.   Place your name and the current date in a box below the map.

3.   Save as *EX14-3* in your name directory on your data disk.

4.   Print if directed by your instructor.

Advanced Tasks 2: Merging

OBJECTIVES

When you finish this chapter you will be able to

- *prepare a word processing document for merging with a database*

- *copy spreadsheet data into a word processing document*

- *insert a border around text in a word processing document*

- *select database records for a merged document*

- *print a merged document*

INTRODUCTION

There will be times when you will want to combine a word processing document with parts of a database or a spreadsheet. If you were using separate programs, it might be a little difficult to produce such a document. With an integrated program such as *WORKS 3.0*, however, you will see how quickly and easily you can combine material generated by different modules. The unifying application is the word processor. In this lesson, you will explore some of the integration capabilities within *WORKS 3.0*.

SETTING THE SCENE

The Fun Factory's income has increased dramatically, and you want to send your managers a letter to inform them of the profitability of the store and of your gratitude for the role they have played in its success. You will create a letter using your new letterhead, paste in the financial data from a spreadsheet, put a border around the financial data, and personalize the letter by inserting each manager's name and address from the *PROFILE* database. Figure 15-1 shows how all the parts will fit together.

GETTING STARTED

The Fun Factory letterhead that you created in the last chapter should be stored on your data disk. You will use that document for this exercise.

IT'S YOUR TURN

1. Launch *WORKS 3.0*.

2. Open the *LTRHD* word processing file from your name directory on your data disk. If you did not do the activity in the last chapter, you can use the *LHEAD* word processing file from the data disk that goes with this book.

WORD PROCESSING FILE

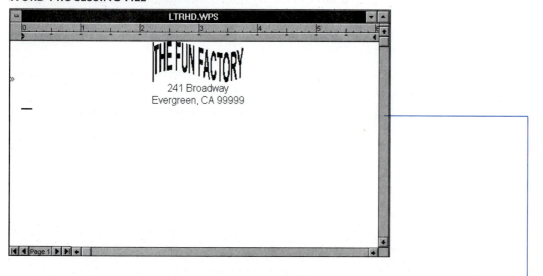

DATABASE FILE

	LAST NAME	FIRST NAME	STREET ADDRESS	CITY	STATE	ZIP	PHONE	BIRTHDAY	DA
1	CARLSON	ROBERTA	575 Pebble Beach Drive	Cupertino	CA	95014	255-6100	February 02	
2	CARRILLO	ANGELA	863 Columbia Drive	San Jose	CA	95130	291-8654	December 16	
3	JACOBSEN	RUSS	283 Campbell Avenue	Campbell	CA	95008	378-1330	June 03	
4	MANSUR	GLORIA	164 Blossom Hill Road	Los Gatos	CA	95030	353-4454	March 14	
5	PRADA	JOSEPHINE	675 Big Basin Way	Saratoga	CA	95070	867-1779	January 02	
6	TYLER	GEOFFREY	1001 No. Bascom Avenue	San Jose	CA	95128	299-4151	May 14	
7	VILLARREAL	RAOUL	3065 Maui Drive	San Jose	CA	95130	289-4050	April 17	
8	WILLIAMS	CORINNE	248 Budd Avenue	Campbell	CA	95008	379-1008	January 16	
9	YEE	WENDY	1864 McFarland Avenue	Saratoga	CA	95070	867-4891	November 01	
10									
11									
12									
13									
14									
15									
16									
17									
18									
19									
20									
21									

Title bar: PROFILE.WDB

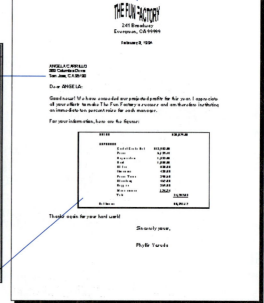

FINISHED LETTER

SPREADSHEET FILE

Title bar: STATEMNT.WKS

	A	B	C	D	E	F	G	H	I
1		*THE FUN FACTORY*							
2		Income Statement							
3		For the Month of November							
4									
5	SALES				$30,079.00				
6									
7	EXPENSES								
8		Cost of Goods Sold		$13,982.00					
9		Payroll		6,129.44					
10		Depreciation		1,322.00					
11		Rent		1,000.00					
12		Utilities		525.00					
13		Insurance		420.00					
14		Payroll Taxes		398.65					
15		Advertising		467.00					
16		Supplies		369.00					
17		Miscellaneous		174.74					
18		Total			24,787.83				
19									
20	NET INCOME				$5,291.17				
21									

FIGURE 15-1

The document opens with The Fun Factory letterhead displayed at the top. To avoid destroying the blank letterhead, you will immediately save it under the name you will use for your completed integrated document.

3. Choose Save As from the FILE menu, and save the file in your name directory on your data disk. Use the file name *MGRRAISE*.

   The title bar changes to reflect the new name, and your screen should resemble the screen shown in Figure 15-2.

FIGURE 15-2

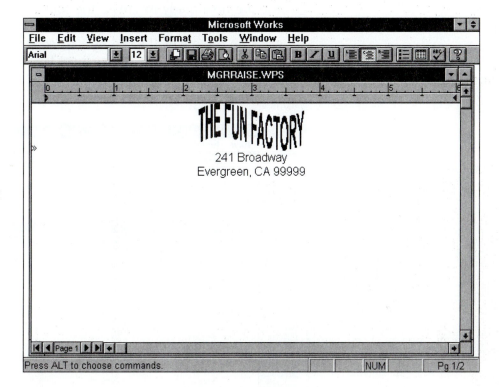

This is the letterhead on which all of your letters will appear. Each letter will include the recipient's name, address, the salutation line, the message, the financial data, and the closing lines. Even though you will send letters to all three of your managers, and the letters will be personalized with the managers' names and addresses plus the correct first name in the salutation line, you will only type the letter once. *WORKS* 3.0 includes a form letter capability that you will use in this exercise.

PREPARING TO CREATE THE FORM LETTER

Your form letter will be sent to managers listed in the *PROFILE* database and will include part of the *STATEMNT* spreadsheet file, as illustrated in Figure 15-1. The number of documents you can have open at one time depends upon the size of the documents and the amount of memory your computer has. You should have no problem having these three files open at the same time.

IT'S YOUR TURN

With *MGRRAISE* already open, you now need to open the database and the spreadsheet.

To open the other two files,

1. Choose Open from the FILE menu, and open the database file *PRO-FILE* from your data disk.

2. Choose Open from the FILE menu, and open the spreadsheet file *STATEMNT* from your name directory on your data disk. If you did not do this exercise, open the *STMENT.WKS* file from the data disk.

You are now ready to create the form letter. If you followed our directions, your screen should look like the one shown in Figure 15-3, with the three files stacked as a *cascade* so the title bars of all three are visible. Because the spreadsheet file was the last one opened, it is the active window.

FIGURE 15-3

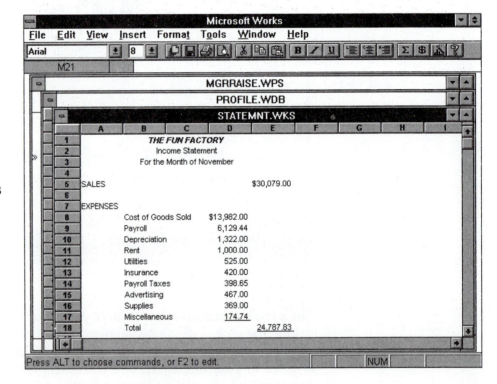

CREATING THE MASTER DOCUMENT

The master document is the integrating document for the form letter. It is created in the word processing document and includes instructions which, when the individual letters are printed, causes names and addresses to be copied from the database document into the individual letters on the letterhead.

IT'S YOUR TURN

To return to the word processing document,

1. Click the *MGRRAISE.WPS* title bar, or choose *MGRRAISE.WPS* from the WINDOW menu.

The database and spreadsheet windows are now not visible.

To insert the date in the letter,

2. Click to the right of the zip code in the letterhead.

   The insertion point will blink immediately following the zip code.

3. Press [ENTER] twice.

   The insertion point will now be blinking in the center of the second line, below the address. The address lines of the letterhead were typed in Arial 12 font, which is too large for the entire letter.

To reduce the font size,

4. Choose 10 from the Font Size drop-down box on the toolbar.

5. Type the current date.

6. Press [ENTER] six times.

   The insertion point is still centered.

To move it to the left margin,

7. Click the LEFT ALIGNMENT button on the toolbar.

You are now in position to insert the database placeholders. *Placeholders* are used to indicate where information from a database is to be inserted. To select the desired fields,

8. Choose Database Field from the INSERT menu.

   The Insert Field dialog box appears on the screen.

9. Click the DATABASE button in the lower right corner of the dialog box.

   The Choose Database dialog box shown in Figure 15-4 appears.

FIGURE 15-4

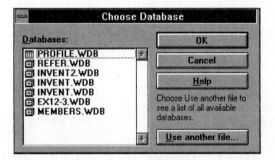

Note the icons preceding the file names. The Open Document icon preceding *PROFILE.WDB* indicates that this file is already open and available. The Closed File Drawer icon preceding the other names indicates that, although these files exist on your data disk, they are not yet available for use.

10. Click *PROFILE.WDB* to choose that database.

11. Click the OK button or press [ENTER].

    You will be returned to the Insert Field dialog box, but this time it will look like Figure 15-5.

In the Fields scrolling box on the left, WORKS 3.0 has listed all the fields in the database. You will now select the fields you want in your word pro-

FIGURE 15-5

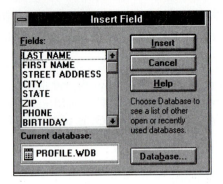

cessing document in the order in which you want them to appear. First you must build up the three address lines at the beginning of the letter.

12. Click FIRST NAME.

13. Click the INSERT button.

> The placeholder <FIRST NAME> appears on the word processing document. If you can't see it, you can move the Insert Field dialog box by dragging on its title bar.

14. Click LAST NAME, then click the INSERT button.

> Note that when you select more than one field on the same line, *WORKS* automatically places a space between the fields. At this point, you must go back to the main document to start a new line for the address lines.

15. Click the CLOSE button.

> You are returned to the word processing window, with the insertion point blinking immediately following the <LAST NAME> placeholder.

To move to the next line to insert the street address,

16. Press [ENTER].

To insert the street address,

17. Choose Database Field from the INSERT menu.

When the Insert Field dialog box appears,

18. Click STREET ADDRESS, then click the INSERT button, followed by the CLOSE button.

> You are back in the word processing window.

19. Press [ENTER] to move to the next line.

> Now you are ready to enter the city, state, and zip code.

20. Choose Database Field from the INSERT menu.

21. Click CITY, then click the INSERT button.

22. Click STATE, then click the INSERT button.

23. Click ZIP, then click the INSERT button.

> These are all the fields you need for the last line of the address.

To return to the word processing document,

24. Click the CLOSE button in the Insert Field dialog box.

    The dialog box goes away, and you are returned to the *MGRRAISE* window.

To place a comma between the city and state,

25. Click to place the insertion point immediately after the chevron (>>) following the City placeholder.

26. Type: , (a comma)

    The placeholders should appear, as shown in Figure 15-6.

FIGURE 15-6

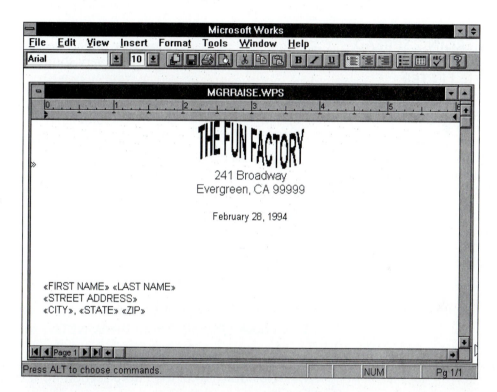

You are now ready to type a personalized salutation, or greeting.

27. Click anywhere to the right of the Zip placeholder to place the insertion point at the end of the last line of the address, or press [END].

28. Press [ENTER] twice.

29. If the font size changed to 12 after doing step 28, pull down the Font Size box on the toolbar and click 10.

30. Type: Dear

31. Press [SPACEBAR] once.

To insert the placeholder for the first name of each recipient at this point,

32. Choose Database Field from the INSERT menu.

33. Click on FIRST NAME, click the INSERT button, then click the CLOSE button.

The extra space that separates placeholders does not get inserted until additional placeholders are placed on a line.

Since the insertion point is in the correct place for the colon that should follow the first name,

34. Type: : (a colon)

35. Press [ENTER] twice.

You have now finished inserting the placeholder codes that will cause data from the *PROFILE* database to be merged with this word processing document. The next step is to type a short introductory message and to integrate data from a spreadsheet document into the letter.

MERGING SPREAD-SHEET DATA INTO THE LETTER

The company has had a good year, largely because of the efforts of your managers. The message you will type is very short.

IT'S YOUR TURN

1. Type the following two paragraphs. Use single spacing, but double space (press [ENTER] twice) between paragraphs.

   Good news! We have exceeded our projected profits for this year. I appreciate all your efforts to make The Fun Factory a success and am therefore instituting an immediate ten percent raise for each manager.

   For your information, here are the figures:

2. Press [ENTER] twice.

At this point, you will paste in the sales and expense figures from the *STATEMNT* file.

3. Choose *STATEMNT* from the WINDOW menu.

   The Income Statement will appear.

4. Scroll down until the entire section from cells A5 to E20 displays.

5. Drag to select the Sales through Net Income lines (cells A5 through E20), as illustrated in Figure 15-7.

6. Choose Copy from the EDIT menu.

To paste the data into the form letter,

7. Choose *MGRRAISE.WPS* from the WINDOW menu, or click on the MGRRAISE title bar.

8. Choose Paste from the EDIT menu.

9. Use the vertical scroll arrows until the entire statement appears on the screen.

   The insertion point will appear at the left edge of the statement and will be noticeable because it is the same height as the statement. The material from the spreadsheet comes into the word processing document as a single object, much like a *DRAW* or a WordArt object. You cannot change anything within the object once it has been trans-

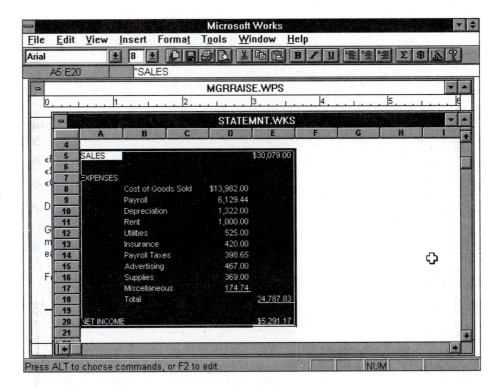

FIGURE 15-7

ferred to the word processing document, but you can position it more attractively. There are more complex ways to transfer data from a spreadsheet so that when the spreadsheet changes, the word processing document will also change, but those methods are beyond the scope of this text. If you are interested, look in the *WORKS* manual or the on-line Help for information on "Linking."

10. Click the CENTER ALIGNMENT button on the toolbar.

    The spreadsheet object will become centered under the second paragraph.

11. Click anywhere to the right of the spreadsheet object.

    The tall insertion point will now blink on the right side of the spreadsheet object.

12. Press [ENTER] twice.

13. Click the LEFT ALIGNMENT button on the toolbar.

14. Type: Thanks again for your hard work!

15. Press [ENTER] twice.

To set a tab stop for the closing lines,

16. Click in the ruler, directly under the three-inch mark.

    The left-tab symbol will appear.

To type the closing lines,

17. Press [TAB] and type: Sincerely yours,

18. Press [ENTER] three times, then press [TAB].

19. Type: (your name)

You will now place a border around the financial data to set it apart from the rest of the letter.

20. Use the vertical scroll bar to bring the complete financial table into view.

21. Click in the center of the table.

    Handles will appear around the table to show that it is selected.

22. Choose Border from the FORMAT menu.

When the Border dialog box appears,

23. Click Outline in the Border block and Double in the Line Style block, then click the OK button or press [ENTER].

    A border will enclose the table and extend from margin to margin.

To bring the sides of the border in closer to the edge of the table,

24. Drag on the Left Indent marker (the bottom half of the double triangle at the left edge of the ruler) to the one-inch mark.

25. Drag the Right Indent marker (the triangle at the right edge of the ruler) to the 5 1/2-inch mark.

    Your screen should resemble the screen shown in Figure 15-8.

FIGURE 15-8

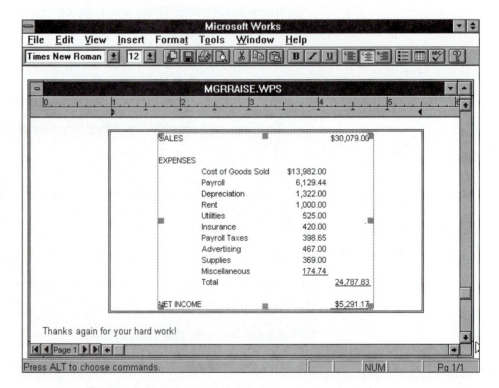

26. Click in the white space above the border to deselect the table.

    Do not be alarmed if you see a faint box outline around the spreadsheet (including handles). These will not print.

You are almost ready to print.

**SELECTING THE
LETTER RECIPIENTS**

The database file contains the names and addresses of all your employees, but this letter should be sent only to the managers. Since all managers are full-time, you will direct *WORKS* to print letters only for those records that contain FT in the Status field.

IT'S YOUR TURN

1. Choose *PROFILE* from the WINDOW menu.

2. Choose Create New Query from the TOOLS menu.

   The New Query dialog box appears.

3. Press [SHIFT] + [TAB] to move the highlight back to the query name text box.

4. Type: Managers

5. Click the down arrow on the right side of the Choose A Field To Compare box, and scroll down the list box until STATUS appears at the bottom of the box.

6. Click STATUS to select it.

   The How To Compare The Field box displays "Is Equal To," which is what you need.

To place the cursor in the Value To Compare The Field To box,

7. Press [TAB] twice, or click in the box.

8. Type: FT

   Your dialog box should now resemble the one shown in Figure 15-9.

FIGURE 15-9

```
┌─────────────────────────────── New Query ───────────────────────────────┐
│                                                                          │
│  Please give this query a name:  │Managers          │                    │
│  Create query sentences below, and then choose Apply Now to see all records that match the criteria. │
│                                                                          │
│   Choose a field to compare:    How to compare the field:     Value to compare the field to: │
│  A. │STATUS          │ ▼     B. │is equal to      │ ▼    E. │FT                │ │
│                                  ○ And                                    │
│                                  ○ Or                                     │
│  F. │                │ ▼     G. │                 │ ▼    I. │                  │ │
│                                  ○ And                                    │
│                                  ○ Or                                     │
│  J. │                │ ▼     K. │                 │ ▼    L. │                  │ │
│   │ Clear │              │ Apply Now │ │ Query View │   │ Cancel │   │ Help │  │
└──────────────────────────────────────────────────────────────────────────┘
```

To select the records that match the stated criteria,

9. Click the APPLY NOW button or press [ENTER].

   The database will now display only the records of managers. If you are in the List view, you will see all three managers listed; if you are in the Form view, the first manager's record will display.

FINISHING UP INTEGRATION

You are almost ready to print and quit this session. As a general practice, it is always a good idea to save your work for a while, even if you think you won't need it again. For example, if you discover a mistake in the spreadsheet, it will be faster to simply change the spreadsheet, copy and paste the appropriate parts, and reprint the letter rather than start from scratch.

IT'S YOUR TURN

To save your word processing document,

1. Choose the *MGRRAISE.WPS* document from the WINDOW menu, or click on its title bar.

2. Choose Save from the FILE menu.

Previewing and printing merged documents is a little different than normal previewing and printing. You have three different printing methods from which to choose. Choose step 3, 4, or 5 if directed to print by your instructor.

3. To view your letters, then print from the Print Preview screen:

   a. Click the PRINT PREVIEW button on the toolbar.

      The Choose Database dialog box will appear so you can once again choose the database for merging with this letter.

   Since *PROFILE.WDB* is already highlighted,

   b. Click OK or press [ENTER].

      The first letter to Angela Carrillo appears on your Print Preview screen. You can zoom in to examine it more closely, if you wish. When you have finished examining your work, note that the NEXT button is active.

   To see the next letter,

   c. Click the NEXT button.

      Now the letter to Gloria Mansur is displayed.

   The NEXT button is still active, so

   d. Click the NEXT button again.

      This time you see a letter addressed to Geoffrey Tyler.

   If you wish to print these letters,

   e. Click the PRINT button on the Print Preview screen.

      Once again, the Choose Database dialog box appears with *PROFILE.WDB* preselected.

   f. Click OK or press [ENTER].

4. To print from the FILE menu without going through the Print Preview screen, simply

   a. Choose Print from the FILE menu.

      When the Print dialog box appears, note that the Print Merge option is already selected.

b. Click the OK button or press [ENTER].

The Choose Database dialog box appears with *PROFILE.WDB* pre-selected.

c. Click the OK button or press [ENTER].

5. To print from the toolbar,

a. Click the PRINT button on the toolbar.

When the Choose Database dialog box appears,

b. Click OK or press [ENTER].

No matter which method you choose, printing commences, and all three letters are printed. You will have personalized letters for each manager, similar to the one illustrated in Figure 15-1.

Right now you have three documents open, but only one of them needs to be saved and you have already done that. The other two should be closed without making changes because they were simply being copied into your merged document.

6. Quit *WORKS,* as directed in previous chapters, and do not save changes to any file but the word processing one.

SUMMARY

Congratulations! You now know how to create a personalized form letter using the word processor and database files. You have also integrated data from the spreadsheet tool into a word processing document using the cut and paste method.

REVIEW QUESTIONS

1. When there is more than one file open in memory, what menu lists the open files and allows you to move quickly between them?

2. What menu and option allows you to put placeholders in a document?

3. What are the steps for printing form letters using the FILE menu?

4. What term is used when more than one file is open and the title bars are visible?

5. What menu and option do you use when you want to display only records showing a specific criterion?

6. What is the unifying *WORKS* application for integration?

EXERCISES

EXERCISE 15-1   Creating a letter with placeholders and merging it with a database

1. Open the *PROFILE* database.

2. Create a simple word processing document with placeholders for First Name, Last Name, Address, City, State, and ZIP.

    a.   Use the *LHEAD* file, if you wish, or make up your own.

    b.   Type the current date two lines below the letterhead.

3.   Return to the *PROFILE* database, and create a query to select people who make $5.75 per hour.

4.   Return to the word processing document.

    a.   Change the font size to 12.

    b.   Type a short paragraph informing the employee of a raise in pay rate.

    c.   Set a left tab at three inches, type an appropriate closing line, and type your name as District Manager.

5.   Type a footer with your name left aligned and the date right aligned.

6.   Save the letter as *EX15-1* in your name directory on your data disk.

7.   Print the document using the PRINT button on the toolbar. (One will print.)

EXERCISE 15-2   Creating a memo to a group of employees in a database and pasting in information from a spreadsheet

1.   Open the file *PROFILE.*

2.   Create a query to select files containing mornings.

3.   Open a new word processing document.

    a.   Use Arial 12.

    b.   Click at the one-inch mark on the ruler to set a left tab for the text following the memo headings.

4.   Create a memo similar to the following using placeholders for First Name and Last Name:

    To: <<First Name>><<Last Name>>

    From: (Your Name)

    Date: (Current Date)

    Subject: Inventory

    (Press [ENTER] twice)

    During the morning shift, please inventory the following items:

5.   Press [ENTER] twice.

6.   Open the file *REORDER* from your data disk.

7.   Copy cells A4 through B13, and paste them into the word processing document.

8.   Center the selected block.

9.   Add a footer with your name on the left and the date on the right.

10.   Save the memo as *EX15-2* in your name directory on your data disk.

11.   Print the memo using the Print Preview screen. (Two should print.)

EXERCISE 15-3 **Create your own letter and letterhead (using WordArt)**

1. Open a new word processing document.

    a. Change the font to Arial 12.

    b. Create a letterhead for The Fun Factory using the skills you learned in Chapter 14 for using WordArt.

    c. Press [ENTER] twice after the letterhead, and type the current date.

2. Use placeholders for the First Name, Last Name, Address, City, State, and ZIP using the *MEMBERS* file from your directory. (If you do not have the file, open the *MEM.WDB* file in the Exercise directory.)

3. Compose a letter to all members living in Campbell about a special discount sale on stuffed animals. Embellish as much as you like.

4. Create a query for all members living in Campbell.

5. Set a left tab at three inches on the ruler to type the following closing lines:

    Sincerely yours,

    (Your Name), Manager

6. Save as *EX15-3* in your name directory on your data disk.

7. Print the document using any method you wish. (Two should print.)

CHAPTER 16

Advanced Tasks 3: Newsletter

OBJECTIVES

When you finish this chapter you will be able to

▪ create a newsletter with multiple columns

▪ import and edit a TIFF file

▪ flow text from column to column

SETTING THE SCENE

In this final lesson, you will create a short newsletter using *WORKS 3.0*. Although the layout features are limited, they will provide you with an introduction to the use of columns, flowing text from column to column, and importing scanned graphics.

The principal of Evergreen Elementary School was happy to work with you on the essay contest and helped you choose three winners. You will present gift certificates to the winners at an award ceremony at the school. In addition, The Fun Factory will publish the students' essays in a special two-page newsletter that will be sent to the homes of all fourth- through sixth-grade students. The completed newsletter is shown in Figure 16-1.

FIGURE 16-1

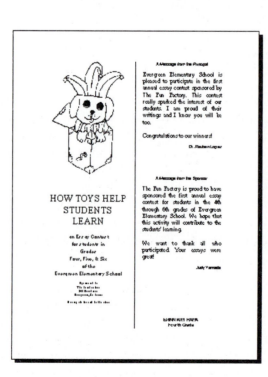

GETTING STARTED

You will begin your newsletter by creating two columns. Notice that the first column contains a picture and the introductory title lines, both of which are taken from files stored on your data disk in the *CONTEST* directory.

IT'S YOUR TURN

1. Launch *WORKS 3.0.*

When the Startup dialog box appears,

2. Open a new word processing document.

CREATING COLUMNS

It is easy to format newspaper-style columns in your word processing documents. In these columns, text flows continuously from the bottom of one column to the top of the next. When you create columns in a word processing document, you can specify the number of columns you want, the amount of space between each column, and whether or not to insert a vertical line between the columns to visually divide them. All columns will be the same width, and all pages of the same document will have the same number of columns.

IT'S YOUR TURN

1. Choose Columns from the FORMAT menu.

The Columns dialog box shown in Figure 16-2 appears with the Number of Columns text box highlighted.

FIGURE 16–2

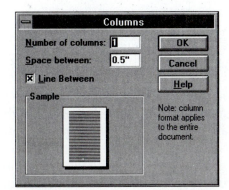

The Space Between option allows you to specify how far apart to place the columns. You will keep the 0.5-inch measurement suggested by *WORKS*. The Line Between option is already checked for you; you will keep that option also, since it will create a clear visual separation between the two columns.

2. Type: 2

That number will replace the 1 in the Number of Columns text box. Although the sample will not immediately change, if you should open this dialog box again, the sample will show two columns.

3. Click OK or press [ENTER].

An information box appears, recommending that you switch to Page Layout view. Page Layout view displays each page in your document as it will look when printed and also allows you to continue editing your document. Page Layout view is especially helpful when working with columns, because you can tell where the text is relative to the columns. In Normal view, you would only see one continuous column.

Since you want Page Layout view,

4. Click YES or press [ENTER].

The Information box goes away and your screen now resembles the one shown in Figure 16-3.

FIGURE 16-3

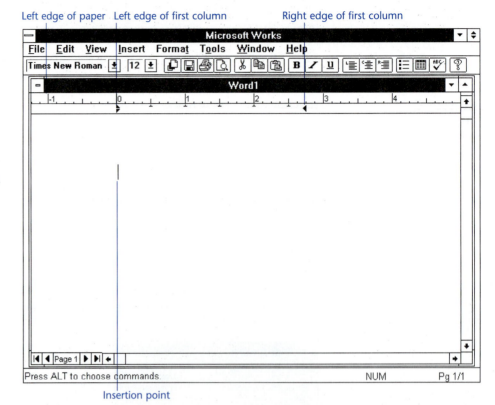

Left edge of paper   Left edge of first column   Right edge of first column

Insertion point

Look at the ruler at the top of your screen. The left edge of the screen (at the –1.25-inch mark on the ruler) represents the left edge of the paper. Since the default margins in *WORKS* are 1.25 inches on the left and right side, the Left Margin marker (at the zero-inch mark on the ruler) shows the beginning of the text area, and the Right Margin marker (at the 2.75-inch mark on the ruler) represents the end of the columns. Both columns in this document will be 2.75 inches wide. You specified 0.5-inch space between columns in the Columns dialog box, which accounts for the amount of available space left unused (on standard 8.5-inch-wide paper) after making allowance for the two columns and the two side margins.

You are now ready to insert the picture.

RESIZING AND INSERTING A DRAWING

As you learned from the last chapter, *MICROSOFT DRAW* is used to insert drawings and clip art into word processing documents. The *CONTEST* directory on your data disk contains a drawing that was done by one of the sixth-grade students at Evergreen Elementary School as a part of her entry. Her drawing depicts a jack-in-the-box, with a dog as the jester. Although her entry did not win, you asked for and have received her permission to use it for your newsletter (you will give her a special prize for her efforts).

You will resize this drawing so it fits into your newsletter column, and you will insert it as the first object in the newsletter.

IT'S YOUR TURN

1. Choose Drawing from the INSERT menu.

   After a few moments, the *MICROSOFT DRAW* window appears in the middle of your screen.

   To enlarge the *DRAW* screen so that there will be no chance for you to select the wrong menu bar,

2. Click the MAXIMIZE button on the *DRAW* window.

   The *DRAW* window now covers the entire screen, including the menu bar for the word processing window which was formerly visible. All your work for the next few steps will be done in the *DRAW* window.

3. Choose Import Picture from the FILE menu.

   The Import Picture dialog box shown in Figure 16-4 appears on your screen.

FIGURE 16-4

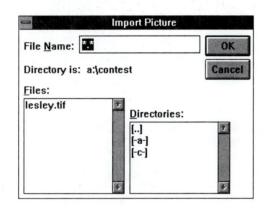

4. If the Files list box does NOT contain the filename *LESLEY.TIF*, double click the root directory or the drive designator for the drive containing the data disk that goes with this book, then double click the *CONTEST* directory.

   The Import Picture dialog box should be similar to Figure 16-4, with the filename *LESLEY.TIF* displayed in the Files list box.

5. Double click the filename *LESLEY.TIF*.

   In a few seconds, your screen should resemble the one shown in Figure 16-5.

Obviously, this picture is too large to fit into one of the newsletter's columns. You will resize it to make it fit.

6. Click once in the vertical scroll bar.

   The screen will scroll up to show the bottom of the picture (see Figure 16-6).

You will use the handle marked in Figure 16-6 to resize the picture. If you drag the handle vertically, the picture will be resized in the vertical dimension; if you drag horizontally, resizing will occur in the horizontal dimension. However, by dragging the handle diagonally, the picture will be resized proportionally in both the vertical and horizontal dimensions.

FIGURE 16-5

FIGURE 16-6

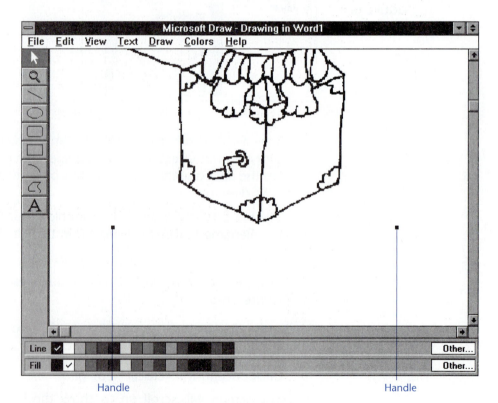

Handle   Handle

Holding down the [SHIFT] key while dragging diagonally will maintain the proportions of the drawing.

7. Move the pointer to the handle on the right side of the screen, and hold the [SHIFT] key and the mouse button down in preparation for dragging.

Note that as soon as you press the mouse button, a dotted line appears around the drawing.

8. Keep pressing down on the [SHIFT] key and the mouse button while you drag the handle <u>diagonally</u> toward the upper left corner of the screen until the pointer is a little above the middle of your screen (see Figure 16-7), then release both.

FIGURE 16-7

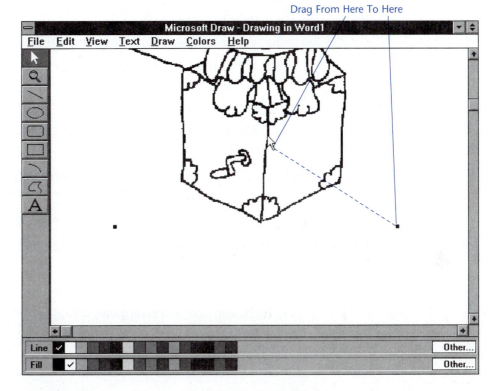

Now you can only see the bottom half of the picture.

9. Click in the vertical scroll bar, immediately above the scroll box.

The picture will scroll into view. It should look somewhat like the picture in Figure 16-8.

FIGURE 16-8

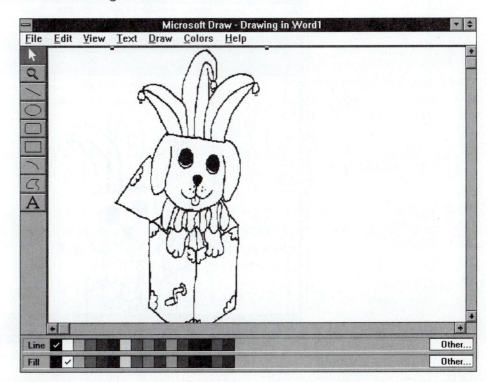

If you are not happy with the way your picture looks, there are several different ways you can change it.

To move the picture so the handles are more accessible,

a. Place the pointer in the middle of the picture, and drag in the direction you wish it to move.

To reduce or enlarge the vertical dimension,

b. Move the pointer to one of the corner handles, and drag up or down.

To reduce or enlarge the horizontal dimension,

c. Move the pointer to one of the corner handles, and drag to the right or the left.

When you are happy with the picture and you think it might fit into the column,

10. Choose Exit, and Return to Word1 from the FILE menu.

A dialog box will appear, asking if you want to update the word processing document.

11. Click the YES button or press [ENTER].

The dialog box will disappear, and the word processing screen should come into view, with the picture placed at the top of the first column. It should look something like the screen shown in Figure 16-9.

12. Click inside the drawing if the handles are not visible.

Note that there are eight handles surrounding the picture now. They show that it is selected.

FIGURE 16-9

13. Examine the picture carefully relative to the right-edge marker for this column. If the picture extends beyond the right-edge marker, drag the horizontal resize button marked in Figure 16-9 to the left, until the right edge of the picture is to the left of the right-edge marker, and your screen resembles the screen shown in Figure 16-9.

With the picture still selected,

14. Click the CENTER ALIGNMENT button on the toolbar.

The picture should appear between the zero and 2.75 inch markings.

15. Click anywhere in the white space to the right of the picture to de-select it.

An insertion point the full height of the picture will start to blink.

16. Press [ENTER] four times.

The picture scrolls up, and a small insertion point is now blinking in the middle of the first column. Since the text that you intend to place in this column will also be centered, you will not change the alignment of the insertion point.

INSERTING THE INTRODUCTORY TEXT

The *CONTEST* directory on your data disk contains all of the text for your newsletter. Among the files is one that serves to introduce the rest of the newsletter. You will insert that file next

IT'S YOUR TURN

1. Open the file named *INTRO.WPS* from the *CONTEST* directory on your data disk.

The unformatted title lines shown in Figure 16-10 will open on your screen.

FIGURE 16-10

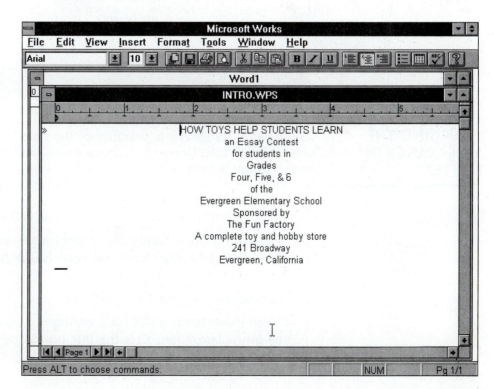

2. Choose Select All from the EDIT menu.

   All the text will become selected.

3. Choose Copy from the EDIT menu.

4. Choose Close from the FILE menu.

   The *INTRO* file will be put away, and the newsletter word processing document will once again appear on your screen, with the insertion point blinking where you left it last.

5. Choose Paste from the EDIT menu.

   The introductory lines appear in your document, four lines below the picture.

6. If necessary scroll down until all of the introductory text is visible on the screen, as shown in Figure 16-11.

FIGURE 16–11

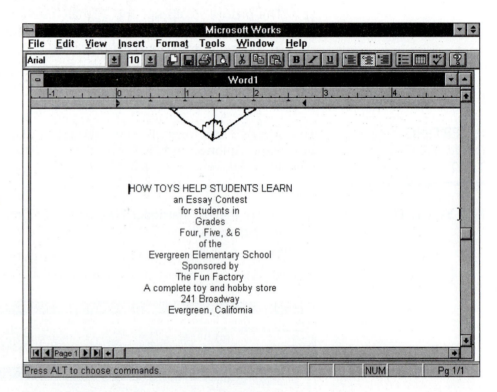

CHANGING THE APPEARANCE OF THE TEXT

You need to change the appearance of the lines in this introductory text so that they will grab the reader's attention, as well as to balance the size and impact of the picture.

IT'S YOUR TURN

1. Select the line "HOW TOYS HELP STUDENTS LEARN."

2. Choose the Times New Roman font (or any font of your choice, if that one is not available) from the Font Name box (currently displaying Arial) on the toolbar.

3. Choose 24 from the Font Size box.

   Since the column is not wide enough to accommodate the entire title in the larger font size, the title now occupies three lines.

To emphasize the information about the contest, the next six lines should be spaced out a little, and their font style should be made bold.

4. Click anywhere in the white space to the left of the line containing "an Essay Contest" to position the insertion point immediately in front of the first letter of that line.

5. Press [ENTER] once.

6. Drag to select the six lines below the title, as shown in Figure 16-12.

FIGURE 16-12

7. Choose Paragraph from the FORMAT menu.

   The Paragraph dialog box appears on the screen.

8. Click the Breaks and Spacing tab if it is not already showing.

   Your screen should look like Figure 16-13, with the insertion point blinking in the Between Lines text box of the Line Spacing box.

To indicate 1.5 line spacing,

9. Type: 1.5

10. Click OK or press [ENTER].

   The lines will spread apart and will continue to be selected.

11. Click the BOLD button on the toolbar.

12. Choose 12 point from the Font Size box.

13. Click anywhere in the white space to deselect the text.

   Notice that there is a mixture of letters and numbers in the grade list.

FIGURE 16-13

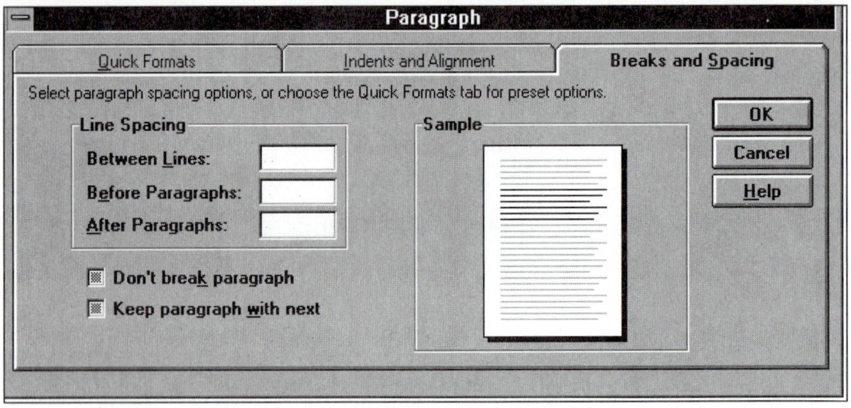

Paragraph

Quick Formats · Indents and Alignment · Breaks and Spacing

Select paragraph spacing options, or choose the Quick Formats tab for preset options.

Line Spacing

Between Lines:

Before Paragraphs:

After Paragraphs:

Sample

☐ Don't break paragraph
☐ Keep paragraph with next

OK
Cancel
Help

To spell out all grade levels,

14. Double click on the 6 to select only that number.

15. Type: Six

16. Use the vertical scroll bar to bring the last line of this introductory text into view, if it is not presently visible.

17. Click to position the insertion point immediately in front of the line "Sponsored by."

18. Press [ENTER] once.

    The line "A complete toy and hobby store" is out of place; it needs to be moved to the end of the introductory text.

19. Select the entire line "A complete toy and hobby store" by moving the cursor into the left margin of that line (the pointer turns into a right pointing arrow) then clicking once.

20. Choose Cut from the EDIT menu ([CTRL] [X]).

CAUTION   If you simply dragged to select the words in step 19, you may have left a blank line in their place, because the invisible paragraph marker at the end of the line was not selected and cut. To eliminate the blank line, simply click on the line and press [BACKSPACE]. (If you have the All Characters option checked in the VIEW menu, you will be able to see the ¶ symbol.)

21. Click to place the insertion point at the end of the line "Evergreen, California."

22. Press [ENTER] twice.

23. Choose Paste from the EDIT menu ([CTRL] [V]).

To de-emphasize your store's lines so the reader's attention will be directed to the importance of the essay contest, you will reformat them in a smaller type.

24. Drag to select the last five lines, starting with "Sponsored by" and ending with "A complete toy and hobby store."

25. Choose Arial from the Font Name and 8 point from the Font Size boxes of the toolbar.

26. Click in the white space on the right side of the last line to deselect.

    The insertion point should be blinking immediately to the right of the last letter in "store."

27. Press [ENTER] until the insertion point jumps to the top of the next column.

You are now ready to insert the text for the second column of the first page.

INSERTING TEXT INTO THE SECOND COLUMN

To complete this page of the newsletter, you will add messages to the parents from the principal of Evergreen Elementary School and from you as the owner of The Fun Factory. The textual material is stored on your data disk. Your job is simply to put everything together and make it look attractive. Review Figure 16-1 to get an idea of the layout of the newsletter.

IT'S YOUR TURN

The insertion point should be blinking at the top (in the middle) of the second column on the first page.

To prepare for the left-aligned messages,

1. Click the LEFT ALIGNMENT button on the toolbar.

2. Open the *PRINCIP.WPS* file from the *CONTEST* directory of your data disk.

    The *PRINCIP.WPS* window will be the active window after the file has opened.

3. Choose Select All from the EDIT menu.

4. Choose Copy from the EDIT menu.

5. Choose Close from the FILE menu.

    The word processing window reappears, with the insertion point blinking at the left side of the second column.

6. Choose Paste from the EDIT menu.

    The principal's message is now inserted in the second column.

7. If you cannot see the right edge of the second column, use the horizontal scroll bar to scroll it into view.

8. Use standard word processing techniques that you have learned previously to select, italicize, and center the first line of the second column, "A Message from the Principal."

You can tell by looking at the Font Name box in the toolbar that this message was saved in Arial font. Arial is a sans serif font. A serif is the extra little horizontal stroke that appears at the top or bottom of the main vertical stroke of a printed letter. Serif fonts are believed to be easier to read in paragraph form, so you will change the body of the principal's message to Times New Roman, if it is available on your system.

9. Drag to select the two paragraphs that make up the body of the principal's message.

10. Choose Times New Roman from the Font Name box on the toolbar, if it is available. If it is not available, just skip this step.

11. Choose 14 from the Font Size box on the toolbar.

The next change you will make is to align the text so it is evenly justified at both margins of the column. Some people call such alignment *fully justified*. *WORKS 3.0* simply calls it *justified.* Because such alignment is not used often, there is no button for it on the toolbar, but it is available from the Paragraph dialog box.

12. Choose Paragraph from the FORMAT menu.

When the Paragraph dialog box appears,

13. Click the Indents and Alignment tab.

Your screen should look like the screen shown in Figure 16-14.

FIGURE 16-14

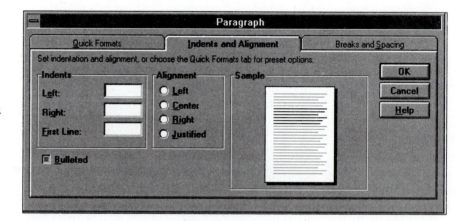

14. Click Justified in the Alignment block of the dialog box.

15. Click OK or press [ENTER].

16. Click anywhere in the white space to deselect the paragraphs.

Your screen should look something like the screen shown in Figure 16-15.

17. Scroll down, if necessary, and click in the white space to the right of the line that contains "Dr. Reuben Lopez."

18. Click the RIGHT ALIGNMENT button on the toolbar.

19. Press [ENTER] eight times.

20. Click the LEFT ALIGNMENT button on the toolbar.

You are ready to insert the sponsor's message.

21. Open the *SPONSOR.WPS* file from the *CONTEST* directory of your data disk.

22. Follow the techniques presented in steps 3 through 18 above to insert the Sponsor's message and format it to match the principal's message.

23. Type your name at the end of the message and right align it.

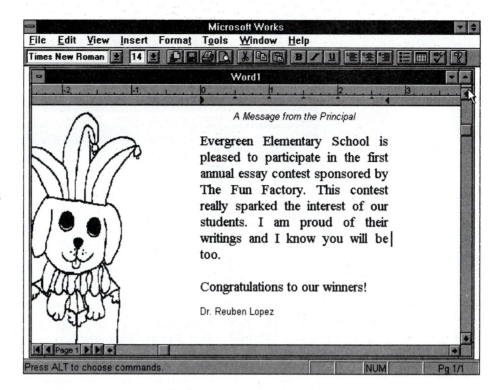

FIGURE 16-15

When you are finished,

24. Press [ENTER] once to move the insertion point to the line following your name.

25. Click the LEFT ALIGNMENT button on the toolbar.

26. Choose Save As from the FILE menu, and save your incomplete newsletter in your name directory on your data disk. Use the file name *NEWSLTR* for saving.

INSERTING THE STUDENTS' ESSAYS

The winning essays are stored on your data disk, ready for you to insert them in the newsletter and format them attractively.

IT'S YOUR TURN

To advance to the second page of the newsletter, the insertion point should be blinking at the left margin of the line immediately following your name.

1. Press [ENTER] until the insertion point moves to the top of the first column on the next page by watching the page number (1) at the lower left of your screen change to 2.

If you enter too many lines, press [BACKSPACE] to move the insertion point to the top of the second page.

2. Open the *WINNERS.WPS* file from the *CONTEST* folder of your data disk, then select, copy and paste the *WINNERS* document into the *NEWSLTR* document.

The *NEWSLTR* document should now be displayed on your screen with the text filling column 1 and the overflow extending into column 2, as shown in Figure 16-16.

FIGURE 16-16

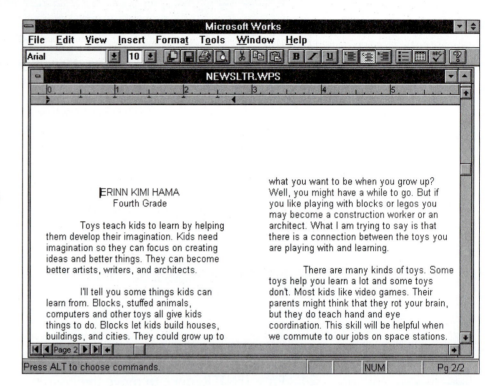

3. Use the skills you learned in the previous section to format the second page of the newsletter as follows:

   a. Make all three titles (the students' names and grade levels) Arial 10, bold style. Leave them centered above the essays.

   b. Make the bodies of all three essays 12 point Times New Roman font. Use the Paragraph dialog box to fully justify the bodies of all three essays.

Now you must give credit to the artist who drew the front page picture.

4. Click to place the insertion point immediately following the line of asterisks at the bottom of the second column.

5. Press [ENTER] twice.

6. Cick the LEFT ALIGNMENT button on the toolbar, if necessary, and use the toolbar to set the font to 12 point, Times New Roman, Bold.

7. Type: Many thanks to Lesley Tanaka of the sixth grade for her wonderful drawing, which appears on the first page.

8. Select the paragraph, and use the Paragraph dialog box to justify it.

That does it. The newsletter is practically finished. To save all your hard work up to now,

9. Choose Save from the FILE menu.

CREATING THE FOOTER

In multiple-page documents, it is desirable to insert footers that identify the document and give the page number. To create the footer for this document,

IT'S YOUR TURN

1. Choose Headers and Footers from the VIEW menu.

When the familiar Headers and Footers dialog box appears,

2. Press [TAB] to advance to the Footer text box.
3. Type: &Lyour name&CPage &P&R&D

   By now, you should recognize the codes to place your name at the left margin with the word page followed by a space and the page number in the center, and the date on the right.

Usually the first page of a multipage document does not contain the page number. You can direct *WORKS* to suppress the number on page one by clicking the option in the dialog box.

4. Click the option No Footer On 1st Page in the lower left corner of the dialog box.
5. Click OK or press [ENTER].

FINISHING UP THE NEWSLETTER

You are now ready to save again and, if required, to print.

IT'S YOUR TURN

1. Choose Save from the FILE menu.
2. If you wish, you can view the newsletter by using the Print Preview screen.
3. Print the newsletter, if requested to do so by your instructor.
4. Close all files.
5. Quit *WORKS,* as directed in previous chapters.

   If a message appears asking if you want to save the clipboard contents, click "No."

SUMMARY

That's it! You have covered all the basic features of *WORKS 3.0.* In this chapter you have imported a TIFF file and created a simple newsletter. We hope you feel comfortable with the program and will explore more advanced features by experimenting, referring to the user's manual, and using the Help menu.

REVIEW QUESTIONS

1. Which *WORKS* module would you use to create the primary document for a newsletter containing columns, text, and pictures?

2. How do you create columns?

3. Which view allows you to see a columnar document as it actually appears when printed?

4. Which menu and option allows you to justify text?

5. How do you insert artwork into a word processing document?

6. How do you prevent a footer from appearing on the title page?

EXERCISE

Create your own two-page newsletter. You may use existing text and graphic files or create your own. You might try three columns. Have fun!

Appendix A
Communications

<table>
<tr>
<td>INTRODUCTION</td>
<td>Computers can "talk" to each other! You can use a properly equipped computer to exchange messages with a friend or to access the data and services of large computers anywhere in the world. Communications capabilities enable you to</td>
</tr>
</table>

- use electronic mail to send messages and files
- search on-line databases for information
- obtain business, finance, and investment information
- conduct electronic conferences
- shop electronically
- connect to your office computer and work from anywhere in the world

WHAT'S NEEDED

To send a message with a personal computer, you will need the following items:

- computer
- modem and its related phone number
- communications software
- telephone line
- cables

Modem is short for modulation/demodulation. A physical device called a modem is needed on the sending computer to change the electronic signals of the computer to sounds that travel over telephone lines. This is called modulation.

Another modem is needed at the receiving end to convert the sound waves back into electronic signals that the computer can understand. This is called demodulation.

There are two types of modems: internal and external. *Internal modems* fit into slots inside the computer's system unit. Most modern *external modems* are small boxes with direct cable connections to the computer and the telephone lines. To better understand how computers communicate, you may want to know how a modem transmits computer data. Personal computers use a combination of eight binary numbers, or bits, to represent one letter. For example, the letter A is represented by the numbers 01000001. When this combination of bits is translated into sound signals, a one is transmitted as a high signal, and a zero is transmitted as a low signal. To send the letter A over telephone lines, eight signals must be sent. The modem sends each signal sequentially (serially) through a device known as an RS-232-C interface. (RS-232-C stands for "Recommended standard number 232, version C.")

One of the identifying features of a modem is the rate at which it transmits and receives data, called the **baud rate**. The baud rates supported by *WORKS 3.0* range from 300 to 19,200. The baud rate of the sending computer must match that of the receiving computer. Before you can begin communications, you must find out the baud rate of the receiving computer. Information services usually publish their modem speed, which you match with your software. You can use your communication software to set the baud rate, as well as several other important settings. Other settings have to do with checking for errors in transmission. You don't have to understand what it all means in order to use it—just type in the proper settings, or parameters, of the modem you are calling.

USING *WORKS 3.0* TO COMMUNICATE

To use the communications module of *WORKS*, you must create a Communications file, adjust the settings that *WORKS* needs to communicate, connect to another computer, transfer information, and disconnect. In this appendix, we give you the general steps to accomplish each of those activities. This appendix is not intended to be a step-by-step tutorial. Because of the diversity of communication connections that can be made, it is impossible for us to anticipate every situation. (Notice that this appendix contains no "It's Your Turn" icons.)

OPENING A COMMUNICATIONS DOCUMENT

You need to create a new *WORKS 3.0* file for each computer or service you want to call. You open a new Communications file the same way you create a new file for any other *WORKS* module: launch *WORKS* and click on the COMMUNICATIONS button of the Startup dialog box to obtain a new Communications document.

When you open a new Communications document, the Easy Connect dialog box appears. You can now either choose from the list of phone numbers in the Easy Connect dialog box (the Phone menu and Easy Connect dialog box list the eight most recent connections), or type the number you want to call. Include a prefix if needed. For example, you may need to dial 9 to access an outside line. At such times, you may also include a comma after the 9 to interject a brief pause that will give the phone system time to access the line. If one comma does not create a long enough pause, you may use as many as you wish.

GETTING READY TO DIAL

If you called someone in another country, you would have to agree on a common language in which to communicate. Similarly, to establish communications between two computers you must find out the settings of the computer you are calling, then adjust your computer settings accordingly so they speak the same language. This is accomplished through the SETTINGS menu.

When you choose the Modem command from the SETTINGS menu, *WORKS* displays the Modem Setup dialog box. Clicking the *test* button in this dialog box allows you to test that the modem is properly connected and is able to receive and respond to the commands *WORKS* sends.

The default modem settings are generic Hayes-compatible settings and can be examined by clicking the ADVANCED button in the Modem Setup dialog box. That button brings up the Modem Settings dialog box showing the current settings. You may change anything you wish, but you should make changes only if your modem requires them. If you do change the settings and then want to restore the default settings, click the RESTORE button in the Modem Settings dialog box. To obtain detailed information about either dialog box, click the HELP button.

Before computers can exchange information, they must follow the same rules or settings. *WORKS* uses standard communication settings used by many information services. These settings can be examined and changed, if necessary, by using the Communication section of the Settings dialog box, which is displayed when you choose Communication from the SETTINGS menu. The following table explains the preset *WORKS* communication settings.

Type of Setting	Default Setting	Description
Port	COM1	The port to which your modem or cable is connected.
Baud Rate	9600	The speed by which information is transferred. Check your modem manual for the baud rates it can use.
Parity	None	Checks for transmission errors.
Ignore Parity	On	If you need to use a Parity setting other than None, you must clear this box, then use the Parity setting you want.
Data Bits	8	The number of bits used to represent a character.
Handshake	Xon/Xoff	Controls data flow from one computer to the other. Xon/Xoff is standard for communicating through modems.
Stop Bits	1	The number of bits used to signal the end of each transmitted character.

CONNECTING AND DISCONNECTING

Be certain that your modem is turned on before you try to connect. Once you have matched your settings with the communicating computer and have chosen or dialed the phone number by using the PHONE menu, the Dial Status dialog box appears, informing you of the progress. If a connection is made, you may start typing your message. If you are calling a computer service, you may be asked for an identification number and password. Follow the instructions received from the service to navigate through your session. When you are finished, log off the service according to its instructions. It is important that you always sign off from an information service before you disconnect; otherwise, you may be charged for the time it takes the service computer to recognize that you have disconnected. To stop communicating with another computer, choose the Hang Up command from the PHONE menu.

SENDING A FILE

Telephone communication charges are made by the minute, so if you wish to send a long message, you will save money by creating your message with a word processor before beginning a session. In communications jargon, that is called creating a file *off line.* When you send a file (TOOLS menu, Send File option), the computer at the other end saves it on disk. You can send files as either text or binary files. Choose the text option when the receiving computer does not have *WORKS* installed; choose the binary option when the other computer has *WORKS* installed.

When you send a file, you must match the transfer protocol used by the other computer (SETTINGS menu, Transfer option). Kermit is the default protocol. It is the slowest protocol but is very reliable and compatible and is designed for transferring files between computers of different types.

GETTING READY TO RECEIVE A FILE

When you are receiving a file (sometimes called ***downloading*** a file), *WORKS* automatically saves the file on your disk as you receive it. You must also make sure the protocols of both computers match. From the TOOLS menu choose Receive File. *WORKS* then displays the Receiving File dialog box and also indicates how the transfer is progressing.

CAPTURING INCOMING TEXT TO A FILE

WORKS displays information as it is exchanged during a communications session. However, as you work the screen may become full, and the information at the top might scroll off the screen. You can capture all or parts of the information you receive by following the procedures outlined in the *WORKS* Help section, "Capture Text Command (Tools Menu)."

AUTOMATIC SIGN-ON

If you are calling a computer service, communication scripts are useful in recording repetitive or time-consuming tasks. Within the TOOLS menu, the Record Script option allows you to choose between two types of scripts: Sign-on scripts for when you connect and sign on to a service and scripts that execute repetitive tasks. The recording procedure is detailed in the *WORKS* Help section, "Recording a Script."

SAVING A COMMUNICATION DOCUMENT

If there are a few numbers you call frequently, creating and using documents that contain the settings for each computer you call will simplify your tasks considerably.

To create and save a communications document, simply open a new Communications document, choose the settings you need to match the other computer, then save the document using a descriptive name that will remind you of the intended receiving computer. The communications extension *.WCM* will distinguish this document from the others. To use this document, open it as you would any other document.

SUMMARY

The *WORKS* communications module contains basic features that enable you to call another computer or bulletin board, connect to a remote mainframe computer, or access information services. Modems can help you communicate with large computers across the country. Companies such as CompuServe, Prodigy, America Online, Dialog, and Dow Jones provide many databases of information, electronic mail services, electronic shopping, and electronic conferences for a fee. Many free, local electronic bulletin boards may be available in your area. You can also use your computer as a terminal to connect to a remote mainframe.

Appendix B
Keyboard Command Summary

Unmodified Function Key Commands by Tool

To do this:	Word Processor	Spreadsheet	Database
Get Help	F1	F1	F1
Edit a cell or field		F2	F2
Toggle Spreadsheet & Chart		F3	
Go to (page/bookmark/cell/field)	F5	F5	F5
Switch to next Pane	F6	F6	F6
Repeat search	F7	F7	F7
Highlight/Extend selection	F8	F8	F8
Paginate Now	F9		
Calculate Now		F9	
Toggle Form/List views			F9
Activate Menu Bar	F10	F10	F10

Modified Function Key Commands by Tool

To do this:	Word Processor	Spreadsheet	Database
Choose The Tutorial	[SHIFT] + F1	[SHIFT] + F1	[SHIFT] + F1
Quit Works	[ALT] + F4	[ALT] + F4	[ALT] + F4
Close Active Document	[CTRL] + F4	[CTRL] + F4	[CTRL] + F4
Move To Next Bookmark	[SHIFT] + F5		
Move To Next Named Range		[SHIFT] + F5	
Switch To Next Document Window	[CTRL] + F6	[CTRL] + F6	[CTRL] + F6
Switch To Previous Pane	[SHIFT] + F6	[SHIFT] + F6	[SHIFT] + F6
Switch To Previous Document Window	[CTRL] + [SHIFT] + F6	[CTRL] + [SHIFT] + F6	[CTRL] + [SHIFT] + F6

To do this:	Word Processor	Spreadsheet	Database
Repeat Format	[SHIFT] + F7	[SHIFT] + F7	[SHIFT] + F7
Highlight A Row		[CTRL] + F8	[CTRL] + F8
Highlight A Column		[SHIFT] + F8	[SHIFT] + F8
Highlight The Entire Document		[CTRL] + [SHIFT] + F8	[CTRL] + [SHIFT] + F8

Keyboard Shortcut Keys by Tool

To obtain the following:	Press	Word Processor	Spreadsheet	Database
Undo Previous Action	[CTRL] + [Z]	X	X	X
Bold	[CTRL] + [B]	X	X	X
Underline	[CTRL] + [U]	X	X	X
Italic	[CTRL] + [I]	X	X	X
Plain text (No format)	[CTRL] + [SPACEBAR]	X	X	X
Cut Selection	[CTRL] + [X]	X	X	X
Copy Selection	[CTRL] + [C]	X	X	X
Paste Selection	[CTRL] + [V]	X	X	X
Left Alignment	[CTRL] + [L]	X	X	X
Right Alignment	[CTRL] + [R]	X	X	X
Center Alignment	[CTRL] + [E]	X	X	X
Justified Alignment	[CTRL] + [J]	X		
General Alignment	[CTRL] + [G]		X	X
Current Date	[CTRL] + [;]	X	X	X
Current Time	[CTRL] + [:] or [CTRL] + [SHIFT] + [;]	X	X	X
Save Active File	[CTRL] + [S]	X	X	X
Print Active File	[CTRL] + [P]	X	X	X

Additional Word Processing Shortcuts

To do this:	Press:
Create Nested Indent	[CTRL] + [N]
Undo Nested Indent	[CTRL] + [M]
Create Hanging Indent	[CTRL] + [H]

To do this:	Press:
Undo Hanging Indent	[CTRL] + [G]
Insert Manual Page Break	[CTRL] + [ENTER]
Insert Non-Breaking Hyphen	[CTRL] + [SHIFT] + [HYPHEN]
Initiate Extension	F8
Select One Word	F8 two times
Select A Sentence	F8 three times
Select A Paragraph	F8 four times
Select Entire File	F8 five times
Remove Selection	[SHIFT] + F8
Stop Extension	[ESC]
Undo	[ALT] + [BACKSPACE]
Move To End Of File	[CTRL] + [END]
Move To Beginning Of File	[CTRL] + [HOME]
Move To End Of Line	[END]
Move To Beginning Of Line	[HOME]
Move To Next Screen	[PAGE DOWN]
Move To Previous Screen	[PAGE UP]
Insert The Filename (When Printed)	[CTRL] + [A]
Insert The Date (When Printed)	[CTRL] + [D]
Insert The Time (When Printed)	[CTRL] + [T]
Single space lines	[CTRL] + [1]
Double space lines	[CTRL] + [2]
Space lines 1.5 lines apart	[CTRL] + [5]
Reduce space before paragraph	[CTRL] + [0] (zero)
Add space before paragraph	[CTRL] + [O] (letter O)

Additional Spreadsheet and Database Shortcuts

To do this:	Press:
Move to beginning of row	[HOME]
Move to end of row	[END]
Move to beginning of file	[CTRL] + [HOME]
Move to end of file	[CTRL] + [END]
Move up one window	[PAGE UP]
Move down one window	[PAGE DOWN]
Move to next field (Database Form view)	[TAB]
Move to previous field (Database Form view)	[SHIFT] + [TAB]

To do this:	Press:
Move to next record (Database Form view)	[CTRL] + [PAGE DOWN]
Move to previous record (Database Form view)	[CTRL] + [PAGE UP]
Comma format	[CTRL] + [COMMA]
Currency format	[CTRL] + [4]
Percent format	[CTRL] + [5]
Create Autosum total	[CTRL] + [M] (in the Spreadsheet only)

Glossary

absolute cell reference In the spreadsheet application, a reference to a cell location that remains unchanged if a formula that contains the reference is copied or moved to a new location. See *Relative reference*.

active cell On a spreadsheet, the currently selected cell, which is boldly outlined on the screen.

address The column letter and row number identifying the location of a cell.

application programs See *application software*.

applications See *application software*.

application software Computer programs that direct the resources and capabilities of the computer and its peripheral devices. Programs include word processing, database management, graphics, and communications. Compare with *system programs*.

argument Value required by a function (enclosed in parentheses).

backup As a verb, to make a duplicate copy of a file or program on a disk in case the original is lost or destroyed. As a noun, the duplicate copy itself is often referred to as the backup.

bar chart A chart containing a series of bars indicating a comparison of numbers within a category.

baud rate A unit for measuring the speed of data transmission.

bit Binary digit. The smallest unit of data stored in a computer. The value of an individual bit is represented by the number one (on) or the number zero (off).

bitmapped objects Designs created by the arrangement of bits, or pixels.

bold Term applied to text that is darker than normal text.

calculated field A field that contains a function or formula based on other fields in that database.

cascade Option in the WINDOWS menu that resizes all open documents so they are all the same size and arranged with their title bars visible.

cell Intersection of a row and column in a spreadsheet.

center tab Centers text at the position of the tab marker.

chevron Character(s) used in *Works* to denote an automatic page break or set off a placeholder (i.e., <<field name>>) when merging a word processing file with a database file.

clicking Positioning the pointer on something, then quickly pressing and releasing the mouse button.

clipboard Portion of computer memory that is reserved for copying text and/or graphics for transfer between or within documents.

close To remove a window from the desktop. When a window is closed, the document it represents is no longer open on the desktop. Closing can be achieved by selecting Close from the FILE menu or by clicking in the window's Close box.

close box Small box in the upper left corner of the active window. When clicked, it closes the window.

column A vertical section containing data in a spreadsheet or database List view.

communications The ability of a computer to send information to and receive information from another computer.

control key A special key [CTRL] on the computer's keyboard that is used in conjunction with other keys to change their normal meaning. The control key usually must be held down while another key is depressed.

copy The process by which selected text is moved to another location without eliminating the original.

CPU The Central Processing Unit. Also called the microprocessor. The part of the computer that directs the flow of information within the computer, performs all calculations, and controls all other components of the computer.

cursor The special mark on the screen that indicates the relative position of the mouse when it is in use. When the cursor (also called a pointer) is in position for the next entry, the mouse button is pressed. If no mouse is available, the cursor shows the position on the screen that will be affected by the next action.

cursor keys The group of keys marked with arrows on the computer's keyboard that can be used to control the position of the cursor on the screen. Also called arrow keys.

cut Selected information is removed from the application and placed on the clipboard.

cut and paste Moving selected information. Removing a portion of text or a picture from one place in a document and copying it elsewhere in the same or another document.

database A collection of data or information concerning one major topic maintained in one central storage place (for example, the telephone book or card catalog at a library) or computer file.

data disk A disk used for storing documents created or altered by the user, such as letters, memos, graphs, etc. Compare with *program disk*.

decimal tab stop Automatically lines up the decimal points in a column of numbers.

default The standard setting or action performed by the software when the user gives no specific direction to the computer.

demodulator Converts the sound waves from phone lines back to digital signals that the computer can understand.

deselect To remove highlighting.

dialog box A special window that requests information. The user must respond before the activity can continue.

directory An index file containing name, location, size, and other information about all of the files contained on a storage medium.

disk A flat, circular piece of plastic (flexible) or metal (rigid) onto which information is recorded magnetically. A flexible disk is also called a floppy. The 3½-inch floppy disk encased in a rigid container is sometimes called a micro-floppy. See also *hard disk*.

disk drive A device that can read information from and write information onto a disk in much the same way that a tape recorder plays from or records onto magnetic tape. Inside the drive, a motor spins the disk, and a read/write head performs the reading or writing operation.

Disk Operating System (DOS) An operating system that allows a computer to use disks for data storage. Many computer manufacturers incorporate the acronym DOS into the name of the operating system for a particular computer (for example, IBM

PC-DOS or MS-DOS for IBM personal computers). See *operating system*.

display (1) As a noun, the screen connected to the computer. See *CRT* or *Monitor*. (2) As a verb, to cause material to appear on the computer screen.

document See *file*.

documentation Written instructions describing how to use computer hardware or software.

DOS See *Disk Operating System*.

dot matrix printer Contains a mechanism consisting of a set of tiny pins that form letters; prints by selecting the appropriate pins to hit the paper through an inked ribbon.

double click Clicking the mouse twice in rapid succession to select or open an item quickly.

double density disk Also called low density or low capacity, to distinguish from high density or high capacity. A 5.25-inch double density disk can hold 360K; a 3.5-inch disk can hold 720K.

download In communications, to receive a program or file sent to your computer by another computer.

dragging Positioning the pointer at the beginning point, holding down the mouse button, moving the mouse to the ending point, then releasing the button.

end-of-file mark A dark solid line (about ¼-inch long) shown always as the last character in every word processing document. You cannot move the insertion point below this mark, and you cannot delete this mark.

endnotes Similar to footnotes, except that footnotes appear at the base of the page where referenced, and endnotes appear at the end of a chapter or document.

extension Term referring to the part of the filename after the period that describes or further identifies the contents of that file.

external modem A small box with direct cable connections to computer and telephone lines.

field Smallest unit of a database record.

file A unit of information that is stored on disk and given a filename. The contents of a file may be anything—a letter, a financial model, a graph, or a program.

first line indent Controls the horizontal positioning of the first line of each paragraph.

floppy disk See *disk*.

font The typeface or design used to print characters (for example, Courier or Arial).

footer Text that appears at the bottom of every page.

footnote Text appearing at the bottom of a page (indicated by a footnote number) or at the end of a document, which credits a quotation, a summary, or a paraphrase.

format As a verb, to prepare the surface of a disk so it can be used for storing data. As a noun, the pattern that must be written on the disk before it can be used for storing data. Different drives require different disk formats. Also used both as a noun and a verb to describe the manner in which text is set up on a page.

formula A rule expressed as an equation.

formula bar In database and spreadsheet modules, that area near the top of the screen where data is typed and edited before being entered into the selected cell.

Form view In database, shows all (or at least a screenful) of the information in a single record.

freeze This option prevents specified rows or columns from disappearing when scrolling through a large spreadsheet.

function A built-in calculation (*WORKS* has 76) that produces a new value from other values called arguments.

function keys [F1] through [F12]. Special keys which, when depressed, will begin some activity as prescribed by the software.

Graphical User Interface (GUI) Pictures and menus that allow control of the computing environment by manipulating the pictures and making choices from the menus. GUIs are usually controlled from a mouse.

handles Small black squares appearing on the corners and sometimes mid-points of an object.

hanging paragraphs The first line of the paragraph begins at the left edge and the rest of the lines begin further to the right.

hard copy Printed material. Also called printouts.

hard disk Fast auxiliary storage capable of storing millions of characters, mounted in its own case or inside a computer.

hardware Refers to the physical components of a computer—e.g., monitor, external hard disk, mouse, keyboard, modem, etc. Contrast with *software*.

header Text that appears at the top of every page.

high density disk Also called high capacity to distinguish from double density, low density, or low ca-

pacity. A 5.25-inch high density disk can hold 1.2MB; a 3.5-inch disk can hold 1.44MB.

I-beam A cursor symbol that marks the present position of the mouse.

icons Screen symbols representing objects, concepts, or messages.

impact printer A device for transferring information from the computer to paper. It contains a printing mechanism that operates by striking the paper through an inked ribbon, much like a typewriter.

indent Distance between the margins and the beginning or end of the lines in a paragraph.

insertion point Blinking vertical line that marks the position for your next action.

integrated program Software that combines two or more applications. *WORKS* is an integrated program that combines word processing, database, spreadsheet, draw, and communication applications. Data are easily exchanged between them.

internal modem Fits into slots inside the computer's system unit. Also see *modem*.

italic Style in which text slants upward to the right. Used to emphasize words, set off book titles, etc.

justification In *WORKS*, pertaining to alignment of text at both left and right margins.

kerning The process of adjusting the space between characters so text appears more evenly spaced.

kilobyte A measure of memory size, often abbreviated as K. One kilobyte (1K) is 1,024 characters or bytes. See *megabyte*.

label Non-numeric entries in a spreadsheet. Calculations cannot be performed on cells containing labels.

landscape Printing horizontally (sideways).

laser printer A non-impact printer using a laser beam and toner to form characters on paper.

launch To start a program.

layout The physical placement of text or data on the printed page.

left-aligned tab Aligns text at the left.

left-indent marker Controls the position on the page where carryover text will begin when the text is wordwrapped. Compare with *first-line indent*.

line chart A chart illustrating trends using lines connecting points that represent numbers.

List view In the database module, this view shows all (or a screenful) of the fields with their content in columns and rows.

low density disk See *double density disk.*

mainframe In terms of physical size, size of memory, and speed of calculations, a large computer—in contrast to a microcomputer (personal computer).

margin Space between the edges of the paper and the printed area. Set in the Print Setup dialog box.

MAXIMIZE button Located at the upper right corner of the window. Clicking it enlarges the window to its maximum size.

MDA Monochrome Display Adapter. Monitor works only with text and cannot handle graphics.

megabyte One million bytes (or one million characters). Commonly abbreviated as MB. See *kilobyte.*

memory See *RAM* and *ROM.*

menu A list of options from which you can choose.

menu bar The bar across the top of the screen that displays the menu names, e.g., FILE.

microprocessor See *CPU.*

MINIMIZE button Located next to the MAXIMIZE button at the upper right corner of the window. Clicking it reduces the active window to an icon usually positioned at the bottom left of the screen with a representative icon.

modem A peripheral device that enables one computer to communicate directly with another computer by using telephone communications channels. MODEM is an acronym for modulator/demodulator. A modem changes the digital electronic signals used by a computer into analog-wave forms that can be transmitted by telephone and vice versa.

monitor A video display connected to the computer and used as an output device. See *CRT.*

monochrome Single color display.

motherboard Main circuit board of a microcomputer.

mouse A pointing device used in connection with graphical user interfaces. The pointer moves in correspondence to the movement of the mouse.

nonimpact printer A device for transferring information from the computer to paper such that the printing mechanism does not physically strike the paper. Examples are ink-jet printers and laser printers.

off line In the communications application, this means that the computer is not electronically connected to another computer.

on line In the communications application, this means that the computer is electronically connected to another computer.

open Bringing a file into the computer's memory and making it ready for use.

operands That which is operated upon by an operator. In the expression "7+6," the 7 and 6 are operands. See *operator.*

operating system A collection of system software that controls the internal operations of the computer and provides certain utility functions to the user. Different operating systems are designed for different computers.

operator In math, any symbol or term indicating that a certain procedure is to be carried out; e.g., the hyphen is used as a minus sign denoting a subtraction activity.

page break Where one page ends and another starts. In word processing documents, automatic page breaks display as a chevron (>) character, and manual page breaks display as a dashed line across the screen.

panes The work areas that appear in *WORKS* when the screen is divided into two or four windows. Each work area can show a different part of the same file.

parity In communications, a form of error checking used to increase the chances that each character has been received correctly.

paste To place a copy of the contents of the clipboard at the insertion point.

peripherals Any hardware that is attached to a computer.

PICT A graphic file format, generally used for object-oriented graphics.

pie chart A chart representing the relationship of parts to a whole.

placeholders In *WORKS,* a field name from a database and the chevrons that surround the field name. During printing, it is replaced by an entry from the appropriate field in the database.

point Measurement used for font height. One point is $\frac{1}{72}$ of an inch.

pointer See *cursor.*

pointing Placing the tip of the pointer (arrow) to the area to be affected.

portrait Printing in the normal vertical mode.

printer The hardware used to obtain printed copies of data produced by the computer.

print preview Found in FILE menu. Lets you see each page of your document (in miniature) before you print.

program A set of directions causing the computer to perform a task. Programs are also called software.

program disk A disk containing a program. Compare with *data disk*.

protect This option prevents the accidental damage or deletion of data in a spreadsheet.

query view In Database, this view is similar to Form view, except it is used for selecting records that contain similar information in one or more fields.

RAM Random Access Memory. The main memory of a computer. All programs are loaded into RAM memory before they can be run. RAM memory is called "volatile" or "temporary," because the programs or data stored there are lost when the computer is turned off.

record A collection of related items of information treated as a unit. Description of an item in a database.

relative reference In the spreadsheet application, a reference to a cell that changes relative to its position if the formula is copied or moved to a new location. See *absolute reference*.

report A printed table showing all or part of the information in a database document. You can have up to eight different reports associated with a single database document.

report view A printed table showing all or part of the information in a database document.

right-indent marker Marks the right edge of the typing line.

right tab Aligns columns of text at the right.

ROM Read Only Memory chip that permanently stores information.

root directory The highest level directory on a disk. Can contain files and/or other directories called subdirectories.

row A horizontal section containing data in a spreadsheet or database List view.

ruler A section of the screen in the word processing and draw applications that is used to control the appearance of the document.

save A common command that tells a computer to store a program or a file from main memory to a disk or tape.

screen The surface portion of a video terminal on which information is displayed.

scroll Process of viewing hidden portions of a large program or file by using the scroll bars on the right side or the bottom of the screen.

scroll bar A vertical or horizontal bar that appears at the right side (vertical) or the bottom (horizontal) of the screen. Some windows may only contain one scroll bar.

scroll box The small box on the scroll bars that indicates the position of the window content relative to the entire document.

select To mark (highlight) text or graphics for editing purposes.

serif font A font that has fine lines projecting out from the ends of main strokes of a letter.

software Another name for programs. Software may be written by the computer user, it may be purchased for a special purpose, or it may be delivered with the computer.

sort Rearrange data according to a predefined schema.

split bars When dividing a window into panes, these bars indicate the split location.

split screen Screen divided into two or four work areas, called windows or panes. Each work area can show a different part of the same file.

spreadsheet A type of program that arranges data and formulas in a matrix of cells.

stacked line chart A chart showing the relationships between the values of the categories and their totals by drawing stacked lines, each of which represents a data series.

status bar Located at the bottom of the screen and indicates such information as page, etc.

style Options such as bold, italic, and underline. Can be applied to any character.

system programs Software that controls the computer and provides common capabilities to all users.

system unit The housing that contains the CPU chip, memory chips, the motherboard, and the disk drives.

tab key Used to move the cursor a predefined number of spaces to the right or between choices in certain windows and dialog boxes.

tab stops Settings on the ruler which you set or that *WORKS* presets to allow you to move to those setting when the tab key is pressed.

template A frequently used form stored as a file that can be used whenever the information varies but not the format.

text editing cluster [HOME], [END], [PGDN], [PGUP], [INS], [DEL]. Used to quickly move through a file or text and to insert and delete data.

tile Resizes all open documents so that all are made visible by arranging them side-by-side or in panes.

title bar The area at the top of a window that contains the document name. If more than one window is open on your screen, you can distinguish the active window by its darkened title bar. The window can be moved by dragging the title bar with the mouse.

toggle key (switch) A key that alternately turns an activity on and off when you press it.

toolbar Bar located above the ruler for mouse users to quickly activate frequently used commands.

tracking *Works'* method of automatically adjusting the spacing between all characters.

undo A command that will reverse the most recent user action.

value In spreadsheet terminology, numeric entries or formulas. Contrast with *label*.

VGA Video Graphics Array. Enables the monitor to display high graphic and text resolutions.

wildcard A special character (*) that stands for any other character or group of characters. A method of handling multiple files without specifying each file by its full, unique name.

window A viewing area of a portion of computer memory as displayed on the video screen. Some programs and computers allow multiple windows to be displayed at the same time so that the viewer can see different files or different parts of the same file at the same time.

wordwrap If a word exceeds the right margin in word processing, the program will automatically move the word to the next line.

write protect A procedure to prevent accidental writing to a disk or tape.

write-protect notch An indentation or opening near the top corners of disks which is used to prevent accidental writing to a disk.

x-axis In charts, the horizontal line usually showing the way the data is classified, such as days, months, years, products, and so on.

y-axis In charts, the vertical line that represents the unit of measurement or amount, such as dollars, number of products sold, and so on.

Answers to Review Questions

CHAPTER 1

1. T 2. F 3. F
4. T 5. F

CHAPTER 2

1. T 2. F 3. T 4. F 5. T
6. T 7. T 8. F 9. F 10. T

CHAPTER 3

1. T 2. T 3. T 4. F 5. T
6. F 7. T 8. T 9. T 10. F

CHAPTER 4

1. F 2. F 3. F 4. F 5. F
6. T 7. F 8. T 9. F 10. F

CHAPTER 5

1. T 2. F 3. T 4. F 5. F
6. F 7. F 8. F 9. T

CHAPTER 6

1. Column letter and row number; column letter
2. FORMAT menu, Number option
3. EDIT menu, Go To option
4. EDIT menu, Clear option; or [BACKSPACE] [ENTER]
5. Right
6. =
7. Formula is created by user; function is pre-defined by *WORKS*
8. 56.7389 in General format; 56.74 in Comma and 2 decimals format

CHAPTER 7

1. FILE menu, Page Setup option
2. Click the Column header letter or use [SHIFT] + [F8]
3. =SUM(F2:F5)
4. Absolute reference shows $ preceding column and row headers
5. EDIT menu, Fill Down option
6. VIEW menu, Formulas option

CHAPTER 8

1. EDIT menu, Cut and Paste options. No
2. EDIT menu, Fill Down option
3. FORMAT menu, Alignment option
4. FORMAT menu, Protection option
5. False

CHAPTER 9

1. TOOLS menu
2. [CTRL] + [X]
3. INSERT menu
4. Save the associated spreadsheet
5. Choose Create New Chart from the TOOLS menu or click Chart button on the toolbar

CHAPTER 10

1. VIEW menu
2. List view; Form view
3. VIEW menu, Apply Query option
4. INSERT menu, Record/Field option
5. Form, List, Report
6. Form, List, Report, Query

CHAPTER 11

1. List
2. Changing column size or changing field size
3. Word processing
4. [TAB]
5. TOOLS menu, Sort Records option

CHAPTER 12

1. Form
2. FORMAT menu (Number option)
3. Query
4. A field whose contents depend on the contents of other fields
5. Report Statistics dialog box (displayed after the New Report dialog box is OK'd)

CHAPTER 13

1. [CTRL]
2. Select a field in the desired record and click the Form view button on the toolbar or press [F9].
3. b. Choose Copy from EDIT menu
   c. Select new record position
4. [CTRL] + [V]
5. Word processing, database

CHAPTER 14

1. Handles appear around the object
2. Hold down [SHIFT] key before dragging
3. Drag the Title bar
4. Crosshair
5. Select the objects (choose Select All option from EDIT menu if appropriate) then choose Group from DRAW menu
6. Select the object, then click "Fill" and the desired color from the color palette

CHAPTER 15

1. WINDOW menu
2. INSERT menu, Database Field option
3. Open the form letter and the associated database. With the letter file active, choose Print from FILE menu, click Print Merge (if necessary) from Print dialog box, choose the appropriate database file and begin printing.
4. Cascade
5. TOOLS menu, Create New Query option
6. Word processing

CHAPTER 16

1. Word processing
2. Choose Columns from FORMAT menu
3. Page Layout
4. FORMAT menu, Paragraph option
5. Choose Drawing from INSERT menu then Import Picture from the FILE menu, or choose ClipArt from the INSERT menu. If you have just drawn the picture, choose Exit and Return from the FILE menu then click YES to update your word processing document.
6. Click "No Footer on 1st page" from Headers and Footers dialog box (VIEW menu)

Index